Do-It-Yourself

HOME RECORDING

BY CHAD JOHNSON

To access audio, visit:
www.halleonard.com/mylibrary

Enter Code
5009-1814-8720-0739

ISBN 978-1-7051-0396-8

Visit Hal Leonard Online at
www.halleonard.com

World headquarters, contact:
Hal Leonard
7777 West Bluemound Road
Milwaukee, WI 53213
Email: info@halleonard.com

In Europe, contact:
Hal Leonard Europe Limited
Dettingen Way
Bury St Edmunds, Suffolk, IP33 3YB
Email: info@halleonardeurope.com

In Australia, contact:
Hal Leonard Australia Pty. Ltd.
4 Lentara Court
Cheltenham, Victoria, 3192 Australia
Email: info@halleonard.com.au

CONTENTS

ABOUT THE AUTHOR

Chad Johnson is a freelance author, editor, and musician. For Hal Leonard Corporation, he's authored over 95 instructional books covering a variety of instruments and topics, including *Guitarist's Guide to Scales Over Chords*, *The Hal Leonard Acoustic Guitar Method*, *Pentatonic Scales for the Guitar: The Essential Guide*, *Ukulele Aerobics*, *All About Ukulele*, *The Hal Leonard 12-String Guitar Method*, *Teach Yourself to Play Bass Guitar*, *Play Like Eric Johnson*, and *Bass Fretboard Workbook*, to name but a few. He's a featured instructor on the DVD *200 Country Guitar Licks* (also published by Hal Leonard) and has toured and performed throughout the East Coast in various bands, sharing the stage with members of Lynyrd Skynyrd, the Allman Brothers Band, and others. He works as a session guitarist, composer/songwriter, and recording engineer when not authoring or editing and currently resides in Franklin, WI with his wife and two children. Feel free to contact him at chadjohnsonguitar@gmail.com with any questions or comments.

Dedication and Acknowledgments

This book is dedicated to my beautiful family—my wife Alli, my son Lennon Ezra, and my daughter Leherie Ireland. Y'all are my favorite part of waking up every day and a continuous source of never-ending joy. I'd also like to dedicate the book to Peter McIan, whose excellent book, *The Musician's Guide to Home Recording*, lit a fire in me and infected me with the recording bug long ago.

Special thanks go to the following companies for their cooperation and support, which helped make this book a reality: AKG, Applied Acoustics Systems, Behringer, Garritan, IK Multimedia, Klark Teknik, MicParts, PreSonus, sE Electronics, Shure, Snark Tuners, Sterling by Music Man, Tascam, TC Electronic, Toontrack, Warm Audio, and Valhalla DSP.

A very special thanks goes to everyone at Hal Leonard for their combined efforts in this project.

Introduction

Welcome to *DIY Home Recording*. With this book, I aim to demonstrate that you don't need a professional studio and thousands (millions?) of dollars to make great-sounding recordings. In fact, you can do so from the comfort of your own home. The advantages afforded to the home recordist today are truly astounding and have leveled the playing field between pro and amateur like never before. With the right know-how and determination, you can produce amazing results with affordable gear that's within nearly everyone's reach.

I should clarify that when I say "affordable," it's in comparison to the "desert island" gear found in professional studios. There are no $5,000 compressors, $3,500 microphones, or $4,000 EQs mentioned in this book. There are a few "clones" of those famous units mentioned, but the vast majority of them fall well under the $1K mark, and many of those pieces of equipment are optional as well. For the most part, the gear mentioned in this book falls under the "prosumer" umbrella. In other words, you're not going to need to take out a second mortgage to outfit your studio.

Before moving forward, I'd like to say just a few more things about the book's goals and your expectations from it:

- The #1 rule of recording is this: *garbage in, garbage out*. It should be understood that, in order for a recording to be effective, the performances and sounds that are recorded need to be of a high caliber.
- I'm going to assume that you're a beginner or intermediate recordist wanting to learn how to record the most common instruments used in popular music, including predominantly vocals, guitars, bass, and keyboards. The recording of a full drumset is not covered in this book, as it is by far the most difficult instrument to record well at home, and the topic would be beyond the scope of this book. However, the use of drum loops, samples, and virtual drums is discussed in detail.
- As should be understood by now, the world of computers is a highly volatile one, and therefore any specifics mentioned in this book with regard to computer software or hardware are likely to become outdated before too long. The best I can hope to do is combat this with updates and revisions in possible future editions of the book.
- I'm just going to say this once. One of the most important things you can do to help you achieve good sounds—with *any* piece of gear or software—is to **read the manual**. (Ok ... I may say that again later as well.)
- Recordings, and music in general, are *subjective arts*. Sometimes, one man's genius is another man's rubbish. This may have to do with the skill of the recordist, musician, composer, etc., or it could just be that a certain song or recording rubs someone the wrong way. You can't please everyone with your music or recordings, so you may as well try to please yourself. (The exception to this, of course, is if you're recording a client, then you should try to please them too, of course!)

Now that all that's out of the way, let's get down to it and have some fun.

How to Use This Book

This book is more of a reference than a method. I'd certainly encourage everyone, regardless of their experience level, to read it cover to cover—just in case there's something new in there for them—but it will no doubt eventually serve as more of a reference in the long run.

If you're brand new to recording, you should absolutely start at the beginning and read it thoroughly. In fact, the complete beginner will likely not want to read it cover to cover at first because they'll need to try out some of the earlier techniques and concepts before they begin to understand some of those found later in the book. The book begins with a good bit of groundwork before we "hit record," and if most of this is old hat to you, feel free to skip ahead a bit.

Most of the instrument chapters are designed to be self-contained, but if and when a certain idea or concept borrows from that of another chapter, you'll be directed to the appropriate page or section.

In the Appendix, you'll find an extensive glossary that covers most of the terms you're likely to come across during your recording adventures. Feel free to consult it as necessary.

About the Recordings

On page 1, you will find a unique code. Go to ***www.halleonard.com/mylibrary*** and enter that code to gain access to the individual audio tracks for download or streaming. Audio tracks are indicated throughout the book by this symbol 🔊.

All of the recordings in this book were done in my home studio, which resides in the basement of my suburban house and was in no way constructed with the slightest regard for acoustics. I've done a good amount to improve this situation in my room, and this type of work is covered in Chapter 2. But just to be clear, this is a home studio through and through! In fact, you may hear a stray noise occasionally in a few tracks that use a microphone. I've decided to leave these in for the most part, as they represent the exact kind of things (someone closing a door, a pet scurrying, etc.) you need to be aware of when you're recording in less-than-professional spaces. Had these been "keeper" tracks, of course, they would need to be re-recorded.

Author's home studio

Here is some general info about the recording gear used in this book:

- **Dell Optiplex 7050 computer**: Windows 11, 32GB RAM, i7 7th Gen. 3.6GHz, 64-bit
- **PreSonus Studio One 6**
- **PreSonus FaderPort 8 control surface**
- **PreSonus Eris E8 studio monitors**
- **Focusrite Clarett 8Pre**: This interface has 8 analog inputs, 10 digital inputs, 10 analog outputs, 10 digital outputs, 2 headphones jacks with separate levels, and MIDI in/out.
- **sE Electronics sE8 small diaphragm condenser mics**: Used on guitars, piano, mandolin, and auxiliary percussion.
- **Warm Audio WA-14 large diaphragm condenser mic**: Used on guitars and vocals.
- **Warm Audio WA-47 large diaphragm tube condenser mic**: Used on vocals.
- **Shure SM7B dynamic mic**: Used on vocals and guitars.
- **Shure SM57 dynamic mic**: Used on guitars.
- **IK Multimedia virtual instruments and effects plug-ins**: Used for recording electric guitars and basses direct (AmpliTube 4) and for adding effects during mixdown (T-RackS).
- **Valhalla DSP plug-ins**: Used for reverb and delay effects.
- **Toontrack software**: Used for all drum tracks (EZdrummer 3), some bass tracks (EZbass), and some keyboard tracks (EZkeys 2).
- **Warm Audio outboard gear**: WA273-EQ two-channel mic preamp, WA76 FET compressor, WA-2A opto-compressor, and EQP-WA tube equalizer.
- **Electric guitars**: Fender Telecaster, Fender Stratocaster, Epiphone SG, Ibanez Artcore AG75 (archtop, flatwound strings).

- **Acoustic guitars**: Gibson J-185 True Vintage, Seagull S6, Seagull Walnut 12 (12-string).
- **Bass guitars**: Sterling by Music Man Stingray Ray25, Fender Precision Bass (flatwound strings).
- **Guitar amps**: Vox AC15.
- **Guitar effects/amp simulator**: Line 6 HX Stomp.
- **Bass amps**: Ampeg Micro-CL.

Other gear will be identified as used. I had a lot of fun creating these recordings, and I hope you find them enjoyable and inspiring as well!

At the end of the book are two original songs demonstrating all the concepts covered in the book. The individual audio track files for these two songs are available for download (see the code on page 1 of this book), so you can practice your mixing skills.

Note: All songs and examples in this book are owned by the author, and therefore, cannot be recreated without the author's express consent.

Chapter 1:
Basic Equipment Checklist

So, you're ready to start recording at home, but you have no idea where to begin. That's what this chapter is for. We're going to break down the home studio into its essential ingredients and look at each piece, its function, and its importance in the overall scheme.

We'll look at two basic setups:

- A **computer-based setup** using a desktop or laptop computer.
- A **mobile device setup** using a tablet or smartphone.

Computer-Based System

Let's start with the system that's completely transformed the way we record music like never before: the computer-based system. Although in professional studios, analog reel-to-reel recorders (i.e., tape recorders) still do see some action—oftentimes implemented in a hybrid system—the personal computer has clearly established itself as the go-to method for recording music, both at home and in pro studios alike.

Item 1: Computer

It's obvious, of course, but it's not quite as obvious as you may think. While many computers are up to the task of recording audio—at least in some capacity—it's common to use a computer dedicated solely to music production above all else. This is because, in a nutshell, recording music is a CPU-intensive process, and the leaner and cleaner your machine is, the more smoothly things will run.

One big thing to consider is whether you want a laptop or desktop system. Both have advantages and disadvantages, so you'll need to identify your needs and make an informed decision.

TOOLBOX

Laptop vs. Desktop

Let's examine a few pros and cons of these two setups:

Desktop

Dell XPS 8930 Tower PC
Courtesy of Dell, Inc.

Pros

- Often have more ports and expandability
- No limit to screen size
- Can be placed in a remote location (a closet, a custom-designed cabinet, etc.) to eliminate mechanical noise (fans, drives, etc.) if necessary

Cons

- Not portable
- Often difficult to access ports (USB, etc.)

Laptop

Apple MacBook Pro
Courtesy of Apple

Pros

- Extremely portable
- Easy access to ports

Cons

- Smaller screen size (though you can use an external monitor)
- No easy way to deal with mechanical noise

TOOLBOX

Mac or PC? Does It Really Matter?

You'll find an endless debate raging in online forums about which platform is better for recording music. But let's just cut to the chase here: it largely doesn't really matter when you're talking about a desktop or laptop computer.

What does matter is the processor and the amount of RAM you have. The faster it is, and the more RAM you have, the more you'll be able to do without having to compromise. Of course, there are physical differences between a Mac and a PC, including the type of ports they use. So you will need to pay attention in this regard when you choose your interface, etc.

Item 2: Audio Interface (A/I)

The *audio interface* is the device that turns your analog signal (from a guitar, microphone, keyboard, etc.) into a digital one so that the computer can work with it. It then turns it back into an analog signal so that it can be played back over the speakers. As such, it features A/D (analog to digital) and D/A (digital to analog) converters for this purpose. You don't need to know exactly how this process works in order to use them; you just need a decent interface that performs well and contains the features you require. Let's look at some of the most important ones.

Number of Analog Inputs: How many tracks do you want to record at once? This is probably the most important thing you need to think about because it's not something you can overcome by upgrading anything. You'll have to buy another piece of gear if you need more inputs. For most home recordists who do everything themselves, two inputs will work just fine.

The Tascam US-2x2 USB Audio and MIDI Interface features two inputs and two outputs.

If you need to record several sources at once, though, and you want to have individual control over the tracks, then you'll need more inputs than that. Interfaces are normally available with an even number of inputs.

Number of Analog Outputs: If you're planning on doing everything "in the box"—i.e., using plug-ins for all your effects and mixing everything entirely within your DAW (Digital Audio Workstation) software—then you'll only really need two outputs (left and right for the stereo mix). This is the most common method for most home recordists. But if you have some outboard gear you'd like to incorporate (a favorite reverb, delay, or compressor unit, for example), then having more outputs allows you to integrate those types of things.

The Celesonic US-20x20 from Tascam provides 10 analog inputs and 10 analog outputs for increased flexibility during tracking and mixing. Digital inputs and outputs are included as well for further possibilities.

Mic Preamps, XLR Inputs, and Phantom Power: Most microphones use "balanced" XLR cables, which contain three connectors. These are sometimes referred to simply as "mic cables."

XLR "mic" cable

Most interfaces contain one or more XLR inputs with a built-in preamp, allowing you to plug the microphone directly into it. Condenser microphones require additional current to operate, which is occasionally supplied by an external power supply that comes with the mic (or a battery inside the mic). Most often, though, it's supplied through the cable via *phantom power*. Be sure to check and see if your interface features phantom power. If it doesn't, you can purchase an external phantom power supply for around $20 or $50 per channel.

MIDI Inputs/Outputs: Many interfaces contain MIDI in and out jacks, which allow you to plug in your MIDI controllers directly to send and receive MIDI data. If your interface doesn't have MIDI jacks, you can easily get a USB-powered MIDI interface. Many MIDI controllers these days also allow you to simply connect to the computer via USB directly.

Computer Connection: As mentioned earlier, you'll find various connections—mostly USB-C today—but others, such as Ethernet and Thunderbolt, are available as well. Be sure you select one that's compatible with your computer system.

Direct Monitoring: This is a feature that allows you to overcome the *latency* issue that's a part of every computer-based recording system. (Latency basically describes the time it takes for a signal to pass from analog to digital and back again.) It allows you to monitor the incoming signal directly after the input instead of waiting for it to make the trip through the computer. It's a very nice feature if your system is not efficient enough to work smoothly with a low latency setting.

Item 3: Software

Next, we have software. Most software programs will fit into one of the following categories:

- The *DAW* (Digital Audio Workstation) program, which can also be called sequencer, recording, or production software
- Effects plug-ins (such as reverb, compression, EQ, etc.)
- Virtual instruments (MIDI-controlled sounds such as piano, strings, drums, etc.)
- Loops and samples (short audio files that can be looped to form a drumbeat or added to your own tracks as you please)
- Samplers (a program you can use to record and/or manipulate samples of your own)

We'll discuss software in much greater detail in Chapter 4.

Item 4: MIDI Controller

Although these border on being instruments (and I said I wasn't going to list instruments), I feel they're a bit unique in that they're incapable of producing any sound on their own. In other words, they have to be *controlling* something else that can make sound. *MIDI* (Musical Instrument Digital Interface) is quite a large topic and beyond the scope of this book, though we'll discuss it enough to get you started. Fortunately, there are plenty of resources out there on the subject when you need to investigate further.

A *MIDI controller* is simply the name for a device we use to input MIDI data. The most common is the MIDI keyboard controller, which usually resembles kind of like a plain-looking electronic keyboard. Although, they can feature a good amount of bells and whistles too.

Akai LPK 25 keyboard controller

By the way, just about any keyboard (with built-in sounds) these days will usually feature a MIDI out jack, which means that it can be used as a MIDI keyboard controller as well. So, if you already have a keyboard with a MIDI out jack, you don't need to buy another one (to start, anyway!).

Item 5: Microphones

If you want to record vocals—or any instrument that you can't plug in somewhere—you'll need a microphone. Mics come in two main categories with regard to the home recordist: *dynamic* and *condenser*. A third type, the *ribbon* mic, is also occasionally used.

Dynamic Mic

A *dynamic* mic is more rugged in construction and is therefore used a great deal in live situations, where lead singers are apt to swing it around by the cable (which is hopefully securely attached!). They're not as detailed in the treble frequencies, especially as a condenser, but they can generally handle higher volume levels without distorting, which makes them good choices for loud guitar amps, drums, rock vocals, etc. The dynamic mics used in this book are the Shure SM57 and the Shure SM7B.

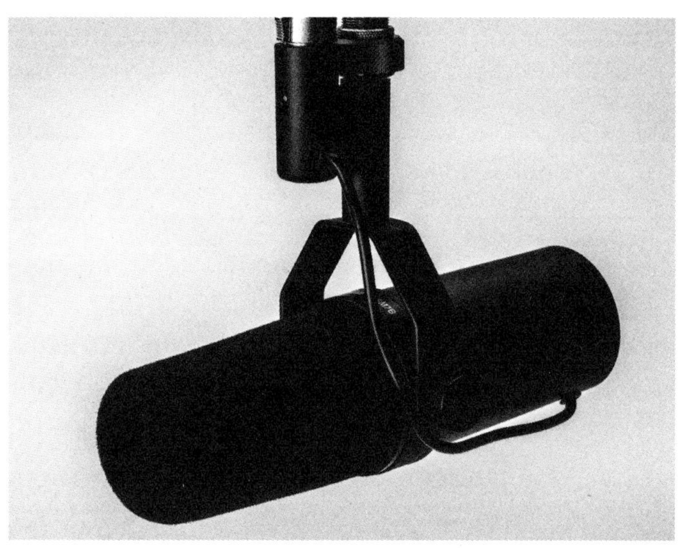

Shure SM7B and Shure SM57.

The WA-14 large diaphragm condenser mic is a reproduction of the famous AKG C414.

Condenser Mic

A *condenser* mic comes in two main categories: *large diaphragm* and *small diaphragm*. As you may have guessed, the large diaphragm is physically larger. It's the prototypical vocal mic you see in photos when someone's singing in a studio. It's also used on guitars, percussion, piano, horns, and other instruments. LDCs are *side-address* microphones, which means you sing (or aim the sound source) into the side of the microphone. The LDC mics used in this book are the Warm Audio WA-47 (a tube mic) and a Warm Audio WA-14.

Small diaphragm mics are usually short and kind of stubby—much like a cigar—and are usually *top-address* (sometimes called *end-address*), meaning you sing or play into the top (or end) of the mic. These are often used when miking an instrument in stereo, such as a piano, guitar, or drum kit. If you intend to do this, it's really nice to have two identical mics (a "matched pair" is best) for this purpose, as it will generally result in a more accurate stereo image of the instrument. The SDC mics used in this book are a matched pair of sE8 mics from sE Electronics.

The sE8 small diaphragm condenser mics from sE Electronics excel on acoustic guitars, pianos, drum overheads, auxiliary percussion, and more.

Condenser microphones use a more delicate mechanism than dynamics do. As such, they're easier to damage and should be handled with great care. There are now many LDC microphones available under the $300 mark, such as the sE2200 from sE Electronics, that would serve the home recordist extremely well.

TOOLBOX

Handy with a Soldering Iron?
If you're the DIY type and want to get the most bang for your buck, you may want to look into building your own microphone from a kit. **MicParts** has many such kits available, including the highly praised T-12, which is endorsed by multi-platinum producer Greg Wells (Adele, Taylor Swift, Pharrell Williams, etc).

The company also offers the T-25 kit, a medium diaphragm condenser that's specifically designed for novice builders. A perfect first-time project for someone with some basic soldering experience, it's a transformer-balanced design that's based on Neumann's KM84 circuit. Coming in at under $300, the mic will surely find many uses around your studio, including vocals, drums, guitars, and more.

I've used several of their modification kits, and I can personally vouch for the high quality of these kits. Not only have the mods made a night-and-day difference, but their instructions are incredibly detailed and easy to follow. To top it all off, their customer service is absolutely top-notch. In short, if you're curious at all about building your own high-quality DIY mic for a very affordable price, I highly recommend you check out MicParts (www.microphone-parts.com).

MicParts T-25 medium diaphragm condenser microphone kit

Ribbon Mic

A *ribbon mic* uses yet another method for capturing sound, and it's generally the most delicate mechanism of all. They're common in pro studios for certain applications, but their prices often make them a pipe dream for the home recordist. However, several affordable models have become available as of late, and if you have a few extra bucks to spare, they can certainly make a valuable addition to your mic locker.

The Avantone Pro CR-14 ribbon mic sounds as good as it looks on many sources and is an incredible value.

TOOLBOX

Polar Patterns

Microphones are placed in different classes also by way of their *polar patterns*. This refers to the directions in which they're most sensitive to sound. There are three basic categories: *cardioid*, *figure eight*, and *omnidirectional*.

A cardioid mic will pick up sound well in the front and to the sides but not from the back of the microphone. Most LDC mics are cardioid, although some of them have switchable patterns including figure eight and/or omnidirectional as well. The most common application for a cardioid mic is vocals.

A figure eight pattern, as its name implies, will pick up sound from the front and back equally, but it will reject sound from the sides of the mic. All ribbon microphones feature this pattern. Figure eight patterns are useful for when you want to record two singers at once onto the same track since they can each stand on opposite sides of the mic.

An omnidirectional microphone will pick up sound equally from all sides. They're used often for ambient recordings—if you just want to pick up the sound of the room with several people gathered in a circle performing live, for example. The results of this will vary with the "sound" of the room, however.

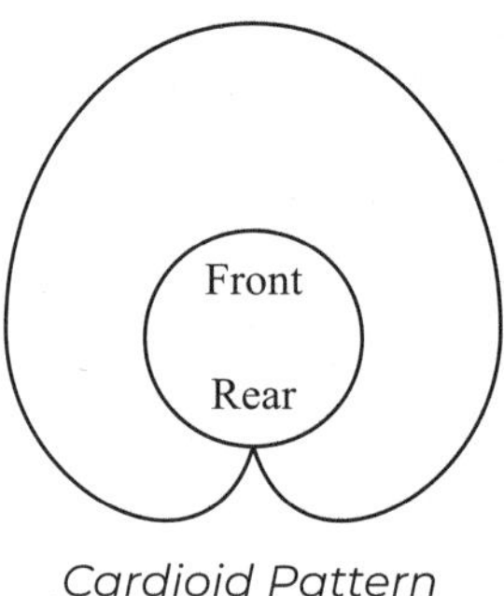

Cardioid Pattern

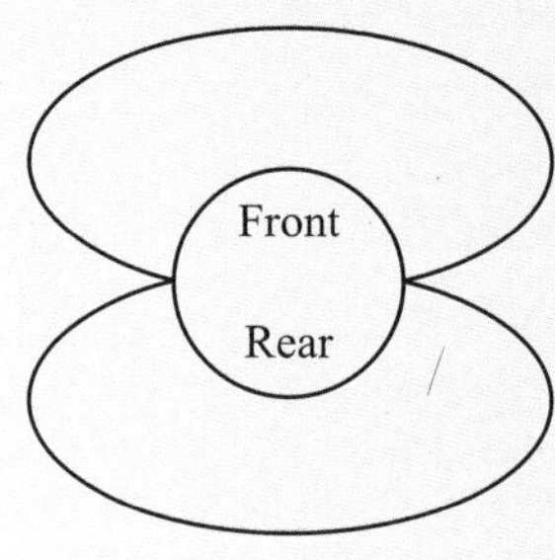

Figure-eight Pattern

Front

Rear

Omnidirectional Pattern

Item 6: Headphones and Studio Monitors (Speakers)

If you're going to be using a microphone at all, you're going to need headphones in order to hear the backing tracks while you record vocals/guitar/piano/etc. on top of them. Headphones will also allow you to hear how your mixes are translating to them, which is very important nowadays considering the sheer number of people who listen to music predominantly on mobile devices. Ideally, you'll want a pair of headphones that are designed for studio use.

AKG K240 Studio Headphones

Studio monitors (speakers) are another important part in obtaining a well-balanced mix. Whereas stereo speakers are designed to make music sound more pleasant, studio monitors are designed to give a much flatter frequency response. This helps you create a mix that will translate better to the many different speakers (and headphones) on which people will eventually hear your music.

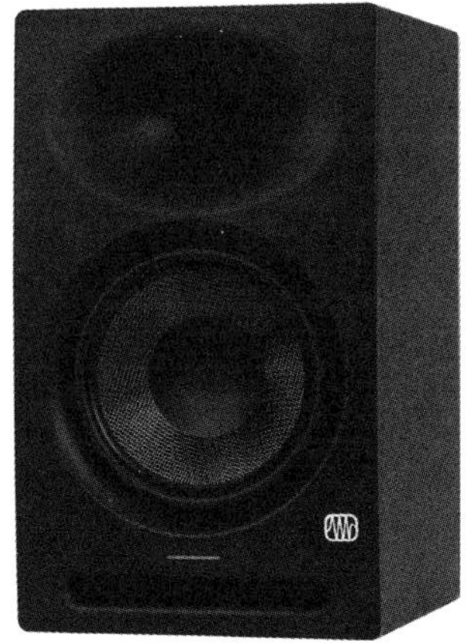

PreSonus Eris Studio 8 Monitor

Monitors come in two flavors: *active* (powered) or *passive* (non-powered). Powered monitors require no amplifier to work because they have one built into them. You can plug them straight into your audio interface's output. Passive monitors require a power amp to work. You would plug your interface's outputs into the power amp and then run speaker wire from the amp to the monitors.

It's also a good idea to have some cheap boombox or desktop computer speakers available as well to reference from time to time. Most professional mixing engineers, including Chris Lord-Alge and Michael Brauer, employ this principle and are constantly referencing the cheap little speakers to make sure they're on the right track.

Item 7: Cables, Stands, and Miscellaneous

All this equipment has to connect in some fashion, so you'll need several different types of cables. Here are the most common types:

XLR Mic Cables

These are the three-conductor cables mentioned earlier under Item 2 (the A/I). You'll use these to connect your mic to the preamp or interface, among other things. XLR cables are excellent at rejecting noise and are the best choice when you need to run long cable lengths. Not only that, but they have male and female ends, which means you can daisy chain two (or more) together if you need to.

XLR "mic" cable

Tourtek Pro Noiseless Instrument Cable by Samson Audio

1/4-inch Instrument Cables

This is your basic guitar cord. It's also known sometimes as a TS (tip-sleeve) cable, which means it has two conductors: hot (the signal, which is found on the tip of the plug) and ground (which is found on the "sleeve" of the plug—the opposite side of the black band from the tip). These are typically used in the studio as longer cables (for plugging in guitars, keyboards, etc.) and as shorter "patch cables" (anywhere from six inches to three feet) for connecting rackmount gear, guitar pedals, etc.

Speaker Cables

These are 1/4-inch cables that are used to connect a guitar or bass amp to the speaker cabinet. Although they look just like a standard guitar cord (and use the TS format), they're different inside. They will usually say "speaker cable" or something similar along the outside of the cable.

These should not be confused with the cables used to connect your studio monitors, which will typically be a normal TS instrument cable, a TRS cable, or an XLR cable (possibly an RCA cable).

RCA Cables

These are two-conductor cables that are normally paired together in a red/white or red/black configuration. Some equipment makes use of RCA jacks, while others use 1/4-inch or XLR jacks. You can also use RCA-to-1/4-inch adapters or vice versa if necessary.

RCA cable

RCA-to-1/4-inch adapters

USB Cables

You'll most likely end up using standard USB cables as well as specialized ones that will usually come with a piece of gear (the male end will be standard, and the female end will be specialized).

Hosa TRS cable

1/4-inch TRS Cables

These look like guitar cables, but they're actually three-conductor cables. You can tell them apart from a normal (TS) guitar cable by the extra band on the end of the plug. "TRS" stands for "tip-ring-sleeve." The "ring" carries the extra signal. These provide a "balanced" signal—like an XLR cable—in a 1/4-inch package. Balanced cables are especially useful for longer cable runs (over 20 or 30 feet, for example) because they're excellent at rejecting noise from RF interference.

Insert cable

Insert Cables

These are most often found in the 1/4-inch format, but they can appear in other forms as well. An insert cable has one plug on one end and two on the other. The single end will be the TRS type, while the other two ends will be the TS type. One of the dual ends will send a signal somewhere, while the other end will return it. They're used to "insert" another piece of gear into the signal path.

Boom mic stand

Stands

Then there are stands, including microphone stands (and mic clips), guitar/bass stands, and keyboard stands (although smaller MIDI controllers can fit on a desk), among others. With regards to mic stands, a *boom mic stand* is especially useful in the studio, as it will allow you access to many more spots than a standard vertical mic stand will.

Miscellaneous

Under the miscellaneous umbrella, you have many little things. Most of these items you'll just end up collecting as you need them. Some of the most common are:

- Power strips/surge protectors
- Picks
- Tuners
- Metronome
- Adapters (male XLR to female 1/4-inch, female XLR to male 1/4-inch, female RCA to male TS, male RCA to female TS, etc. You'll no doubt pick these up as you find the need for them, eventually ending up with a whole shoebox full of them.)
- Cable ties
- Capos
- Flash drive
- Flashlight
- Electrical tape
- Etc., etc.

That just about wraps it up for the basics. It may seem like a lot, but let's do a quick review. Basically, we've got:

- Computer
- Audio interface
- MIDI controller
- Microphone(s)
- Software
- Headphones/Speakers
- Cables/Stands

TOOLBOX

But Do I Really Need ...?

Even though this is a basic equipment checklist, there are some of you for whom one or more of these items may be optional. For example, if you plan to record nothing but acoustic guitar and vocals, then you don't really need a MIDI controller or any virtual instrument software. Or maybe you only plan to record instrumental electronic music for the foreseeable future. If that's the case, then you don't need to spend your money on a microphone right now. So, if you can't foresee a use for something on the list, feel free to skip it for now.

Mobile Device Setup

Tascam released the first "Portastudio," the 144, back in 1979 with a price tag of around $1,000. This was a cassette-based four-track recorder, and it changed the music world forever. For the first time, a music recording system could truly be called portable. Bruce Springsteen famously recorded his #3 album, *Nebraska*, on this machine in 1982. It measured 18 by 15 inches and weighed 20 pounds (the Tascam recorder, not the Springsteen record!).

Fast forward to today, and you have portable studios that fit into the palm of your hand with more flexibility and processing options for a fraction of the price. There are still several dedicated portable studios on the market, but ever since smartphones and tablets took over the planet, the portable recording trend has been steadily moving that way. And you can achieve phenomenal results if you play to the platform's strengths.

TOOLBOX

Pros and Cons of a Smartphone/Tablet Studio

Considering that most people already own a usable device, a smartphone or tablet-based studio could be the biggest bang-for-buck studio of all. Of course, they're not for everybody or every situation. Let's look at the pros and cons.

Pros

- You probably already own a suitable device.
- The software apps are very inexpensive, relatively speaking, when compared to home computer setups, with usable DAW apps ranging anywhere from free to about $30 on the top end.
- Since you are used to carrying this device around, it's even that much more portable.
- It's fun to feel as though you're getting some serious use out of the thing beyond email and texts.

Cons

- You generally won't have the flexibility of a home-based setup with regard to things like automation, signal routing, etc.
- You may have other limitations, such as maximum track count, effects, etc.
- Your interface options may be limited, depending on your chosen platform. Apple has the upper hand with regards to this, with numerous dedicated accessories made for smartphone/tablet recording.
- The screen will obviously be smaller than your full-size monitor, and the adjusting of parameters may be a bit more cumbersome as well.

A Word on Platforms

At the moment, there are basically two routes you can go with regards to the mobile platform: Apple iOS or Android. This is because Apple is currently the only company with dedicated hardware interfaces specifically built for mobile devices, such as their iPhone and iPad. Things haven't yet been standardized for Android, Windows, etc., and therefore it's a bit more prickly with regards to functionality on these devices.

At the time of this writing, the Android platform still suffers from latency issues, whereas Apple pretty much has it licked. This makes Apple the clear frontrunner (for the time) in the world of mobile device audio production.

Item 1: Mobile Device

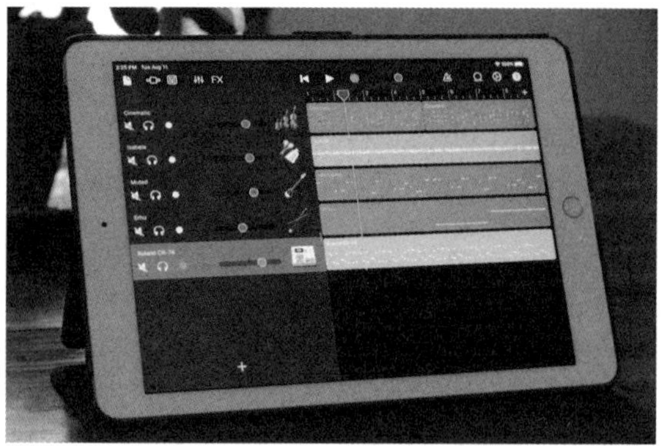

Apple iPad running GarageBand

As with computers, the faster your mobile device is—and the more memory it has—the better it will be for recording audio.

Just about any app will run on a tablet or a phone, so there's no advantage to using one over the other in that regard. The smaller screens on a phone can make editing a bit cumbersome, so most people prefer a tablet. Once you add in an audio interface, a mic and cable, and some headphones, etc., you've just about negated the extra bit of portability that the phone affords, so you may as well go for the bigger screen.

Item 2: Interfaces

Apple got the head start in the mobile recording world, and thus there are numerous devices on the market for this purpose. IK Multimedia leads the charge in this regard with interfaces dedicated to microphones, MIDI, guitar/bass, or all three combined, not to mention guitar pedals, stands, clips, accessories, etc. But other manufacturers, such as Tascam and Line 6, produce similar products.

The iRig PRO DUO I/O from IK Multimedia is a full-featured two-channel audio/MIDI interface for iOS, Android, or Mac/PC.

Copyright IK Multimedia, used with permission

The Tascam IXR is a robust two-channel audio/MIDI interface for iOS, Mac, and PC devices with an ultra-slim design that can easily be moved from desktop to backpack.

Item 3: Recording Apps

There are numerous recording apps available for both platforms that run the gamut from a basic four-track recorder to a full-featured DAW. The good news is that the most expensive of these only reaches around $20 (although some do feature optional in-app purchases for more flexibility, etc.).

iOS

- GarageBand (Apple)
- Logic Pro for iPad (Apple)
- Music Studio (Alexander Gross)
- MultiTrack DAW (Harmonicdog)
- AmpliTube for iPad (IK Multimedia) (Though predominantly a guitar amp simulator, it can be upgraded via in-app purchase to include a Studio feature that allows for eight-track recording on iPad and four on iPhone.)
- Auria (WaveMachine Labs)

Android

- Audio Evolution Mobile (eXtream Software)
- FL Studio Mobile (Image-Line)
- Recording Studio Pro (Glauco)
- J4T Multitrack Recorder (Jaytronix)
- FourTracks Pro (NomadicWhales.com)

Cross-Platform

- n-Track Studio Multitrack Recorder (n-Track Software)

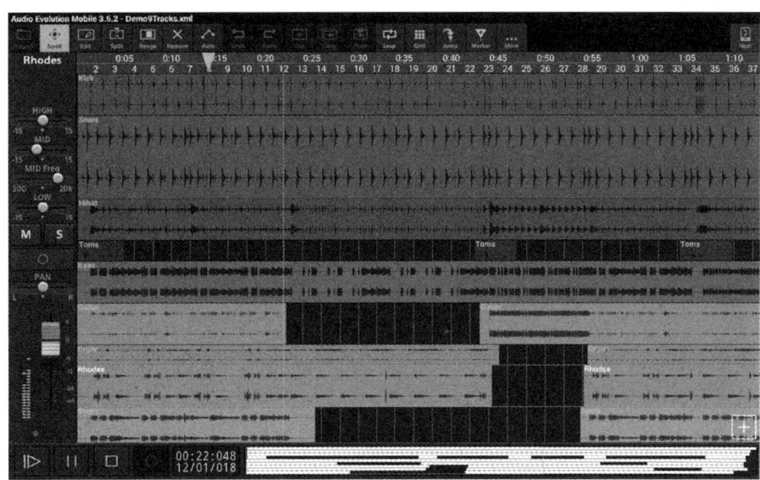

eXtream's Audio Evolution Mobile is a fully-loaded audio production app for Android.

Remaining Items

Everything else—MIDI controllers, microphones, miscellaneous, etc.—is basically the same as with the computer-based setup. Of course, if portability is of paramount importance, then you'll want to keep this in mind when selecting your other gear (smaller MIDI controllers, etc.).

In summary, if portability is your prime factor, you'd be doing yourself an injustice by not checking out the mobile device recording studio. It may take a bit of getting used to at first, and there may be a slight learning curve, but once you're up and running, you can have a very powerful system on your hands capable of producing professional sounds just about anywhere you find yourself.

TOOLBOX

Heads Up for the Mobile User

From this point in the book, we'll be dealing exclusively with computer (laptop or desktop) recording and won't reference mobile devices again. However, most of what we cover will be applicable to mobile devices. Depending on the mobile DAW app you're using, you may not have all the features discussed, but you should have most. Regardless, all of the techniques we cover regarding miking, EQ, effects, mixing, etc., will be applicable to mobile device users as well.

Chapter 2:
Choosing Your Space and How to Treat It

If you're really new to recording, and your head's still reeling a bit from the barrage of equipment listed in the first chapter, don't fret. We'll look much more closely at all of it in the coming chapters. So now that you have a general picture of what kind of gear you're going to be using, let's have a look at where you'll be using it. This chapter is all about choosing where your studio will be and how to make the most out of that space.

For some of you, there may not be a choice. It may be, by default, your 11x8-foot bedroom or nothing. Or possibly you have a finished (or somewhat finished) basement that's yours for the taking. No matter which room you set up shop in, they will most likely all have one thing in common: unfortunately, they were not built or designed with music production in mind. This means that the sound you're hearing through your speakers is not very accurate.

TOOLBOX

A Pro Studio Is More than Just Pro Equipment and Atmosphere!
Professional studios have rooms constructed specifically with acoustics in mind from the ground up. This often means, among other things, they avoid parallel walls. The rooms are often "tuned" (with the use of diffusers, absorbers, and other acoustic manipulative devices) with the aid of a professional acoustical engineer. For the vast majority of us home recordists, this is not a luxury we can afford (it's not cheap!). If, however, you have the opportunity to construct your own home studio—whether it be renovating an existing home or building a separate structure on your acreage—then you'll definitely want to thoroughly research the topic with books/videos/etc. that are dedicated to the topic of studio construction.

Don't Be Square

If at all possible, you *really* want to avoid a room that's perfectly square-shaped. (The absolutely worst shape for a room would be a perfect cube.) The good news is that we can go a long way to make these bedrooms or basements fairly decent in terms of recording and mixing music. Is it going to rival a fully professional, "spare no expense" studio designed from the ground up? No, of course not. But the truth is that it doesn't need to. For our purposes, it just needs to be pretty good, and we can get there without spending a fortune either.

TOOLBOX

One Room or Two? (or Three?)
Many home studios exist entirely within the confines of one room. By this, I mean that the music is not only recorded there, but it's also mixed. In this case, the "control room" (the room with the monitors, mixing desk, etc.) is also the "studio," or "recording room." Others have a dedicated control room (perhaps a bedroom) with another room serving as the "studio." This may be an adjoining living room or den, perhaps. Others may even convert a large adjoining closet into a makeshift vocal booth. This is something that's practical on a temporary basis too, as we'll see later.

However, feel free to try out many different rooms for recording if you're feeling adventurous. You may find that the study, with wooden floors, lots of bookshelves to diffuse the sound a bit, and a higher ceiling, sounds nice for recording solo acoustic guitar. Or maybe the large, tiled bathroom has a cool slap-back echo to it that works well for electric guitars.

Basic Layout: Control Room

We'll look at separate recording rooms in a bit, but let's start with the control room. There are several basic layout features that are common to nearly every control room, including symmetry, listening position, and acoustic treatment.

Monitor Placement

You want to place your monitors along the short wall in a rectangular room, and they should ideally be several feet from the wall. They should be set at ear height (when you're sitting) and pointing toward you. As such, they're normally placed on stands or on top of a desk. They should also be symmetrical regarding their distance to the side (long) walls. Below are several different commonly shaped rooms and the (approximate) ideal monitor placement and listening position.

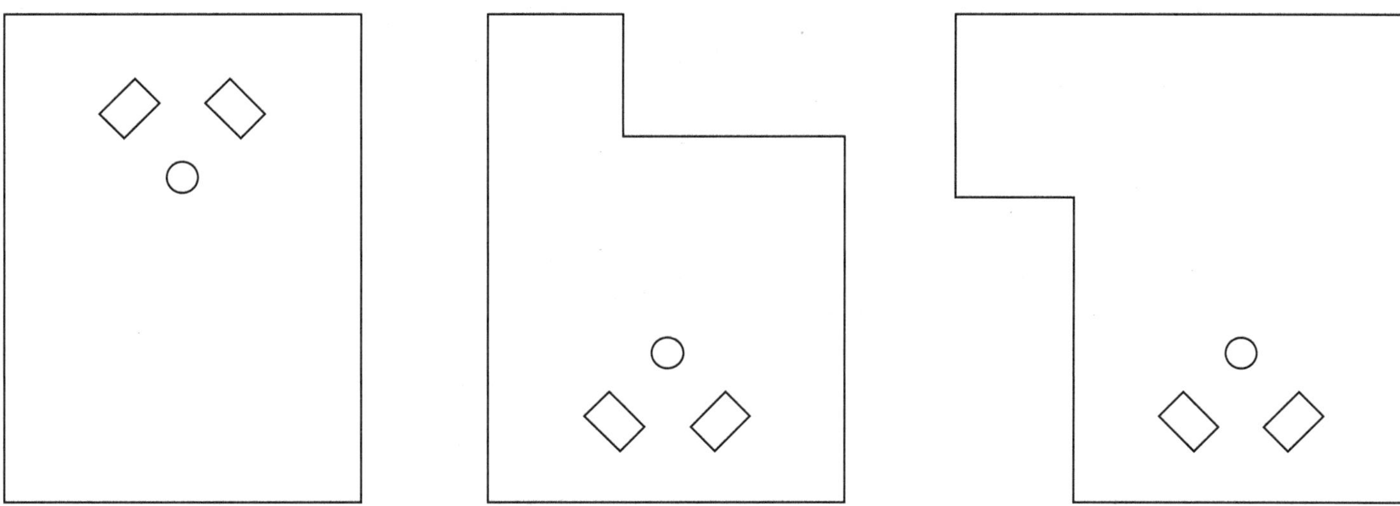

The monitors should form an equilateral triangle with your head as you sit in the listening position. This is referred to as *near-field monitoring*, and the idea is to be physically close to the monitors so that the sound of the "room" is minimized when listening to the speakers.

Specifically, your ideal listening position will usually be at 38% of the length of the long walls. In other words, if your room was 10x8 feet, you'd want to be facing an eight-foot wall with your head approximately 3.8 feet from it and directly centered between the long (10-foot) walls.

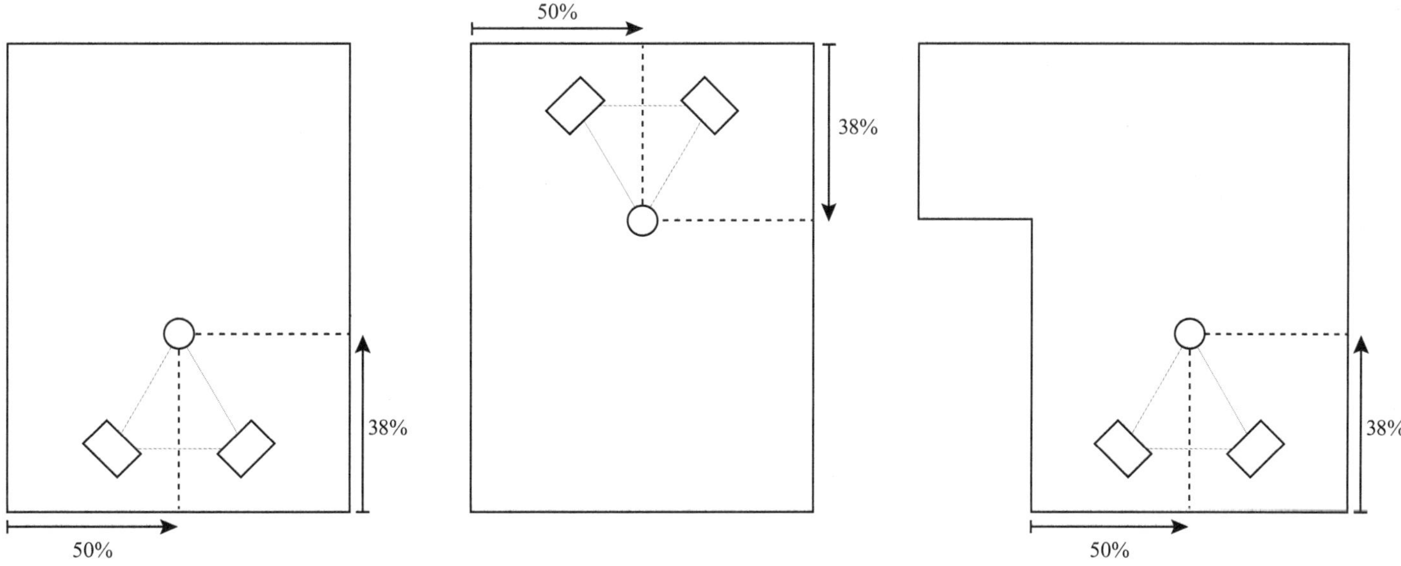

The reason that this number (38%) is standard is that it places you in a certain spot that's fairly devoid of nulls or peaks with regard to frequency buildup. However, it's not a rule. Feel free to try other spots if you'd like as well. One benefit to having space behind your desk, however, is that it allows you walking room back there, which is always nice when you need to check for a loose connection, hook up a new piece of gear, etc.

TOOLBOX

Phantom Image

Once you get your monitors positioned, you can check for proper stereo imaging by playing a mono signal (such as a single guitar or vocal track) and panning it to the center. The signal should appear to be coming from directly between the speakers. This is called a "phantom image" and is one of the fun phenomena of stereo sound. You can try slowly panning the signal to hard left and all the way to hard right to follow it from speaker to speaker. This is also a nice way to test your monitors. The signal should be the same volume when panned hard left as it is hard right.

Quieting the Noise

Computers can tend to get a little noisy at times, so it should also be mentioned that, if using a desktop computer, you should try to place the machine a good distance away from your listening position if possible. Pro studios solve this issue by keeping all the noisy equipment in a separate room, but that's not always an option for the home recordist (although, if you're single, it's probably not out of the question). An adjoining closet is an option, assuming you allow for some ventilation to prevent the machine from overheating.

Alternatively, some people choose to place the machine inside a specially designed-enclosure to eliminate most of the noise. There are several companies that make these, but they can get really pricey. If you're handy, you can build your own with plans found online.

However, before you go to all these lengths, make sure that it's a problem in the first place! Fortunately, I've never had to mess with much of this, as the fan in my computer is relatively quiet.

TOOLBOX

Other Noise Culprits

Aside from the computer, there are several other leading contributors to noise in the studio:

- **Air conditioner/heater:** This is a big one, and having lived in Texas for most of my life, it was by far the biggest thorn in my side. Removing the vent from the ceiling will *significantly* cut down the noise in your room. In fact, if the main AC unit in my house wasn't located right outside my window, this tweak alone would make my room quiet enough for recording even fingerpicked acoustic guitar.
- **Clocks:** This is especially true of a cheap, plastic $8 special. They'll usually tick loudly enough to be picked up by a condenser. The easiest way to deal with this is to avoid those types of clocks—i.e., use a digital one—or simply move it to another room or cover it with a blanket during recording.
- **Cars, pets, and other domestic disturbances:** Unfortunately, unless you're up for a major construction overhaul of your space (or you're designing a studio from the ground up), there's not a whole lot you can do if sound is leaking in through a window from the outside world. Aside from filling the window and blocking it off (you can research online how to do this in a non-permanent fashion if you'd like), you may just have to try to schedule your session at the quietest times.
- **Refrigerators and other household appliances:** If your studio is located in a den next to the kitchen, the fridge may very well be loud enough to creep into the mics. Many of my vocal takes throughout the years (in various home studios) have begun with "Remember to turn the fridge back on!" Always listen through headphones before recording a new track with a mic, as this will reveal the noise floor much more dramatically than with speakers.
- **Weather:** A heavy rain will almost certainly be audible, so unless you're recording a cranked guitar amp or something similar, you may have to wait it out. However, if you have mics set up ready to go and it starts thundering, don't miss your chance to open your window briefly and record a bit of it! It's a very cool sound.

Acoustic Treatment

This is a big one. As mentioned earlier, houses are not designed with mixing in mind, so we've got the odds stacked against us from the beginning. By far the most neglected puzzle piece in terms of getting pro sounds from a home studio lies in *acoustic treatment*. That bears repeating: **the lack of acoustic treatment—not the gear!—is by far the most common problem in home studios.** So, what do we mean by acoustic treatment? Well, there are two main types: soundproofing, and sound treatment.

Soundproofing involves keeping sounds from getting into or out of a room. This is not easy to do, fairly expensive, and very labor-intensive. The short story is that it's not something that a home recordist will deal with unless they're planning on renovating their home or building from scratch. Basements are a bit better in this regard, but sound will still leak in through the ceiling or windows.

Sound treatment deals with the way sound reacts within a certain room. We don't want sound waves to bounce back and forth between parallel walls or bounce endlessly around the room because this will greatly affect the frequencies we hear while we're mixing/recording. This is why, although our song may sound great when we're listening in our room in our mixing chair, it can sound completely different in your car or at your friend's house. This is where acoustic treatment comes in. There are two main categories we'll discuss: absorption and diffusion.

Absorption

Absorption deals with absorbing sound waves. This helps to prevent them from bouncing all over the room. Ideally, we'd like to hear only the sound coming from the speakers straight to our ears. In an untreated room, however, this is not what's happening at all. We use absorption mostly in the control room, because we want to try and create a *reflection-free zone* for the listening position.

So, what we'll do is place absorbers at these first reflective points to help stop the sound from bouncing off the wall to our head. This means we'll place absorbers on each wall and one larger one on the ceiling (large enough to account for both speakers).

Here's where these five spots would be located in a typical bedroom-style control room:

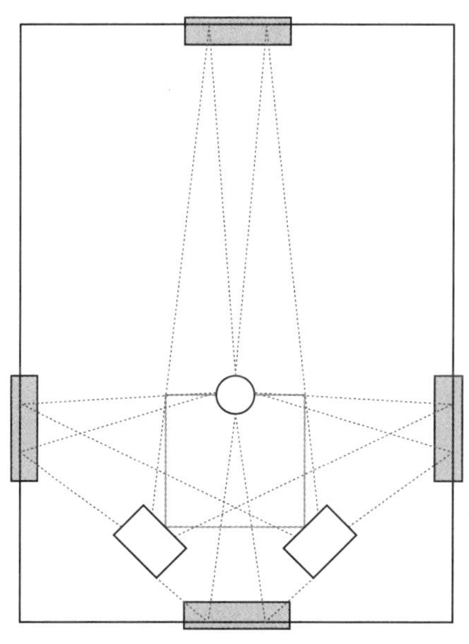

These panels can be made of various materials, including acoustic foam, rigid fiberglass, or mineral wool, among others. Soft, fluffy furniture, such as a sofa or futon, can also provide some absorption as well. Generally speaking, the denser the material, the better it will be at absorbing lower frequencies. Materials that are known for absorbing fairly well throughout the frequency spectrum are known as *broadband absorbers*, and rigid fiberglass and mineral wool are two such materials.

A two-inch thick panel of a broadband absorptive material is usually adequate for each of these reflective points. It's recommended that you mount them a few inches away from the wall, as the space between the rear of the panel and the wall will aid in lower frequency absorption. The ceiling panel (or "cloud" as it's commonly called) should also hang down several inches or more from the ceiling. Make sure to position each one accurately so that you're adequately covering the reflective points on the wall/ceiling.

TOOLBOX

Buy or DIY?

There are numerous companies that sell these types of panels (and numerous ones that sell acoustic foam as well). Unfortunately, they can get pricey pretty quickly. The foam starts off fairly affordable. However, you get what you pay for, and the affordable foam pieces aren't terribly effective at the lower frequencies. You can expect to pay anywhere from $60 to $300 or more for a broadband panel measuring 48x24x2 inches. When you start to add that up (not to mention the shipping charges if you're not near a company), it can quickly turn into an expensive venture. And that's not even including bass traps, which we'll look at next.

This is the reason I suggest that, if you have it in you to DIY *anything*, acoustic treatment is the area to do it. You can easily save yourself *hundreds* or *thousands* of dollars by doing the work yourself, and you can end up with a perfectly decent-sounding control room. And to be honest, I think it's kind of fun! (See Appendix for information on this.)

Homemade absorption panels

Bass Traps

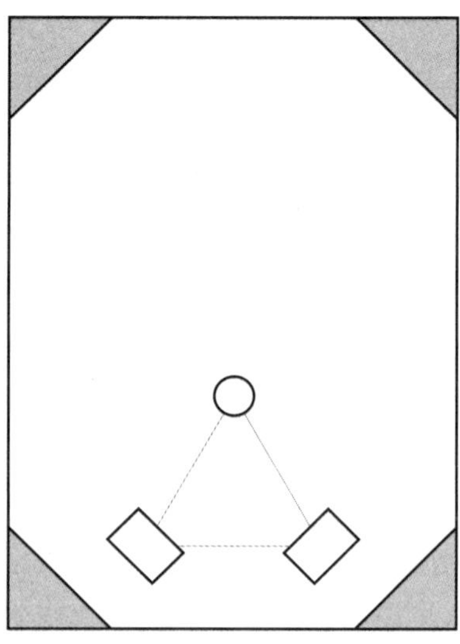

Unfortunately, early reflections aren't the only thing we have to tame in the control room. Bass response is also a big problem in the home studio control room. This can really mess with your monitoring experience and result in poor mixing decisions. Enter the *bass trap*. The purpose of a bass trap, which we place in the corners of the room, is to absorb the extra bass frequencies that build up.

Again, you can buy ready-made traps, but they are very expensive. Lucky for us, though, you can make pretty decent ones on your own. It's actually done the same way as the panels; it's just that instead of two inches thick, bass traps should be at least four inches thick (the thicker the better). Ideally they should span from floor to ceiling, but anything and everything helps. If you follow the advice in the Appendix, you can build four decent, full-size bass traps for around $100–$120. How's that for frugal?

TOOLBOX

What About the Door?

If your control room is in a bedroom, there's a very good chance that the entry door will be in one of the four corners. If that's the case, what do you do about that bass trap? That's a good question. There are several possibilities:

- **You don't have a bass trap in that corner**: This is the least desirable option.
- **You rig up some sort of apparatus, allowing the trap to slide into place as the door is closed and retreat behind the door when the door is opened**: This is the most impressive option, but it's the most difficult.
- **You have a temporary bass trap that can easily be moved into place when you need it**: This is the most practical option.

I use the third method. It works great as long as you work out some system in which you make sure no one will come barging in without knocking. Otherwise, you could end up with a crashing bass trap on your hands!

Diffusion

Diffusion deals with scattering, or breaking up, sound waves, which helps avoid standing waves and resonant frequencies (the buildup of certain frequencies due to the natural resonance of the room). We generally use diffusion a bit more in the "live" or "recording room" (if you have a two-room setup) because we're usually trying to create a room with a natural, even-sounding decay in that instance. This is why you'll often see funny-shaped structures hanging from the ceiling or walls in a musical theater. These are most often diffusers of some sort. We'll talk a bit more about diffusion in a bit.

Tips for a Live Room

If you'd like to be able to record several people at once, you may not be able to fit them into your control room. In this situation, you may want to use an adjacent den or living room as your "live room." In this room, we usually want it to sound fairly balanced throughout the room, meaning that we want *some* reflections, but we want them to be scattered.

Ideal Rooms

The ideal room for this type of thing is a fairly large space—the bigger, the better—with hard floors and a high ceiling. You sometimes see this type of room in the ground-level living area of a two-story house. Of course, unless you live alone, the chances of you making use of this type of room for recording exclusively are pretty slim. (But it may be roomy enough to just temporarily move a few pieces of furniture out of the way when the need arises.)

Author's studio, opposite wall from studio desk

If the walls are filled with bookshelves, dressers, entertainment centers, sofas, etc., you may just end up with a pretty nice-sounding room on your hands naturally. Filled bookshelves make very decent diffusers, as does anything solid with curved or jagged surfaces. If you have access to this type of space, try making some recordings in it and see how it sounds. You can use close mics and also "room mics" to pick up some of the ambience of the room and blend it to taste. (We'll talk much more about this idea in later chapters.)

Bass Traps

Even though we do want ambience in a live room, bass traps in the corners are usually still a good idea if you can swing it. You can experiment with the amount to see if you can get away with less, but you'll most likely want to do the same as in the control room.

Diffusion

What you want to try to do is avoid parallel surfaces when possible. In this regard, if you place a diffuser on one wall, then it's not parallel with the opposing wall. So you don't need to have diffusers opposite each other. As mentioned, there are several objects found within the home that can make good diffusers, and a filled bookshelf is one of them.

Absorption

Aside from the scattering of panels along two of the walls perhaps, you'll most likely want to use absorptive panels in your live room if your ceiling is the standard height of eight feet (or close to it). This is simply too short to produce useable reflections. Therefore, it's best to hang two-inch thick panels—much like the "cloud" in the control room—covering most of the ceiling and therefore making it "acoustically invisible," so to speak. In fact, a low, absorptive ceiling is not all that different from a very high, diffusive ceiling when it comes to the sound.

Absorptive ceiling panels

Other Concerns for the Live Room

There are some other concerns in a live room besides the acoustics; these are the more logistic ones, like getting cables and headphones out there, etc. You could just run the mic cables (and headphone extension cables if necessary) under the door as needed, but if you'd like to have more of a permanent setup, here are some tips:

- **Mount a snake to the wall and send it through a small hole in the wall (assuming the live room is adjacent to the control room)**: You can make the hole look halfway nice by simply adding a wooden border around it.
- **Add a headphone amp on a shelf near the snake and run the cable to the control room**: If you have the ability and/or need to generate different mixes for numerous performers, you can have several line mixers (with four or six channels, for example) with headphone jacks, so that each person can tailor the mix as they see fit; drums could be mono on channel 1, bass on 2, etc. (More on this later in the book.)
- **Run some RCA cables out to a simple stereo system in the live room that can be used as a simple playback system or a talkback system**: This can be an inexpensive old boombox even, as it's not meant for critical listening.

You can get as fancy as you'd like with this type of thing. You'll have to evaluate your particular needs and go from there.

TOOLBOX

Live End/Dead End

If you have a decent-sized control room—say, 20 feet or longer—another option is a *live end/dead end* arrangement. In this scenario, you'd set up one end of the room as a typical control room, creating a reflective-free zone for the listening position. But on the opposite end, you could add diffusers, a hard floor, and absorptive panels on the ceiling to create a live end to the room. Granted, this won't really be generating any reverb, but it will generate some ambience, which is especially nice when recording acoustic instruments.

Other aspects of studio treatment include creating a vocal/isolation booth—both permanent or temporary—and we'll look specifically at that idea in Chapter 10.

Chapter 3: Wish-List Equipment

Beyond the basics listed in Chapter 1, there are still plenty of other pieces of gear you could add to your arsenal if you so desired or needed. In this chapter, we'll take a look at the most common. You may want to come back to this chapter after you've gotten your feet wet a bit and have discovered what you like, hate, lack, or lust for in the world of home studio gear.

Item 1: Outboard (Hardware) Signal Processors

In this category, I'm including any type of hardware processor, such as rack-mountable effect units, compressors, equalizers, etc. (It could also apply to guitar effect pedals for that matter.)

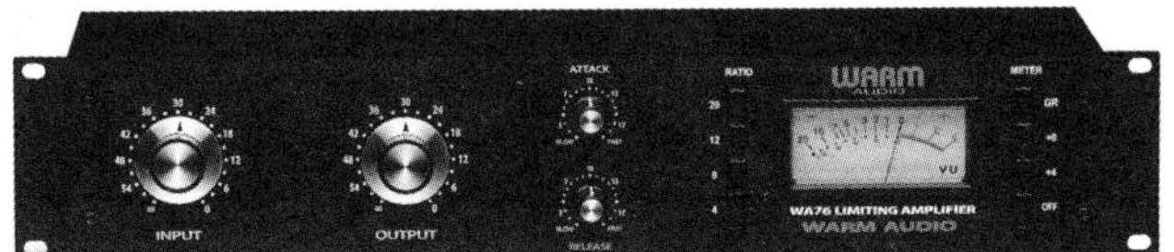

Vintage style compressors, such as the WA76 and WA-2A from Warm Audio, are popular outboard items.

TOOLBOX

Meet Mr. Patchbay

If you end up getting several different pieces of outboard gear, a *patchbay* can certainly make your life easier. This is a rack-mountable unit that's filled with nothing but jacks on the front and the back. Simply put, they allow you to bring all your gear's input and output jacks to a common place (the patchbay), so you don't need to get behind your gear every time you want to connect your processor (reverb, EQ, compressor, etc.) to a different place.

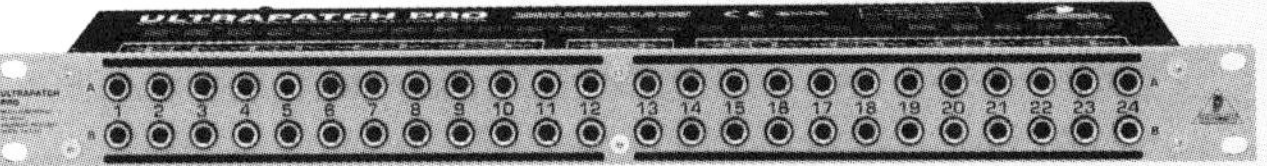

Behringer Ultrapatch Pro PX3000 48-point balanced patchbay

Item 2: External Mic Preamps or Channel Strips

Another extremely common piece of outboard gear is the external *mic preamp* or *channel strip*. What's the difference? Well, a channel strip is simply a mic preamp (or "pre") with a bunch of extra goodies built in, such as a compressor/limiter, equalizer, de-esser, exciter, etc., or any combination thereof. Mic pres (including the ones in the audio interface) can all sound noticeably different, and many people like to have several for the purpose of flexibility.

The Studio Channel, from PreSonus, combines a tube microphone preamp, a compressor, and a three-band EQ in one rack unit.

See Chapter 11 for more on outboard processors and preamps, etc.

Item 3: Additional Mics

Lots of mics sound significantly different, which means they're useful for different things. This isn't to say that you need a mic locker with 40 or 50 different mics in it (which isn't uncommon in pro studios), but at least one decent LDC (large-diaphragm condenser), one SDC (small-diaphragm condenser), and one dynamic would be a nice start. After you feel (if ever) that you've outgrown those, you can start thinking about expanding your collection. An identical pair of SDCs, for example, is especially nice for recording something in stereo.

Item 4: Additional MIDI Controllers

Another common MIDI controller is the percussion pad type, which is most often used for programming drum parts. You can generally control dynamics better than with a MIDI keyboard, and you're able to think more like a drummer in general. (We'll talk more about this in Chapter 9.)

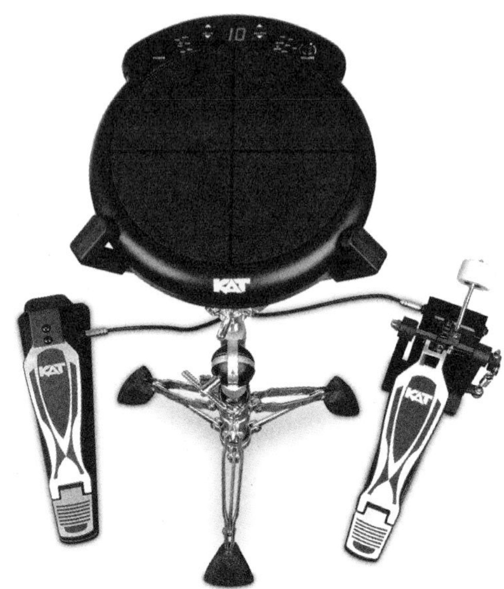

KAT KTMP1 Multipad Drum & Percussion Pad Sound Module

Other types of MIDI controllers include:

- **Pad controllers**: contain many smaller pads (usually 16 or more) and often knobs/faders, allowing you to access a large amount of samples, effects, etc.
- **Wind controller**: allows control of MIDI wind instruments, such as saxophone, clarinet, etc., with a familiar-feeling interface

PreSonus ATOM USB MIDI pad controller

Item 5: External Mixer

If you have an interface with only two inputs, for example, but you need to record a sound source with more than two channels (such as a drumset), you can use a mixer to "submix" a bunch of channels down to two. The big downside to this is that, once you've recorded the drums, you'll lose the ability to control the relative level of each drum (i.e., make the snare louder) because you'll have recorded the whole kit just as a stereo source. But, if you absolutely want real drums, but you don't have an A/I with a bunch of inputs, sometimes it's the only way.

Soundcraft EPM8 analog mixer

Other uses for a mixer include allowing yourself to listen to several different sources (your CPU stereo mix, aux input such as an iPod, etc.) through the same speakers and/or hearing your CPU mix through different sets of speakers for reference. Some mixers, such as the Tascam Model 16, even serve as an A/I as well, in a sense combining the role of an A/I and a control surface.

Item 6: Control Surface

A *control surface* is a nice way to bridge the power of the software DAW to the analog feel of a mixer. Most of them work via MIDI and USB connection, and they allow you to control the features of your software DAW program with actual knobs, faders, buttons, etc. They range in complexity from fairly basic models, such as the single-fader PreSonus Faderport, to incredibly sophisticated models with enough buttons and gadgets to just about negate the need for your mouse altogether.

Many of them will come from the factory already configured to work with particular DAW programs, but most of them can be configured to work with just about any. There's often a bit of a learning curve, however, with this type of thing, so you may have to do a few online searches here and there to get everything running smoothly. The X Touch from Behringer is a full-featured control surface with motorized faders, scribble strips, a jog wheel, and an LED display that will increase your workflow and provide you with incredible tactile control over countless DAW features.

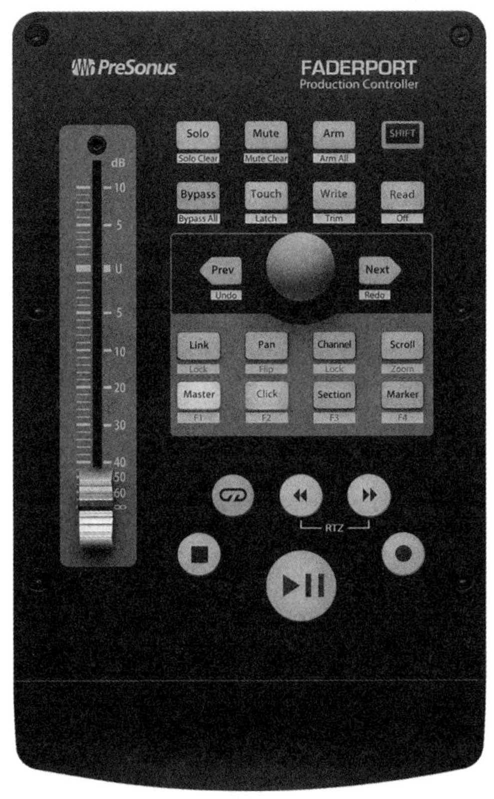

The PreSonus FaderPort Production Controller includes a motorized fader and allows tactile control of numerous DAW functions, including volume, pan, automation, navigation, and much more.

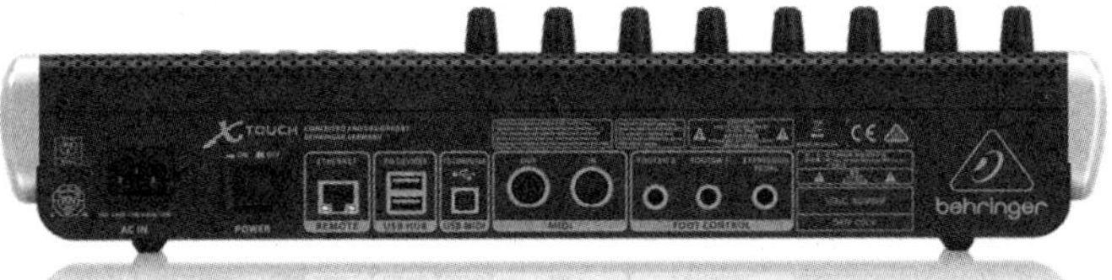

The X Touch from Behringer contains nine motorized faders, eight endless rotary encoders, a jog wheel, and a slew of buttons, many of which can be assigned custom functions, depending on your particular DAW.

OSC (open source control) is another common protocol for controlling DAWs and is particularly useful for wireless applications with a tablet or phone. There are dozens of apps available for this (for both iOS and Android), and set-up isn't too difficult. It's a great solution if you're recording on your own and want to be able to control your DAW while you're in the next room or something.

Chapter 4: Anatomy of a DAW

In this chapter, we'll examine the aspects of the DAW (Digital Audio Workstation) so you can get acquainted with its basic functionality. While every program is slightly different (and there's always a learning curve when moving to a new system), the basic operating procedure from one to the next is the same; they just may have slightly different names and/or keyboard shortcuts for the processes.

Inputs and Outputs

The audio signals enter and exit your system through your audio interface, which can be one of many different types and include many different features. See Chapter 1 for details on audio interfaces.

DAW Program/Sequencer/Recorder

The most commonly used music production program, and the industry standard, is Pro Tools. However, there are dozens of alternatives now that are widely used throughout the recording world. Some of the most common include GarageBand, Logic Pro, Digital Performer, Sonar, Reason, Cubase, Studio One, Nuendo, Reaper, Ableton Live, and FL Studio, to name but a few.

Effect Plug-ins

Another extremely common type of software is that of effect *plug-ins*. These are basically "virtual" versions of all the effects that used to only be available in rackmount or pedal format, such as reverb, delay, EQ, compression, etc. (We'll look much more closely at effects in Chapter 13.) Many DAW programs come with many effects, but you can also buy them individually one at a time, filling up your "virtual rack" as necessary.

Studio One Compressor plug-in

TOOLBOX

Mac OS vs. Windows Again!

Although the vast majority of effect plug-ins (and virtual instruments) are available in both Mac and PC formats, the files are often not compatible. In other words, whereas most PC plug-ins come in a VST format, most Apple plug-ins come in an AU format. This is a simplification, because it's really more reliant on the DAW program, but certain DAW programs will only run on one or the other (Mac or PC). Here's a brief summary of the most common plug-in formats and compatibility:

- **VST (Virtual Studio Technology)**: Windows and Mac OS
- **AU (Audio Units)**: Mac OS
- **RTAS (Real Time Audio Suite)**: Windows and Mac OS
- **DirectX**: Windows
- **DSSI**: Windows, Mac OS, Linux
- **LADSPA**: Windows, Mac OS, Linux
- **LV2**: Linux

It should be noted, though, that even though a program may be offered in VST format for both Mac and Windows, for example, you'll need to download the specific version associated with your platform.

Generally speaking, you'll have a folder in which all your plug-ins are kept. There will be a setting in your DAW that allows you to specify this location. Whenever your DAW boots up, it will check this folder and load all the plug-ins, making them available for you to use.

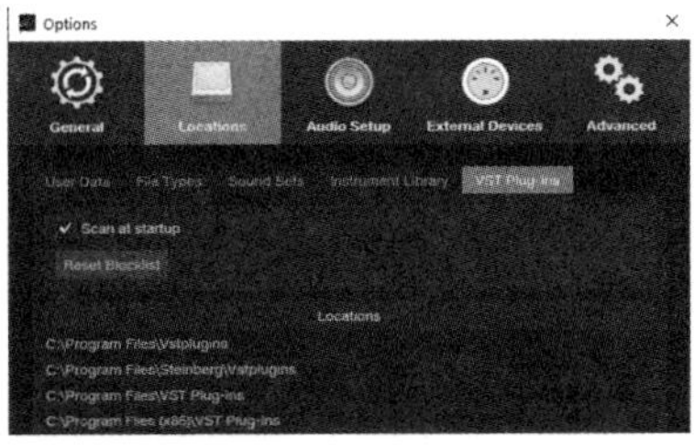

In Studio One, the VST folder location is specified in the Setup menu.

If you try to run too many plugs simultaneously, your system can become sluggish, and the audio can become glitchy. Most DAW programs will have a performance meter that allows you to see which programs are using the most memory. There are ways around this, however, and we'll talk more about that in Chapter 13.

Virtual Instrument Plug-ins

The Mojito virtual synth plug-in in Studio One.

This is where the MIDI controller comes in. There's a myriad of virtual instruments, controlled via MIDI, that mimic the sound of just about any type of instrument you can imagine—from an organ to an upright bass and anything in between. As with effects plug-ins, virtual instruments are generally kept in the same folder and are available in various formats for Mac and PC platforms.

DAW Layout

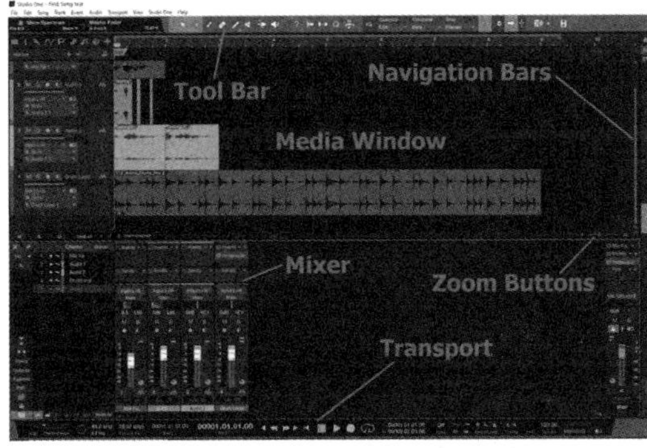

Typical screen layout in Studio One.

Now that we've got a broad picture of what's going on within the DAW program, let's see how it ticks. There are several different sections of the screen where various features exist and functions are performed. Again, each program may be slightly different, so these areas may be named slightly differently, but many of them are roughly the same with only slight variation.

Menu Bar

Just as with a word processor, you'll normally have a *menu bar* along the top that will include multiple pull-down menus.

Tool Bar

Underneath the menu bar is often a *tool bar*, which generally consists of graphic icon shortcuts of the most commonly used menu items. This can usually be customized to include the functions you'd like.

Track Control Panels

These areas give you various controls over each track in your project, allowing you to name each track, arm/disarm them for recording, add plug-ins, etc.

Main Window/Waveform Display/Media Window

This window goes by several different names, but it's easy to spot because it's normally the focal point of any DAW. It displays the waveforms of the audio tracks and the MIDI data for any MIDI tracks. It's the part of the screen you'll most often use for editing since most operations involve manipulating one or more of these waveforms. You can also usually import audio/MIDI files by dragging and dropping them onto this window.

Zoom Buttons and Navigation Bars

These will appear along the side and bottom of the media window and allow for zooming in vertically/horizontally or scrolling through your project along its length. All of these functions can also be controlled by various mouse movements or command (shortcut) keys.

Timeline

The *timeline* runs along the top of the media window and lets you know where you are within your project. You can set it to display measures and beats, minutes and seconds, or both.

Transport

The *transport* is the collection of buttons, such as play, record, etc., that mimic the functions of old tape machine recorders.

Mixer

Generally placed along the bottom of the screen, the *mixer* is just that: a virtual mixer that resembles its real-life counterpart. Each vertical channel allows in-depth control of track features, and each will typically display the level meter as well. The main mix channel is normally found on the far bottom right corner.

TOOLBOX

No Way Around the Manual

For those who don't like reading manuals, learning to use a new DAW may not be all that fun. These programs are so powerful and flexible that the manuals can easily run 500 or 1,000 pages or more. Granted, you certainly won't be using most of the features described in a comprehensive manual on a regular basis, but you will no doubt have to crack open the manual many times to get up and running at first.

Templates

If you find that you generally end up recording the same group of instruments for each song, you can create a *template* to save time. This way, you just start the DAW, load the template, and there you are—all your plug-ins, levels, panning, etc., are all set the way you saved them. Then you would simply save the song under a new name.

Metronome (or Click)

As mentioned earlier, the timeline can display minutes/seconds/frames or measures/beats (or both). While the minutes/seconds display is helpful for scoring a movie or commercial, the measures/beats display is more helpful when recording a typical pop song. Every DAW has a metronome or click track that can be turned on or off. After setting the project's tempo, you can record your basic tracks along with this click track so that the measures/beats display will correctly align with your song.

A Brief Look at Signal Flow

The idea of *signal flow* was a bit easier to grasp in the days of tape because most of the elements (recorder, mixer, etc.) were separate pieces of gear. With a DAW, however, much of the signal flow is virtual, so you can't trace any physical cables. However, the idea is the same, and that's what we'll look at here. Let's boil the signal flow down to its most basic state:

1. A signal enters an input of the A/I.
2. The signal is sent to the recorder and recorded on the appropriate track.
3. The signal is played back from its track on the recorder.
4. The signal is possibly manipulated (via EQ and/or effects).
5. The signal arrives at the main mix.

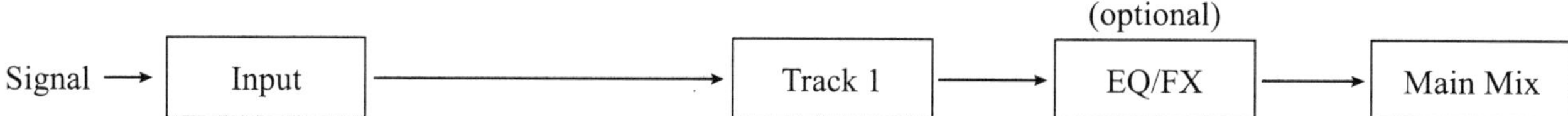

This is quite an oversimplification of the process, but essentially, that's what's happening. Now let's fill in some of the blanks to see how this works in an actual DAW.

1. A Signal Enters the Input

Let's say this is a microphone recording a voice. You plug the mic into channel 1 of your interface and adjust the trim to a good recording level. Create a new track, select channel 1 of your interface as the input device, and arm the track for recording.

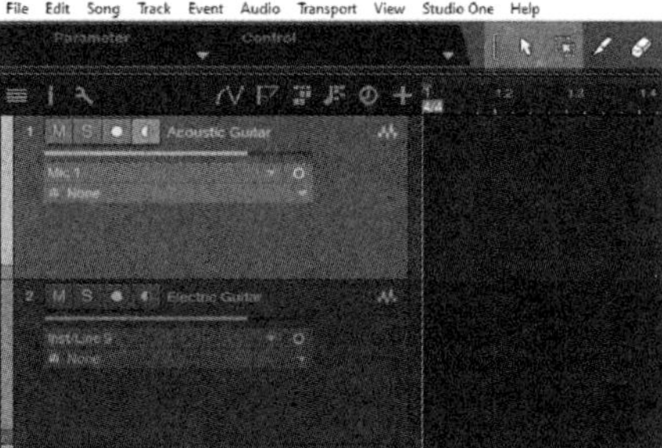

Track 1 is armed, and the input level is good.

2. The Signal Is Sent to the Recorder and Recorded on the Appropriate Track

Since we've assigned our channel 1 interface input to Track 1, the signal will then be recorded onto Track 1. You can then disarm Track 1.

The signal is recorded to Track 1.

3. The Signal Is Played Back from Its Track on the Recorder

At this point, you'll be monitoring the playback signal from Track 1, and it will be displayed on Track 1's level meter.

4. The Signal Is Possibly Manipulated (via EQ and/or Effects)

You have the option of EQ-ing the signal or adding effects via plug-ins. (External hardware effects are also a possibility, which will be covered later.)

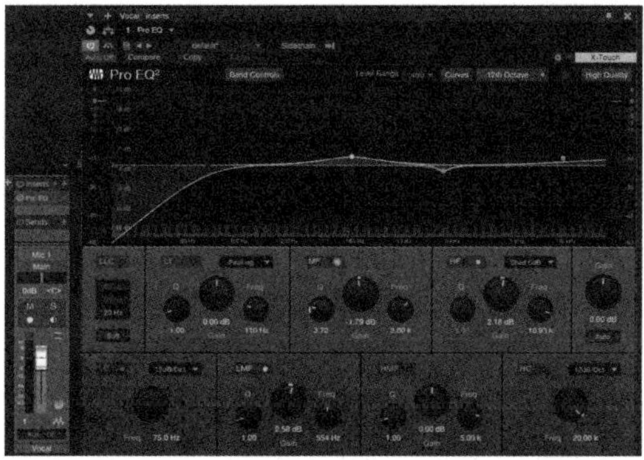

An EQ plug-in has been inserted on Track 1.

5. The Signal Arrives at the Main Mix

After all is said and done, the signal usually reaches its main destination: the main mix. (Signals can also be routed to other destinations, but this just illustrates a typical scenario.)

Now that we have a basic idea of what's going on, let's look at some of the other possible stops along the way.

Sends and Buses

After you've recorded a few tracks and gotten your feet wet with adding effects to tracks via plug-ins, you're eventually going to want to look at using *effects sends* and *buses*. These two terms have a relationship akin to a square and rectangle. In the same way that all squares are rectangles, but not all rectangles are squares, we can say that all effects sends are buses, but not all buses are effects sends. (Note that some people spell "bus" as "buss." They mean the same thing.) But let's look specifically at the idea of effects sends first.

Effects Sends

So, let's say you just recorded a piano on Track 1 and want to add some reverb to it. The seemingly easiest method is to insert a reverb plug-in on Track 1. On the reverb's interface, there will usually be a mix knob that allows you to adjust the output anywhere from completely dry (0 percent, or no reverb) to completely wet (100 percent, or only the reverb signal). A typical value may be anywhere from 10 to 40 percent depending on the reverb's parameters. And there you have it! You have added reverb to your track, and it sounds great.

This is an example of a *series signal path* because the piano signal passes completely through the reverb and comes out the other end before carrying on to the main mix.

Reverb plug-in inserted onto Track 1.

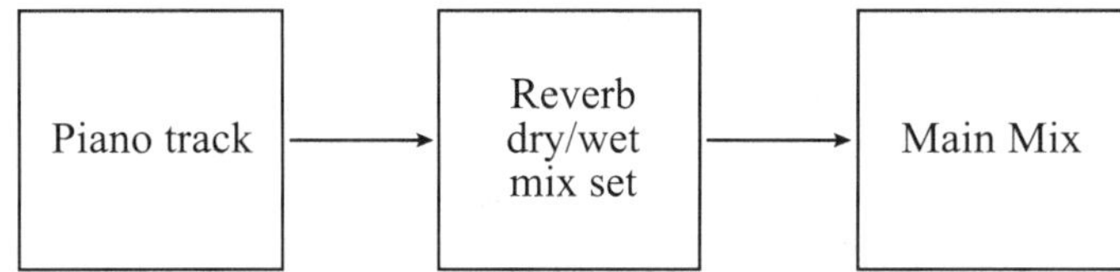

Now, let's say you decide to record two more tracks: a guitar and a shaker. You decide that you want them to have the same reverb as the piano to create the same musical "space." You could repeat the above procedure for tracks 2 (guitar) and 3 (shaker), which would result in three tracks, each with their own reverb plug-in added.

The problem with this method is that plug-ins eat CPU resources. Depending on your computer's specs and the particular plug-in, you could begin to experience glitches if you continue to stack up plug-in upon plug-in. The solution? An effects send!

Here's another way to accomplish the same thing without using nearly as much CPU power:

1. Remove the reverb plug-in from each track.
2. Now create an effects track and name it "Reverb."
3. Add the reverb plug-in to the effects track and set its mix at 100 percent wet.
4. At this point, you'll need to consult the manual of your particular DAW to find out how to create a send on a track. Once you figure out how to do this, create a send for tracks 1, 2, and 3. Their destination should be the reverb track.
5. For each send, you'll have a send level, which controls how much of the signal you want sent to the reverb. Studio One defaults to 0 dB, which, with the reverb set at 100 percent like we have it, will result in a very wet signal, so you'll most likely want to lower it a good bit.

Now, if you want more reverb on the guitar than the other two tracks, simply raise the guitar's send level. You can then use the reverb track's fader to control the overall level of the reverb.

This is an example of a *parallel signal path* because the piano, guitar, and shaker signals are split, sent to the reverb, and then joined again with their dry signals at the main mix.

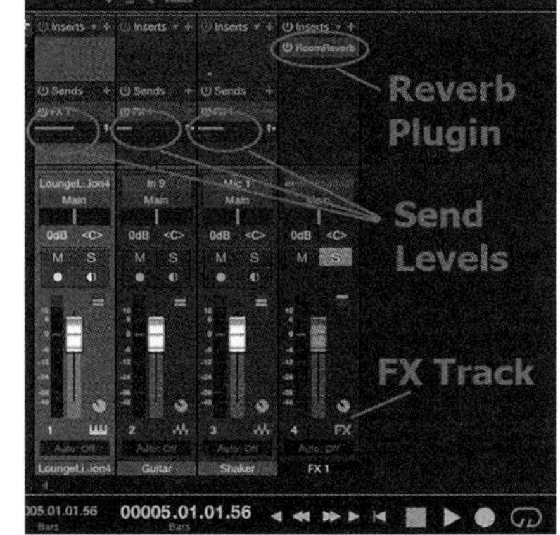

Though all three tracks are being sent to the same reverb, they each have different amounts applied.

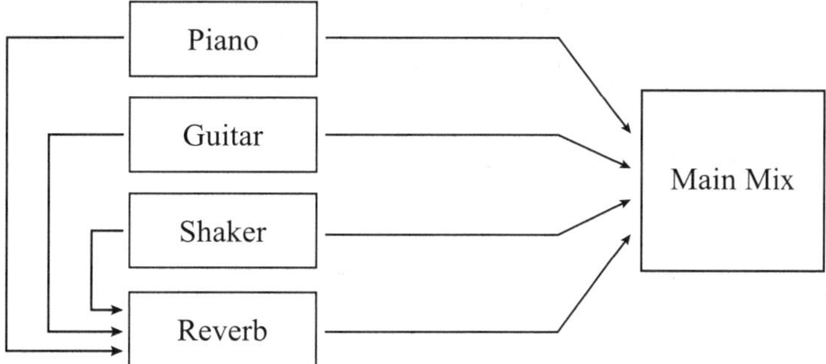

Buses

One of the most common buses is the *submix* bus. The idea here is simple: you want to control the volume of several tracks with only one fader. Drum buses are extremely prevalent because you're often dealing with 8 or more tracks (kick, snare top, snare bottom, high tom, mid tom, etc.) for one instrument. This is similar to an effects send, but there's one difference:

1. First, create a new bus track and name it "Drum bus."
2. Then create sends from each drum track to the Drum bus track. Make sure they're only sent to the Drum bus and not to the main mix as well. This is done differently depending on your DAW, so consult the manual if necessary. All of the drum tracks will now take a detour through the Drum bus track.
3. You then use the send levels for each drum track to adjust the mix that's being sent to the Drum bus. The Drum bus track fader then becomes the overall volume control for the whole drumset, and *its* signal is sent to the main mix.

This is another example of a series signal path because the drum tracks are passing completely through the bus and then on to the main mix.

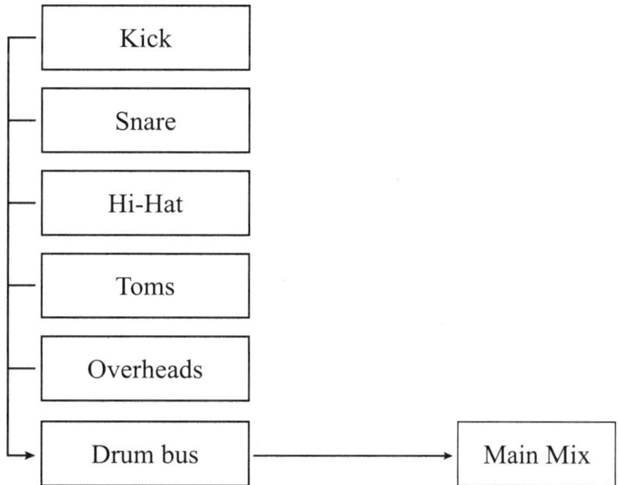

TOOLBOX

Extra Credit!
If the bus track were a stereo track, you would also be able to specify the *panning* on the individual drum tracks too. And, if you felt so inclined, you could then process this bus track with compression (a common practice), reverb, etc., which would affect the whole drum kit. You could even then send *this* bus track to a reverb bus track that had been setup for the rest of the instruments too!

There are plenty of other routing options that are possible within a DAW, but this is a good primer on the most commonly used features. As you learn your particular system, you'll no doubt learn the most effective way to use it for your unique needs.

Chapter 5:

Getting Your Feet Wet—Recording Your First Song

If you've managed to read the entire book without skipping to this chapter, I commend your sticktoitiveness. I know that some of this stuff isn't exactly like reading a best-selling fiction novel, but what can I say? Recording is a big world, and there's a lot to learn!

In this chapter, we're going to make a simple four-track recording to get some hands-on familiarity with the basic operation of a recording studio. I'll use an acoustic guitar, an electric guitar, a synth, and a bass. The reason for this instrumentation is to cover several different recording processes:

- The **acoustic guitar** will be recorded with a condenser microphone.
- The **electric guitar** will be recorded directly using an amp simulator device.
- The **synth** will be recorded using a MIDI controller and an external synth or sound module.
- The **bass** will be recorded using the direct out jack of a bass amplifier.

We'll record the instruments in the order listed above, but there's no rule with regard to this. Feel free to mix it up if you'd like. This chapter is about having fun while learning the ropes of your rig. We're not aiming to make a stellar piece of art here. I realize, of course, that many of you may not be able to record each of these instruments (or may not want to!), so feel free to make substitutions if you'd like.

TOOLBOX

On the Level

Back in the days of analog—i.e., recording to tape—you wanted to make sure to record as "hot" as possible to avoid tape hiss. With digital recording, tape hiss isn't a concern anymore. What is a concern is *digital distortion*. This occurs when the signal level breaches 0 dB, and it results in a nasty, unpleasant distortion.

Therefore, it's a good idea to leave plenty of headroom when first recording your tracks. Try to get your peaks around -15dB or so, and that should be fine. We can always bring up the tracks later (and we will), but if you record too hot and end up breaching 0 dB, you can ruin a take forever.

Step 1: System Setup

The first step, if you've not already done it, is to make the physical connections of your system. Yours may differ slightly depending on your particular situation, but it shouldn't be too far off. Make all these connections with the power off on all components to be safe.

1. Plug the outputs (or channel 1 and 2 outputs if your interface has more than two) from your interface into your monitors. (If you're not using powered monitors, you would plug the interface outputs into your power amp and then run speaker wires from the power amp to the monitors.) The output plugs on your interface will likely be 1/4-inch or RCA type, and your monitors should have one of those types of inputs available. (Most powered monitors have more than one type of input jack.)
2. Plug your interface into your computer via USB/Firewire/Thunderbolt cable. Follow the instructions for your interface to get it installed correctly.
3. Plug a pair of headphones into the interface's headphone jack.

There are other connections we'll need to make along the way, but they're specific to the various tracks we're recording, so we'll cover them as needed. Test the system quickly by playing some music through your computer to make sure you can hear it through your speakers. If not, you may need to set your interface as the default sound device of your computer.

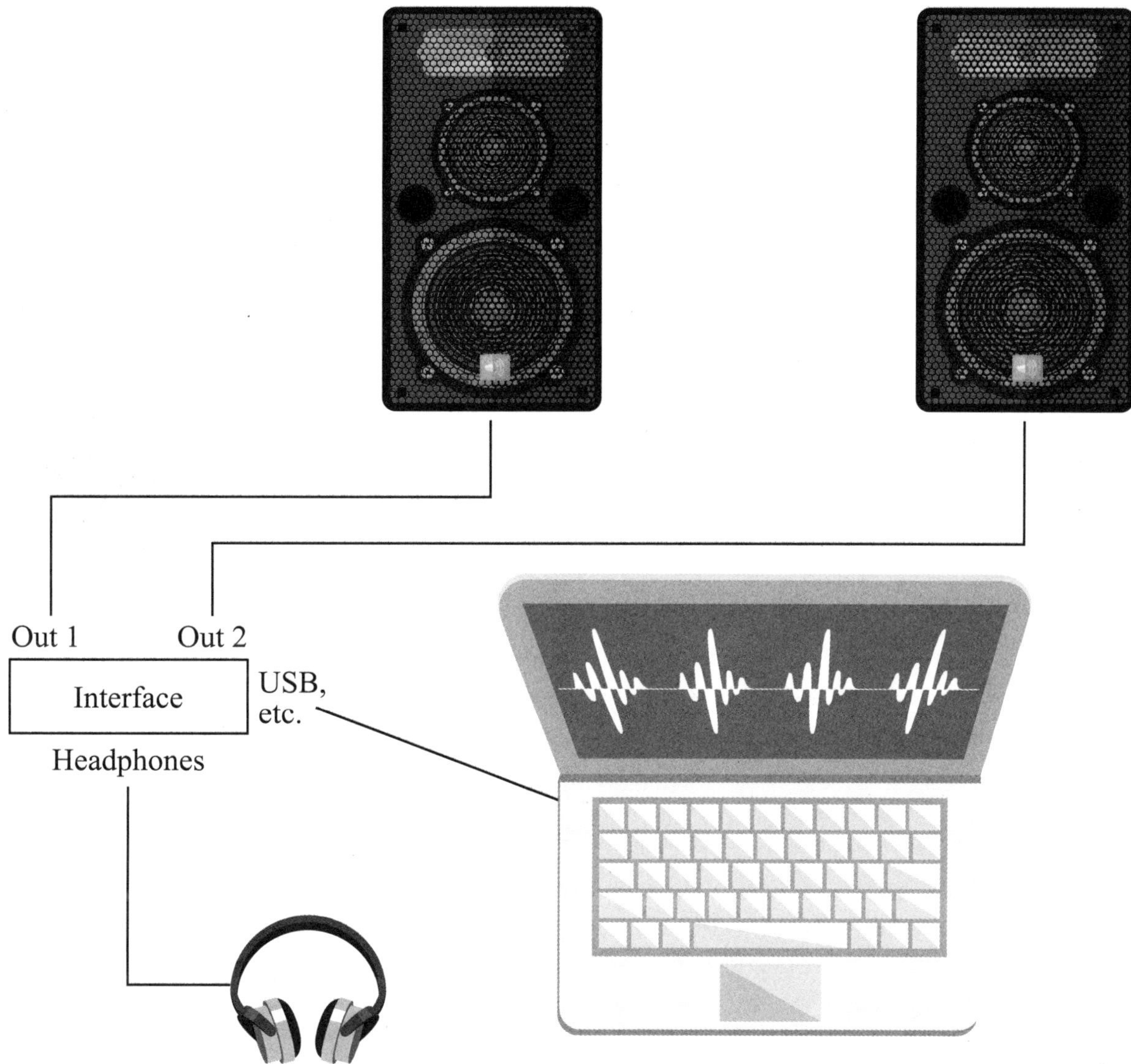

TOOLBOX

System Sounds and Other Tweaks

If you're using a computer that's specifically dedicated to your recording, then it's best to turn off all system sounds in your operating system, as these can sometimes create glitches in your recording software. It's rare, but it only takes one time to ruin the best vocal take of your life!

There are usually several other tweaks you can make to help improve the performance of a recording-dedicated computer. Unfortunately, it's beyond the scope of this book to cover them, but you can easily read about them online.

Step 2: Project Setup

The first thing we need to do is create a new song (or it may be called a *project*). This should be fairly self-explanatory but check your manual if necessary. Then, we need to make a few decisions: the name of the song, the time signature, and the tempo. For our purposes, we'll call it "First Song," it will be in 4/4, and the tempo will be 100 bpm (beats per minute). Make sure the metronome (or click) is turned on.

Note: I use Studio One as my DAW, and therefore, the screenshots I use will come from that program. Consult your DAW's manual as necessary.

TOOLBOX

Where Are My Files?
The first thing you need to do on a DAW system is make sure you know where the files are going to be saved. Consult your manual if necessary. You can, of course, change this location later, but be sure you know where to look in the beginning!

The next step is to add four tracks. Name them as follows (or adjust them according to your instruments):

- Acoustic Guitar
- Electric Guitar
- Synth
- Bass

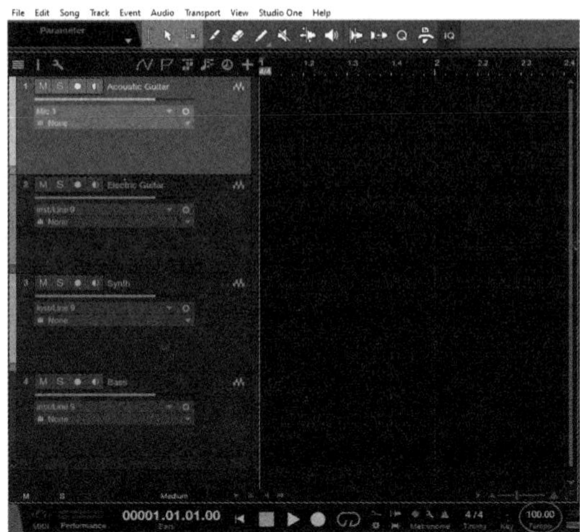

New project in Studio One with a 4/4 time signature, a tempo of 100 bpm, and four tracks added.

Step 3: Recording Track 1

Our first track is going to be an acoustic guitar, and we'll record it with a condenser mic. It doesn't matter right now which kind of condenser mic you're using, as we're just learning the basic idea. You don't need to worry too much about mic placement right now, but a good starting point is pointing toward the neck/body joint about a foot away. After reading the important sidebar on phantom power, run a mic cable from your microphone to a mic input (preamp) on your interface.

TOOLBOX

Important Note Regarding Phantom Power!
Never plug your condenser microphone into (or unplug it from) an interface or preamp while phantom power is on. *Always* switch off phantom power first, wait five seconds or so, and then plug in the mic. After the mic is connected, you can then switch on phantom power. To unplug the mic, do the reverse: turn off phantom power, wait five seconds, and then unplug the mic. In other words, always make sure phantom power is turned off (for at least five seconds) when *connecting or disconnecting* the cable from the mic to or from the input jack of the interface or preamp.

Before you record anything, you'll want to make sure your instruments are in tune. The guitar could be in tune with itself, but if it's not tuned to A440, then you'll either have to tune every other instrument from thereon to the guitar or re-record the guitar (tuned to A440 of course!). Try to use the same tuner for all the instruments, as this can make a slight difference.

Make sure your speakers are turned down or off at this point to avoid possible feedback issues if you're recording in your control room. After you've set up the mic in position, plug it into channel 1 on your interface and turn on phantom power.

TOOLBOX

Feedback Issues and Speaker Bleed

Pro studios are set up with separate control rooms and recording rooms. In a home studio, however, the control room and recording room are often one and the same. If this is the case, there's an issue that comes up when using a mic. You usually don't want your control room speakers on because:

- At worst, depending on the position, level, and orientation of the microphone, you could get some nasty feedback through the speakers.
- At the least, if the speakers are turned up too loud, the microphone will pick up the sound of the speakers bleeding into the vocal/acoustic/etc. track, which we generally don't want. (We'll talk a bit more about this in Chapter 10 when we discuss recording vocals.)

The simplest solution is to simply turn off your monitors (or power amp if using non-powered monitors) while you're recording with a mic. However, this can get a bit tedious, especially if you're doing everything by yourself.

Some interfaces will have a separate headphone level and output level, which allows you to turn the *output* knob down while you have a mic track armed and then turn it back up when the track is disarmed. On other interfaces, though, the output knob affects the volume of both the headphones and the signal sent to the output jacks. What to do then? Again, you could turn off your speakers, but there's another way.

The **TC Electronic Level Pilot** is the answer. This little unit is basically a volume control that you can insert between the output of your interface and your monitors. So, you can have the volume up on your interface if necessary to be able to hear your headphones, but you can then turn down your monitors all the way with the Level Pilot.

TC Level Pilot Desktop Volume Control

You'll then need to assign the correct input to track 1. On a DAW, this is usually done with a pull-down menu on the track control panel, but refer to the manual if necessary. Make sure that you have *input monitor* enabled (if it's not done automatically), as this will allow you to hear what you're recording on track 1 as you're recording it. This is usually done with a switch on the track control panel. Now arm the track by placing it in record enable mode.

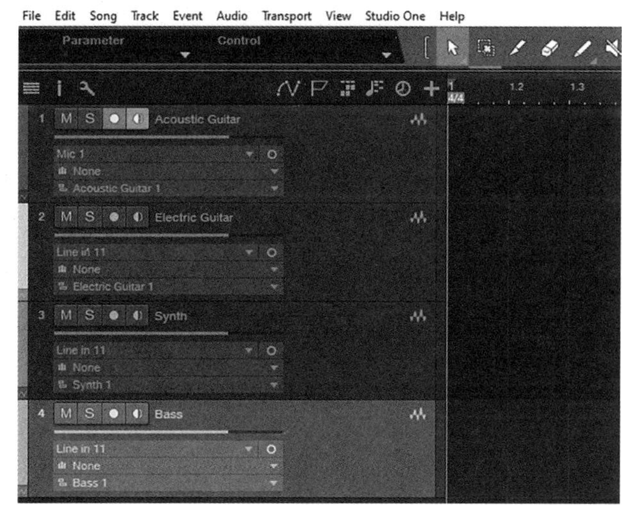

Studio One: "First Song" with track 1 input assigned (mic 1) and armed for recording.

Turn the input/trim knob on channel 1 of your interface up to about the 12 o'clock position to start. Sit in playing position and strum the guitar a few times, making sure the OL (overload) indicator on your interface doesn't light. Make sure the fader on track 1 of your DAW is in the nominal position (0 dB). If you put on headphones, you should now be able to hear the sound of the mic. Strum the guitar some more and watch the signal on track 1 of the DAW, making sure that the level doesn't reach above the -15 dB marker (roughly) on the peaks. Adjust the trim knob on your interface more if necessary to achieve a healthy level.

TOOLBOX

Setting Levels

Note that the trim knob on your audio interface is independent of any level in your DAW. Turning up the fader on Channel 1 of your DAW, for example, will have no effect on the level of the input signal. It's important that you set that properly on your audio interface, as that will ensure you have the appropriate level being sent to the recorder within your DAW. The channel fader on your DAW will only affect the volume that you hear through your speakers or headphones.

TOOLBOX

Click Bleed?

It's a good idea when recording with a mic to check for click bleed before you start recording real takes. This can be done by sitting in playing position and recording with the metronome enabled. Record a few seconds, stop, and then turn off the metronome on the DAW or recorder. Then disarm the track (so you're not hearing the mic anymore) and listen back to what you've recorded. If you can hear the click, then it's too loud in your phones and is bleeding into the mic.

There are three possible remedies:

- Use close-backed headphones if you're not already.
- Turn down the volume of the metronome in your DAW.
- Choose an alternate sound for the click if possible that doesn't bleed as much.

Once you have a good level on the acoustic guitar and there is no bleed from the click, you're ready to record the track. Depending on your DAW's default setting, there may be a *pre-roll* set. This means that when the click is enabled and record is pressed, it will count out several beats (often four) before it actually starts recording. (The mobile version of GarageBand defaults to this behavior, for example.)

Start recording, allow a measure or two of lead-in, and start playing! After you've recorded, you should be able to see the audio file in the media window. If you mess up, simply undo the recording and try again. Once you have a satisfactory take, you're ready to move on to the next track. Disarm track 1 (i.e., take it out of record-ready mode), turn off phantom power on your interface, wait five or ten seconds, and then unplug the mic cable.

TRACK 1: Acoustic guitar recorded to track 1

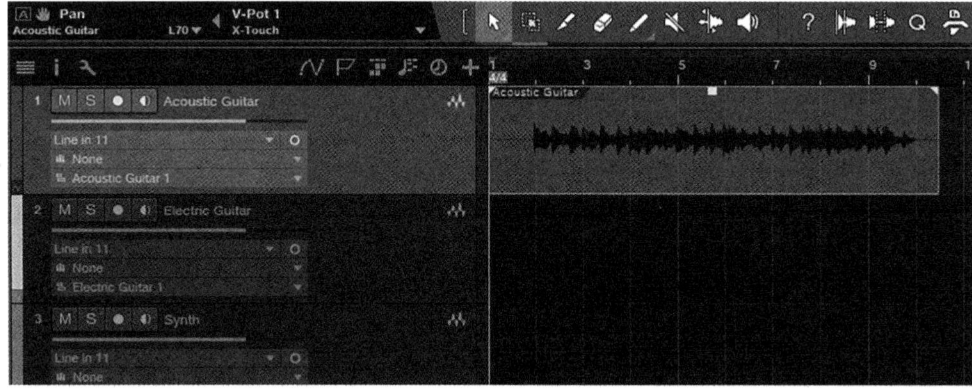

First track recorded.

Step 4: Overdubbing Track 2

Now that you've recorded the acoustic guitar, it's time to overdub the electric guitar on track 2. Turn your speakers on (or turn the volume up). We're going to record the electric guitar using an external amp simulation device. This can be a modeling amp with built-in effects and a direct out jack (such as a Line 6 Spider V60 or Vox Valvetronix VT100X), or a multi-effects unit with amp simulation capabilities, such as the Line 6 HX Stomp.

Line 6 HX Stomp Multi-Effects Processor Pedal

Plug your guitar into the input of the device. Run a guitar cable from the direct out of the device (use the left/mono output if there is more than one) to a 1/4-inch line input on your interface. Since the effect unit will be sending a line level signal to your interface, make sure you select the line level option for your input, if applicable.

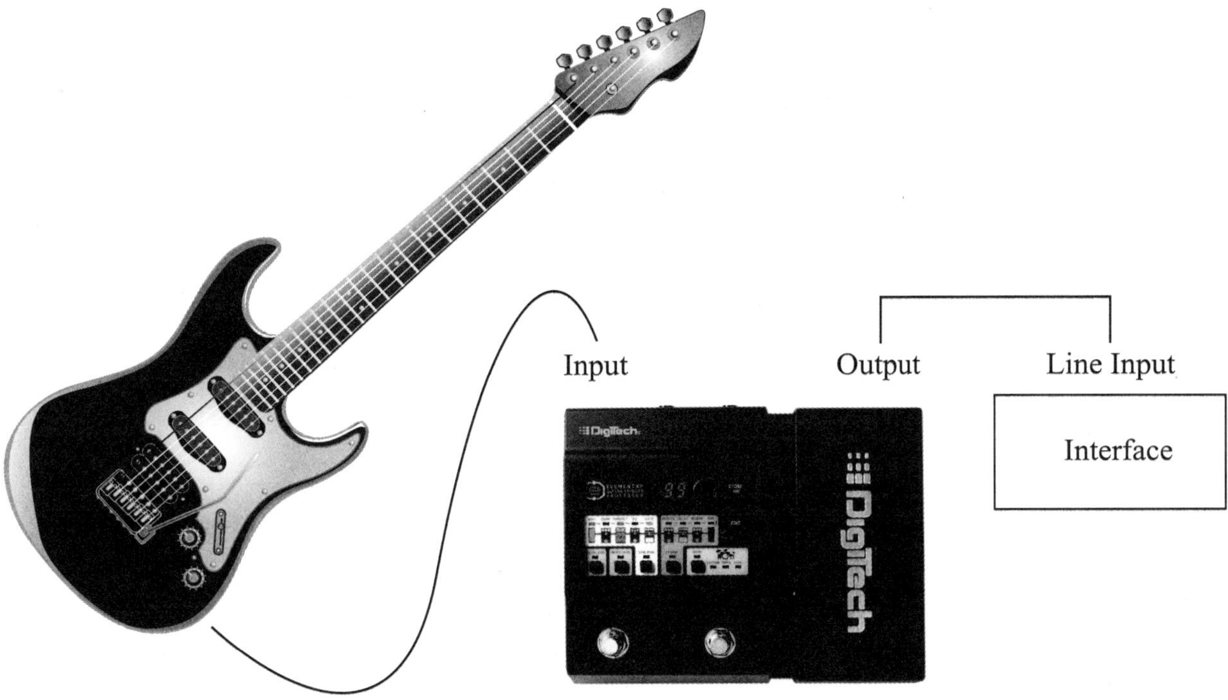

Assign the input from the interface to track 2. Turn up the output level on the amp simulator, arm track 2 for recording, and enable input monitoring. You should now be able to see the recording level and hear the guitar through your monitors. Select the sound you'd like on the amp simulator and adjust the volume so that you're getting a good level going into the DAW, with the peaks going no higher than -15 dB to be safe.

Make sure track 1's fader (acoustic guitar) is turned up and press play. This will allow you to check the level of the acoustic vs. the electric. Adjust the mix (i.e., turn track 1 up or down) as necessary until you reach the desired level for each. When you've got a good mix, rewind to the beginning and hit record.

Again, if you mess up, hit undo (one of the benefits of digital recording) and try again. Once you're satisfied, disarm track 2, rewind to the top, and give it a listen.

"First Song" with tracks 1 and 2 panned L and R.

TRACK 2: Tracks 1 and 2

At this point, you can make the first of many mixing decisions: *panning*. (You could do so after track 1 as well, but when there's only one instrument, there's really no reason to.) Let's try panning the acoustic guitar to the left (about the 9 o'clock position) and the electric guitar to the right (about the 3 o'clock position). This will help make each instrument more distinguishable and easily heard.

TRACK 3: Tracks 1 and 2 panned left and right

Step 5: Overdubbing Track 3

Now let's overdub a synth line using an external synth or sound module. In this way, we'll be treating the synth as a normal audio instrument rather than a MIDI track within the DAW. (We'll cover MIDI later.) For this, we can just use an external synth with its own onboard sounds or use a MIDI controller to play sounds from a sound module or synth, such as the Behringer Model D.

If necessary, plug a MIDI cable from the MIDI output of the controller to the MIDI input of the sound module. Then run an audio cable from the output of the sound module/synth to one of the input channels on your interface/recorder. Again, this will be a line level signal, so make the appropriate adjustments on your interface if necessary.

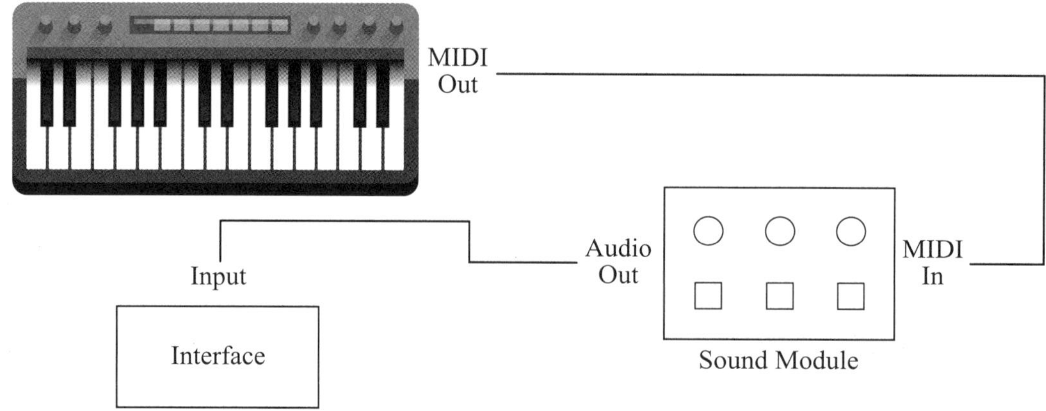

Assign the input from the interface to track 3 in your DAW. Turn up the output level on the synth and play some notes, adjusting the trim on your interface to get a good level. Arm track 3 for recording, enable input monitoring, and you should now be able to see the recording level and hear the synth through your monitors. Select the sound you'd like on the synth and double-check the level going into the DAW.

Play back the track and adjust the mix if necessary, making sure you can hear your synth above the guitars. Once you've got it the way you'd like it, rewind back to the top, hit record, and play your heart out. Since the synth is our lead instrument, we're going to leave it panned up the middle for now.

TRACK 4: Acoustic guitar, electric guitar, and synth

Step 6: Overdubbing Track 4

Finally, let's overdub some bass to tie it all together. We're going to plug our bass into a bass amp and then run from the direct out into the interface. This will require a bass amp with a direct out jack (not all of them have this). For this recording, I'll use an Ampeg Micro-CL bass amp.

Plug your bass into your bass amp and then run a cable from your amp's direct out jack to one of the input channels on your interface. (Again, use a standard input on the interface—not a guitar/bass direct input—as the signal will already be line level.)

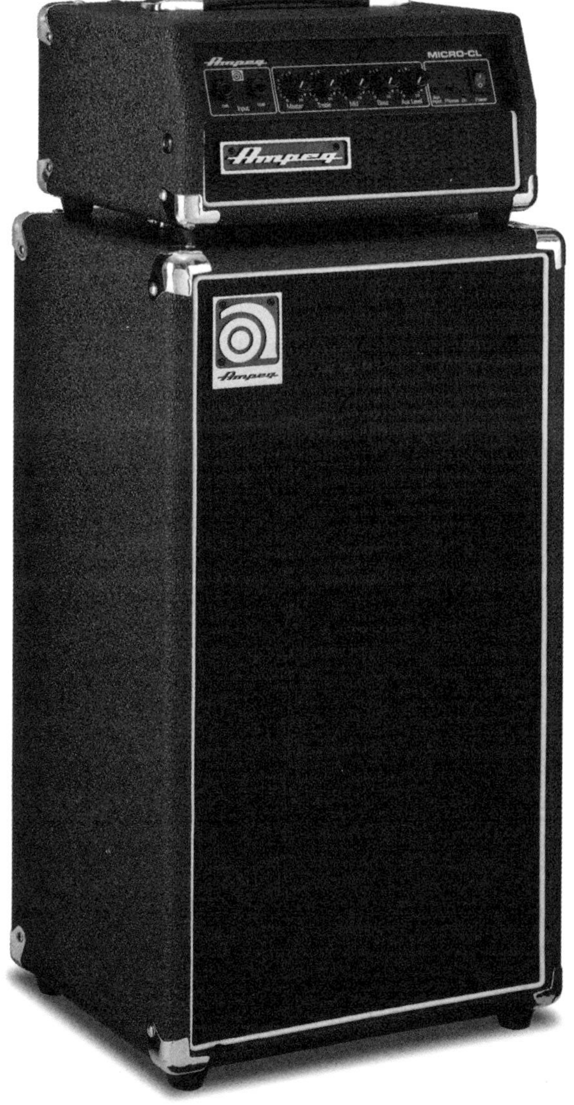

Ampeg Micro-CL

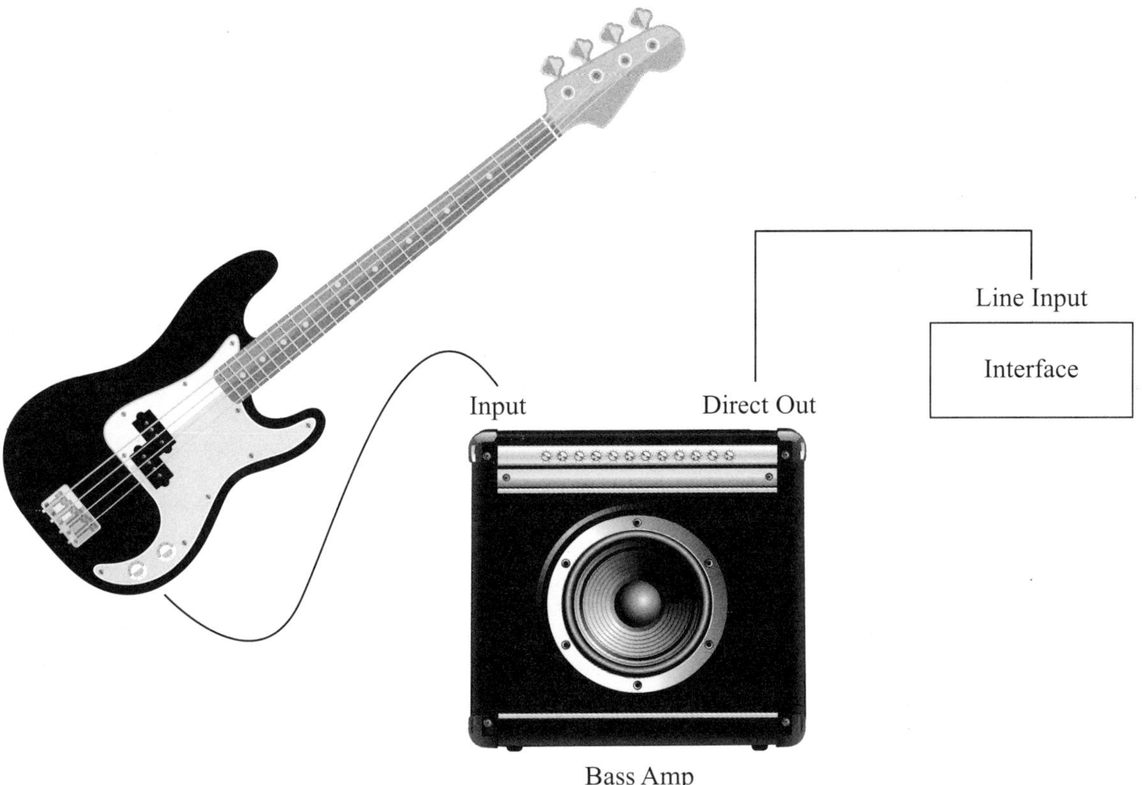

Assign the input from the interface to track 4 in your DAW. Play a few notes on your bass, slowly turning up the amp volume and adjusting the trim on the interface as necessary to avoid overload. Arm track 4, enable input monitoring, and you should be able to hear the bass through your monitors. Double-check the level going into the DAW.

Play back the track and adjust the mix if necessary, making sure you can hear your bass amidst the other instruments. Once you've got it the way you'd like it, rewind back to the top and record the bass.

TRACK 5: Acoustic guitar, electric guitar, synth, and bass

That's it for the tracking! In case you haven't yet, turn off the metronome and give it a listen without it.

Step 7: Editing

We're going to keep the editing phase very simple here and basically just clean up the tracks. This means getting rid of any extraneous noises at the beginning and end of the track (or possibly in the middle of a track if you're not playing for a significant length of time). We'll examine editing more in-depth in Chapter 12.

This is where you really start to see the power of digital audio. In order to clean up the noise at the beginning of track 1 (acoustic guitar), for example, we simply need to select the track item (just by clicking on it usually) and place the cursor at the point just before the audio begins. You can zoom in a bit on the horizontal axis to get a bit more precise if you'd like.

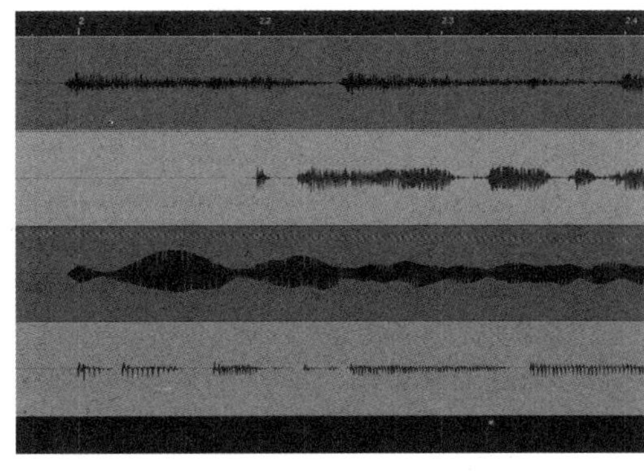

Zooming in allows for more precise editing points.

TOOLBOX

Snap/Grid Settings

If your DAW is not letting you place the cursor in specific points and it keeps moving to one beat or the next, it's likely that you have the "snap" option enabled (it may have different names in other DAWs). This is a setting in which the cursor will "snap" like a magnet to the nearest beat (or whichever division you have set). Although this is very helpful in certain instances (such as when dealing with loops or MIDI tracks), it doesn't allow enough precision for cleaning up tracks. So turn it off for this process.

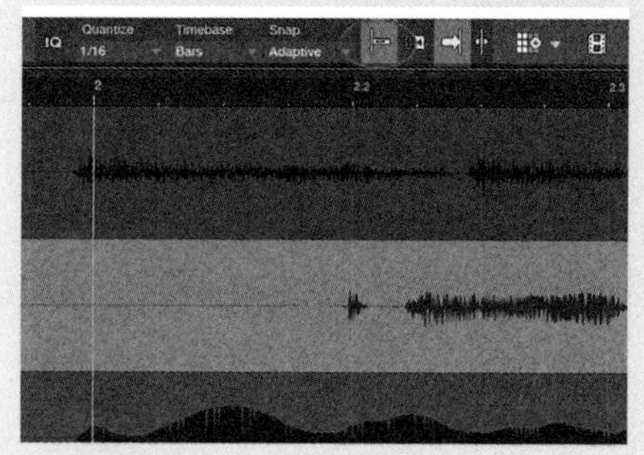

With the "snap" function on (note circled icon in toolbar), the cursor will always snap to the grid. For more precise editing, turn this feature off.

Once you have the cursor in the right spot (just before the first strum begins), you just need to *split* or *cut* the audio item. In Studio One, ALT-X is the default command key for this, or you can find the same action listed in a menu. (Consult the manual for your particular DAW.) Once you do this, you'll have two items. Simply select the first item (click on it) and delete it. (The delete key usually does this.)

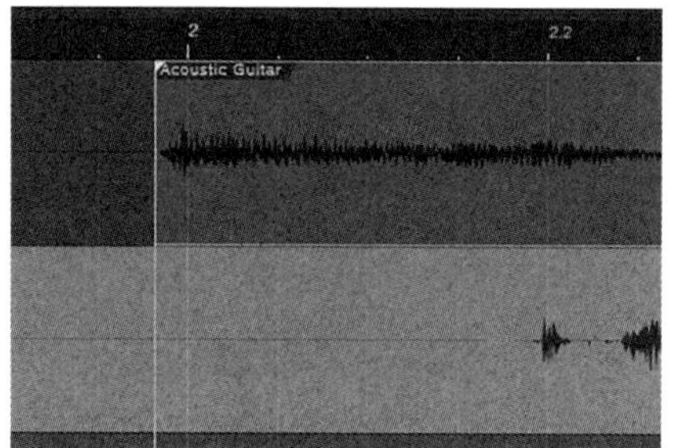

Track 1 (acoustic guitar) is split just before the first strum begins.

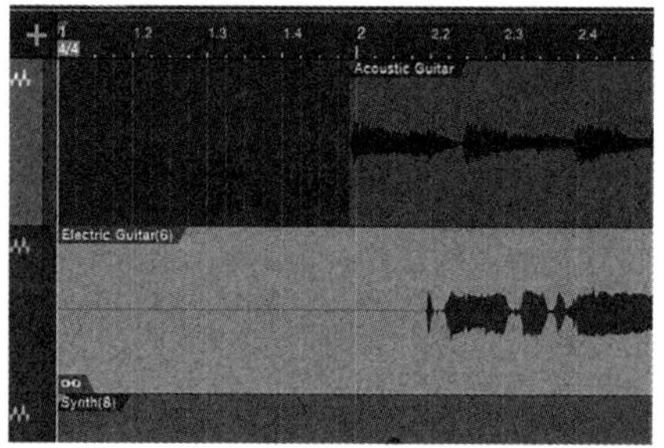

The first item (with intro noise) is deleted.

To hear the result of what we've done, click the solo button for track 1. This will often have "solo" or "S" on it and can usually be found on the track control panel or in the mixer section (or both, likely). Once you've soloed the acoustic track, it will be the only instrument you hear. Play it from the beginning, and you should hear absolute silence until the first strum—the magic of digital editing!

TRACK 6: Acoustic guitar track soloed and trimmed

Now repeat the same process for each of the other tracks, and you should end up with something like this:

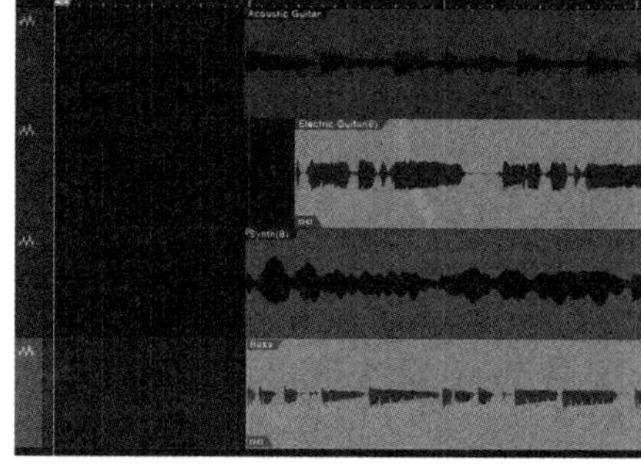

Cleaning for all four tracks is complete.

Step 8: Mixing

So, you've got your tracks recorded and edited, and now it's time to mix them down to a stereo file that can be played in your car, on your mobile device, etc. As with the editing step, we're not going to spend a lot of time on mixing at this stage, because we'll be covering it in depth when we get to Chapter 13. But we'll look at a few basic concepts here.

Panning and Volume Adjustments

Let's first look at panning and volume (or level) adjustments. Take a moment to move the panning around and experiment with different ideas to see what you think. There are no rules in this regard, so if something strikes your fancy, go with it!

For example, here are several different mixes at this point with different panning configurations:

TRACK 7: Acoustic guitar: middle, Electric guitar: hard right (all the way), Synth: hard left, Bass: middle

TRACK 8: Acoustic guitar: hard left, Electric guitar: 10 o'clock, Synth: 2 o'clock, Bass: hard right

 **TRACK 9:** Acoustic guitar: hard right, Electric guitar: hard right, Synth: hard left, Bass: hard left

With regard to the levels of the tracks, one thing to be aware of is the level on the master fader. You want to make sure the song never breaches the 0 dB marker, as this would risk digital distortion, which is not a pretty sound. Play the song and watch the master meter. Ideally, you want the peaks to stay below the -6 dB range, as this will give the mastering engineer plenty of room to work.

If the peaks are rising much further than that, don't pull the master fader down; it should always be left at 0 dB for most applications. Just pull all the track faders down by the same amount. On a DAW, there are two easy ways to do this:

- Select all four tracks (via the mixer or track control panels), pull the fader down for one, and all four will move in sync. Or:
- You can usually enter the exact fader value via the keyboard with most DAWs. You can simply lower them all by the same number (-2 dB, for example). If you have all the tracks selected when you do this, they should all move down by the same amount.

Adding Effects

After you've got the panning and levels worked out, you may want to add a bit of ambience to the tracks so they don't sound so dry and close. *Reverb* is a very common effect for giving instruments a sense of space and making them feel as though they're situated together. So, we're going to use one reverb and add it to all the instruments.

Instead of adding a plug-in for each track, we're going to create an *effect send* and only use one plug-in (see page 32, "Sends and Buses," for an introduction to this idea). You'll likely have to consult your manual to see how these steps are performed in your DAW.

1. Add an effects track and name it "Reverb."
2. Select a reverb effect for the track. For our purposes, I'll use a simple reverb patch that comes with Studio One called Room Reverb. Leave it set for 100% wet (effect).
3. Create a send for each track and route them to it (Reverb).

If you press play now, you'll most likely hear that all of the tracks are heavily drenched in reverb.

 **TRACK 10:** All four tracks very wet with reverb

In order to dial the reverb back a bit, you have two options:

- Turn down track 5's fader. This will lower the level of reverb on all four tracks evenly. Or:
- Turn down the send level of each track until the desired amount of reverb is reached.

All four tracks are being routed to track 5 (Reverb).

We're going to use the second option because we want to vary the amount of reverb that each track has.

TOOLBOX

Reverb Tips

Again, there are no rules with regard to effects, but there are some conventions. Here are some with regard to reverb.

- The less reverb a track has, the more in-your-face it will sound. The more reverb it has, the farther away it will sound.
- You will usually hear more reverb in your headphones than you will through your speakers, so be sure to listen to your mix on both to make sure you're not overdoing it.
- Bass-frequency instruments, such as a bass guitar or kick drum, generally don't sound as good with a lot of reverb because they tend to become muddy. These instruments usually receive the least amount of reverb of all, if any.
- Related to the previous point, reverb itself can tend to muddy up things in the low end, so it's very common, especially when applying it to instruments in a full mix, to add a hi-pass filter on a reverb. This means you're essentially EQ-ing out the bass frequencies of the reverb. Which frequency you choose to place the filter at is a matter of taste and depends on the instrumentation. It could be as low as 200 Hz or as high as 1K or higher. Experiment and see what sounds best.
- A very basic guide to applying reverb when you want a fairly "natural" sound is to add it until you can clearly hear it and then back it off just a tad.

Here's another listen to our mix with a more realistic reverb level for the tracks. The amount ranges from the synth (most) down to the bass (almost none).

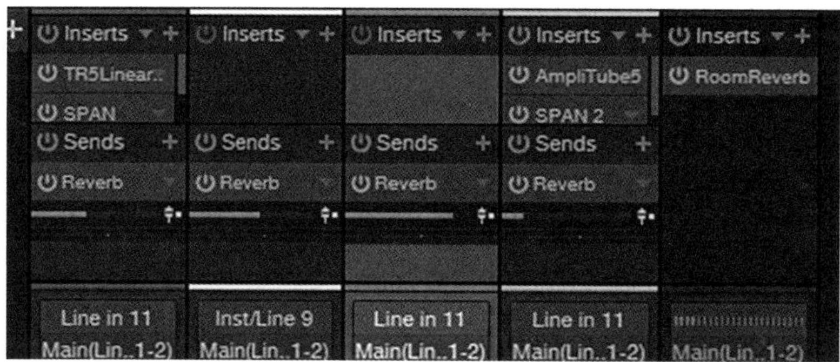

Reverb levels after being adjusted.

TRACK 11: Reverb levels adjusted

Again, this is only a fraction of what's entailed in the mixing process. We didn't get into EQ, compression, or any other effects, not to mention fancier things like automation, etc. We'll take a look at those things and more in Chapter 13.

For now, congratulations on recording, editing, and mixing your very first song!

Chapter 6: Recording Guitars

Is there anyone who doesn't love a great guitar sound? After all, if there's one instrument that's basically *the* sound of rock 'n' roll, it would have to be the guitar. With the numerous options available today, there's never been a better time to get stellar guitar tones out of a home studio.

Electric Guitars

The electric guitar is capable of a massive variety of tones—from rip-roaring distortion to sparkling clean and everything in between. In order to get the desired sound, it helps to use the proper tools. If you're trying to record super-heavy distorted guitars but you're using a Pignose portable amplifier and a Fender Telecaster, you're likely to be disappointed. On the other hand, that same setup could excel if you wanted to record some Mississippi Delta-style blues guitar.

Certainly, there are guitars, such as a Gibson Les Paul and Fender Stratocasters (and various guitars based on them), that can do many things well, just as there are versatile amps. But there are also instruments, amps, etc., that are more specialized. So, with regards to purchasing gear, if you're going to need to cover a wide variety of styles and you're working on a budget, keep that in mind when choosing your tools.

A good Strat-style guitar, such as this ESP LTD ST-203, is very versatile in the studio.

I'll be using various electric guitars for the tracks in this book (see "About the Recordings").

TOOLBOX

First Things First!
Before you record anything, always remember to tune up with a tuner! Just because you tuned up two days ago doesn't mean you don't have to today!

There are several options for recording electric guitars today, and they each have their own advantages and setbacks. But they can all yield terrific-sounding guitar tracks. The decision on which to use will depend on your own specific needs, situation, and budget. We're going to break it down into three main categories:

- Miking an amplifier
- Recording direct with an external amp simulation device
- Recording direct with an amp simulation plug-in

Miking an Amplifier

Let's start out with the oldest, most well-established method of them all: *miking an amplifier*. Not surprisingly, this is often the preferred method for older players who grew up doing this for years before "amp simulation" became a catchphrase.

Lower wattage tube amps, such as the Vox AC15C1 (left) and the Fender '57 Custom Champ (right), are common in home studios because they can generate natural-sounding tube distortion without peeling the paint off the walls.

TOOLBOX

Shake, Rattle, and Rock 'n' Roll
One thing you'll want to pay attention to when setting up to record an amp is mechanical noise. This is especially true when recording a loud amp. Make sure nothing is rattling or shaking while the amplifier is making sound. This includes the amp cabinet itself (possibly a loose screw somewhere, tube, etc.), anything sitting on top of the amp, or anything on the walls, such as clocks, etc.

With the increasing popularity of amp simulators over the past 15 years, some younger recordists these days may have never even tried miking an amp. If you fall into this category, I'd encourage you to give it a shot, as it can be a really rewarding experience when done well.

TOOLBOX

Recording Procedure
The most basic method is to simply aim a mic at your amp, plug it into your interface, arm the track(s), and set your levels. However, it's quite common to track guitars (regardless of recording method) with compression as well. See Chapters 11 and 13 for details on this. Since we're using a dynamic mic, phantom power is not needed.

Single Microphone Techniques: Dynamic Mics

Perhaps the most common method of miking a guitar amplifier is that of *close-miking* with a dynamic mic, such as a Shure SM57 or SM7B, Sennheiser MD 421, or Electro-Voice RE20. The Shure SM57, in particular, is one of the best bangs for the buck in the recording world. It can be had for around $90 new (about $50 used) and is an undisputed staple on many sound sources—most notably guitar amps and snare drums.

One common method is to place the mic a few inches from the grill, on-axis—i.e., directly perpendicular to the grill—and a few inches to the side of the speaker cone. It's also common to lift the amp off the floor by placing it on a chair, stool, etc.

For this first example, we'll compare two different dynamic mics: a Shure SM57 and a Shure SM7B. The amp will be sitting on a small desk several feet away from the short wall of my room. Since I'm going for a somewhat distorted tone here, I've got the amp cranked a good bit (about 7 or 8). These recordings will be completely dry with no reverb or any other effects added.

Vox AC15 close-miked with a Shure SM57 dynamic microphone.

Vox AC15 amp close-miked with a Shure SM7B dynamic microphone.

TRACK 12: Vox AC15 close-miked with SM57

TRACK 13: Vox AC15 close-miked with SM7B

As you can hear, the SM7B—in the same position as the SM57—will have a bit more bass response, among other things.

And now let's hear what happens when I simply pull the mics away from the amp about two feet. Not only does the tone drastically change, but you can really start to hear the room showing up on the recording. (This will be even more pronounced in headphones.)

TRACK 14: Vox AC15 miked with SM57 pulled back two feet

TRACK 15: Vox AC15 miked with SM7B pulled back two feet

TOOLBOX

Role of the Room

By miking an amp closely (with a dynamic), you're minimizing the sound that the room will have on the recording. The *farther you move the mic* from the amp, the *more room you will hear* on the recording. This can be a good thing or bad thing, depending on how your room sounds. You'll also hear less bass response the farther you move the mic due to *proximity effect*. (See page 79 for more on this.)

If you'd like to further minimize the room on the recording, or you need to isolate the guitar track from sound leaking from other instruments (if recording several people at once, for instance), you can surround the amp with baffles or use a prefabricated device, such as the CAD Acousti-Shield AS16.

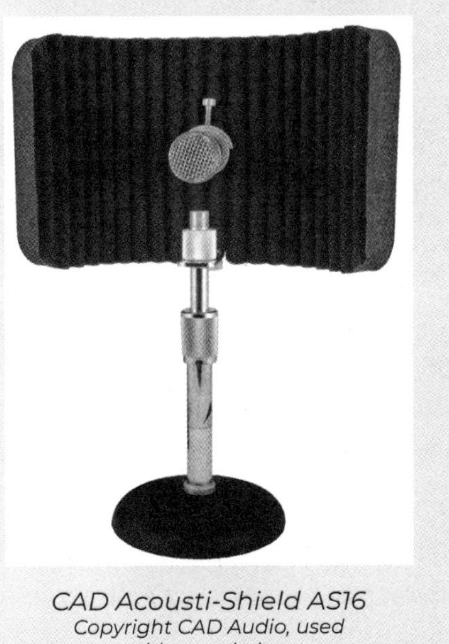

CAD Acousti-Shield AS16
Copyright CAD Audio, used with permission.

Compare this recording with Track 12.

TRACK 16: Close-miking with CAD Acousti-Shield AS16 and SM57

Let's now hear the same thing, only this time the amp will be in a very dead-sounding closet with a carpeted floor and gobos on most of the walls. I've also moved the mics about one inch farther to the side from the center of the cone, resulting in a little less bite. Compare these tracks to tracks 12 and 13.

TRACK 17: **Vox AC15 in dead closet miked with SM57**

TRACK 18: **Vox AC15 in dead closet miked with SM7B**

It should be clear that there are many variables in the sound of a miked amplifier. Moving the mic even an inch—not to mention changing mics—makes a very noticeable difference in the sound.

TOOLBOX

Other Variations on the Single Dynamic Mic

Aside from the method(s) I just demonstrated, there are several other common techniques for a single dynamic mic, including:

- **Off-axis**: By varying the angle of the mic respective to the grill, you'll alter the tone. Generally speaking, on-axis will provide the brightest tone; the more off-axis you move the mic, the darker and bassier the tone will become.
- **Different areas of the speaker**: While the cone will produce the most biting, present tone, moving toward the edge of the speaker will result in a smoother tone.
- **Varying distance from grill**: I demonstrated the difference between a few inches and two feet, but there's obviously a lot of leeway between those two. Six inches is a common distance as well.

It's well worth it to spend several hours recording the same guitar riff with many different setups (on-axis mic, off-axis mic, varying distance, varying amps, different guitars, etc.) so you can learn *your equipment*. (A looper pedal is *very* handy for this purpose, since it will play the riff for you *exactly* the same each time!)

Single Microphone Techniques: Condenser Mics

Another option is the condenser mic, which will usually give a slightly more detailed sound. Regarding mic technique, it's not terribly different from that of a dynamic. However, if you're recording *very* loud guitars, you'll probably want to engage the pad (attenuator) on the condenser mic—if it has one—to be sure no damage will come to the mic's delicate diaphragm mechanism.

Let's have a listen to the sound of the Vox AC15 amp close-miked with a Warm Audio WA-14 mic.

TRACK 19: **Vox AC15 miked with WA-14 condenser mic**

And here's the same mic pulled out about two feet from the amp. With a condenser mic, the room is even more apparent with this setting than when using a dynamic. This makes the condenser mic the obvious choice for when you want to deliberately add an ambient "room" sound to the track.

TRACK 20: **Vox AC15 miked with WA-14 condenser two feet back**

Dual Microphone Techniques

It's also very common to blend a dynamic mic with a condenser mic to form a composite sound. In this instance, you could record both signals to one track (pre-mixed), or you can record each mic to its own track and blend them at mixdown. If you have the resources, the second option will give you more flexibility, including the ability to fix any phasing issues should they occur (see "Don't Forget About Phase!" later this chapter).

Both mics can be set close to the grill, or one can be close and one far away to pick up more ambience. When placing both mics the same distance from the amp, remember that the *diaphragms*—not the grills—are the deciding factor. If you can align both diaphragms, you shouldn't have any phasing issues.

Let's combine a Shure SM57 (close-miked on the cone) with a WA-14 a few inches to the side. In the audio track, you'll hear the riff played three times: once using only the SM57, once using only the WA-14, and then once with both of them combined.

TRACK 21: Vox AC15 miked with SM57 and WA-14

And now, let's do the same thing, but this time we'll pull the WA-14 about three feet back and one foot above the Shure mic. Notice the added ambience from the room.

TRACK 22: Vox AC15 miked with SM57 (close) and WA-14 (three feet back)

On these tracks, I blended the dynamic and condenser mics about 50/50, but you can vary the mix as necessary. If you want more "bite" to the track, you might blend more of the dynamic. If you want more "body" or maybe more "air," you might add more of the condenser. Again, experiment to see what sounds best.

Recording Direct with an External Amp Modeling Device

One alternative to miking an amp is to use an external amp simulation device. If you get the recording bug at 2:30 AM and just *have* to lay down that distorted riff, an amp simulator will allow you to do so with no sound at all other than that bleeding from your headphones. Amp simulators have come a long way since their introduction decades ago, and it's now entirely possible to get completely realistic-sounding tracks using them.

TOOLBOX

Recording Procedure

Plug your guitar into the amp modeler and run a cord from the modeler's output into a 1/4-inch line input on your interface. Don't use the "guitar/bass" (high impedance) input on your interface, as this signal will already be coming in at line level. Arm the track and set the levels. (Note: If you plan on using stereo effects on the device, you will run cords from both the left and right outputs into two channels on your interface. You'd then assign them to two tracks and pan those tracks left and right to achieve the stereo spread.)

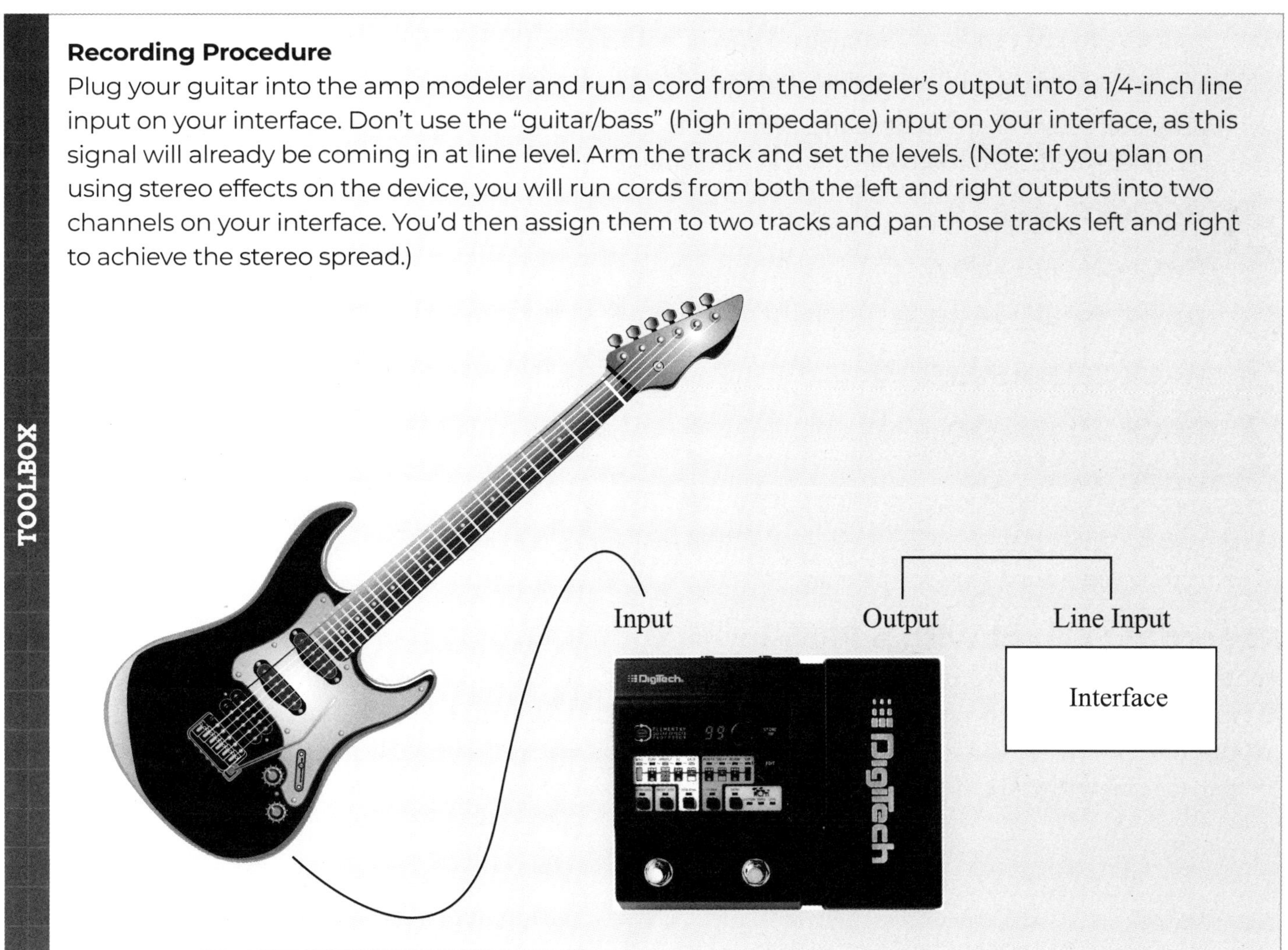

Amp modelers come in various formats, including tabletop, rackmount, and pedals. Be aware, though, that not all multi-effect pedals have built-in amp modelers—some just contain effects—so be sure to check this feature before purchasing!

Line 6 HX Stomp

Hotone Ampero

There are also many modelers in full-fledged amp format as well, such as the Line 6 Spider series, Peavey Vypyr series, etc. These amps all feature built-in effects and amp simulation, and you can run a line from their direct out jack into your interface when wanting to record direct.

You can choose to print some of the onboard effects (such as reverb, delay, phaser, etc.), or you can record them totally dry (using only the amp/cab simulation) and add effects on mixdown.

Let's take a look at several different sounds from the Line 6 HX Stomp to get a glimpse at its versatility. All of the effects (if added) on these tracks come from the HX Stomp.

TRACK 23: Essex A30

TRACK 24: Beach Fuzz

TRACK 25: ArchetypeLed

TRACK 26: Matchstick

TRACK 27: VoltageQueen

TRACK 28: TexasJS

As you can see, these little guys can pack quite a bit of tone into a very manageable size. Again, though, be sure you have the tone you want before you commit!

Recording Direct with a Plug-in

Another common way to record electric guitars direct is with software—i.e., an *amp modeling plug-in*. This affords the most versatility of all because you can record the guitar part with the amp sound you want, but you don't have to print the effect while you record it (although you can if you want). If you decide later that there's too much distortion, for example, you can change the tone completely.

TOOLBOX

Recording Procedure
Plug your guitar into your interface's dedicated guitar/bass (high impedance) input if it has one. If you don't have one, you should run through a DI box first. Then run an XLR cable from the DI box into the XLR input on the interface. Assign the input to a track, arm it, and check your guitar's level.

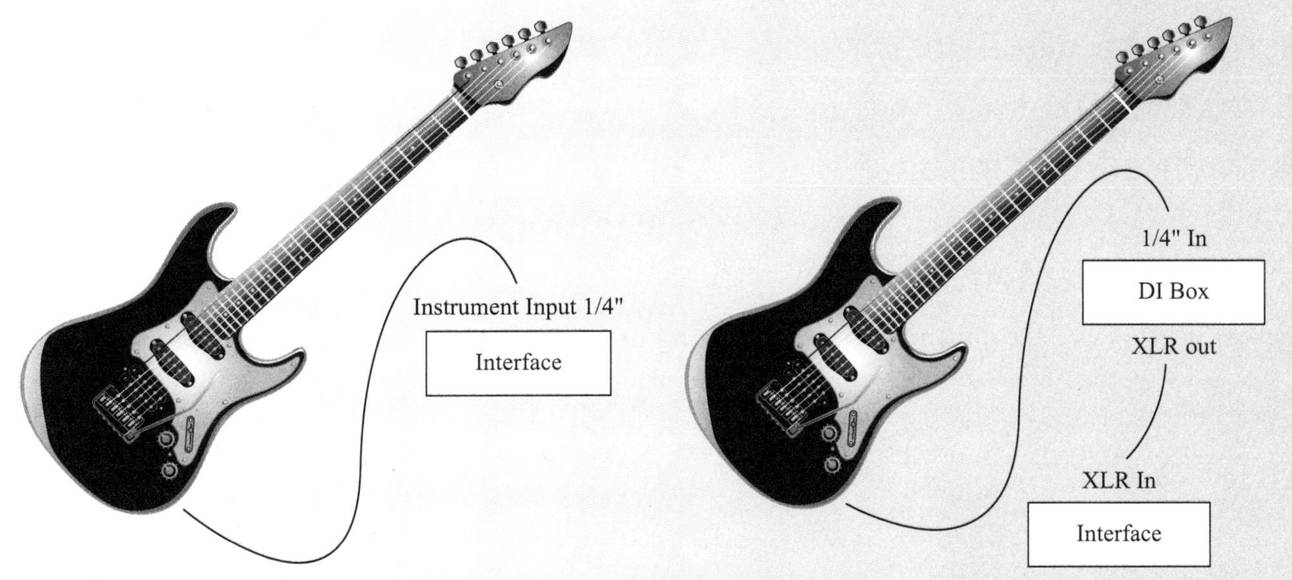

Select your amp modeling plug-in and check your levels once more before recording. (Consult your software's manual for the finer details of tone-shaping, including setting the levels within the plug-in.) This method allows you to monitor (listen to) the amp modeling effect while you record, but it *won't print the effect to the track.*

There are many great-sounding affordable amp modeling plug-ins on the market, including IK Multimedia's AmpliTube and Line 6's Helix Native, among others. They all feature fairly similar capabilities, but their user interfaces and functionality differ, as well as their sounds. For the direct recordings in this book, I used AmpliTube 4 from IK Multimedia, which allows for amazing control of an arsenal of amps and effects.

IK Multimedia AmpliTube 4

Copyright IK Multimedia, used with permission.

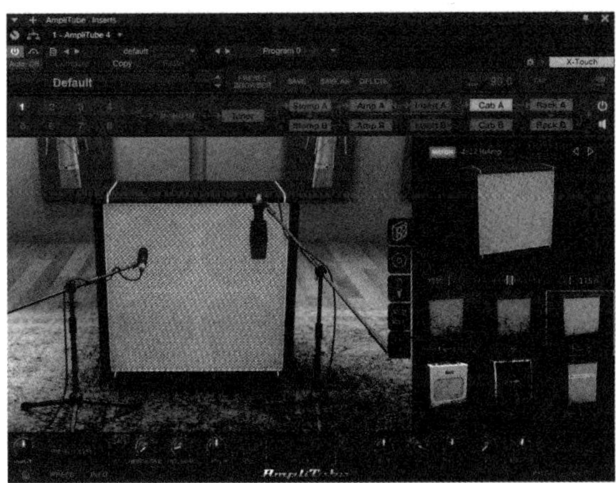

IK Multimedia's AmpliTube 4 lets you completely customize your speaker cabinet configuration, including mic choice(s) and location, room type, and more.

Let's take a listen to some of the amp models and effects within AmpliTube 4. All of the effects (reverb, delay, etc.) heard here will come from the plug-in.

TRACK 29: 65 Twin

TRACK 30: A Dirty Blue One

TRACK 31: Brit 8000

TRACK 32: American Dirty Tremolo

TRACK 33: Dual Metal Mesa Attack

TRACK 34: Dirty Ballad

Acoustic Guitars

Whether it's the sole accompaniment in a folk song or simply a background texture, the acoustic guitar has been a mainstay in the recording world since the beginning. As an instrument, it's an invaluable addition to anyone's studio.

A nice dreadnought acoustic, like this Martin D-10E, is a very versatile studio instrument.

A 12-string acoustic, such as a Seagull Walnut 12, is ideal for creating lush strumming textures.

There are three different methods we'll discuss:

- Miking the guitar
- Recording direct (if your guitar has a pickup)
- Blending a mic with a direct signal

Miking the Guitar

Probably the most commonly used method in pro studios is that of miking the acoustic guitar. It tends to produce the most natural sound of all and is therefore the favorite of many (myself included).

TOOLBOX

Recording Procedure

Condenser microphones are the standard for acoustic guitars (although there are certainly some dynamics that can sound very nice as well), and both LDCs and SDCs are used frequently. Simply set up the mic(s), plug it into your interface, and engage phantom power (if using a condenser). Arm the track, set the level, and you're good to go. Since you're using a microphone, you'll need to wear headphones if you're recording in your control room.

The type of mic you use when it's the sole source depends on the type of sound you want. Generally speaking, a LDC will tend to produce a fuller-bodied sound with more bottom end. A SDC mic will generally produce a bit less bass and slightly accentuate the highs. Again, though, these are broad generalizations and should not be taken as a rule of any sort.

Single Microphone Technique: SDC

For all the SDC recordings in this book, I'm using the sE8 mic from sE Electronics. This is a fantastic-sounding yet affordable small diaphragm condenser that shines on acoustic guitars (along with pianos, drums, and many other sources), making it an excellent value for the home studio. (You can get a matched pair for under $500!)

When using one mic, a common method is to place it about a foot away and aim it roughly at the neck/body joint. The farther you move the mic/aim it toward the soundhole, the more bass you'll hear. Don't be afraid to try out several different locations when looking for the sweet spot; it'll usually be slightly different for every guitar.

The sE8 small diaphragm condenser mic from sE Electronics.

Gibson J-185 True Vintage miked with a sE8 SDC microphone.

For these tracks, I'm using a sE8 from sE Electronics and a Gibson J-185 True Vintage. Remember that most SDC mics are end-address (like your typical dynamic mic). The mic is slightly off-axis here, but it's still aimed at the neck-body joint.

TRACK 35: SDC (sE8) aimed at neck/body joint: strumming

TRACK 36: SDC (sE8) aimed at neck/body joint: fingerpicking

To illustrate the effect of mic placement, let's hear the same thing but with the mic moved: first it will be moved a few inches closer to the soundhole and then a few inches more up the neck. Compare these with Tracks 35 and 36.

TRACK 37: SDC (sE8) moved toward soundhole: strumming

TRACK 38: SDC (sE8) moved toward soundhole: fingerpicking

TRACK 39: SDC (sE8) moved toward neck: strumming

TRACK 40: SDC (sE8) moved toward neck: fingerpicking

As you can hear, though the differences may be subtle at times, they're clearly there. It definitely pays off to spend an extra few minutes trying to get the sound right from the beginning.

Single Microphone Technique: Dynamic

To compare, let's hear the sound of the Shure SM7B, which is a dynamic mic, on the same guitar aimed at the neck/body joint.

TRACK 41: Dynamic (Shure SM7B) aimed at neck/body joint: strumming

TRACK 42: Dynamic (Shure SM7B) aimed at neck/body joint: fingerpicking

It's a different sound, but it's a very useable one in the right circumstances.

TOOLBOX

Don't Forget to "Pick" the Right Pick!

The difference the plectrum's thickness makes, on acoustic guitar especially, can be quite profound and should not be overlooked. Generally speaking, thinner picks usually sound a bit more jangly or feathery when strumming than thicker ones do. Thicker picks are nice if you want a beefier, more rattling tone from the acoustic.

To hear the difference, check out this example, which features the same strumming pattern played twice: first with a thicker pick (1 mm) and then again with a thinner one (.6 mm).

TRACK 43: Acoustic guitar strumming pattern with thick and thin picks

Single Microphone Technique: LDC

A LDC will often sound nice when positioned slightly behind the bridge, about a foot away from the body. This will generally produce a bigger sound, so you'll want to make sure it's not taking up too much room in the mix if there are other instruments in the same basic frequency range. Let's hear the WA-14 in this position to hear the change in tone.

Gibson J-185 True Vintage miked with a Warm Audio WA-14 LDC microphone.

TRACK 44: LDC (WA-14) aimed slightly behind bridge: strumming

TRACK 45: LDC (WA-14) aimed slightly behind bridge: fingerpicking

That was with the mic set to cardioid mode. Let's have a listen to the same thing with the mic set to omnidirectional mode.

TRACK 46: LDC (WA-14) aimed slightly behind bridge: strumming - omnidirectional pattern

TRACK 47: LDC (WA-14) aimed slightly behind bridge: fingerpicking - omnidirectional pattern

As you can hear, you'll pick up a lot more room ambience in omni mode. If you have a nice-sounding room, you can choose to include it in the track if you're going for a very natural sound.

Now let's hear the LDC mic aimed at the neck/body joint. Compare these to tracks 44 and 45 to hear the difference mic placement can make.

TRACK 48: LDC (WA-14) aimed at neck/body joint: strumming

TRACK 49: LDC (WA-14) aimed at neck/body joint: fingerpicking

Dual Microphone Technique: SDC and SDC

It's also common to combine the two mic approaches—the neck/body joint and behind the bridge—to form one composite sound with the characteristics of both. (This is especially common in solo guitar recordings, where you want the guitar to fill up as much sonic space as possible.) Two SDC mics are common for this task. Ideally, you'll assign each mic to its own track so that you'll have complete control over each during mixdown.

It's common to pan the mics left and right, especially for solo guitar recordings. This is where having a matched pair of SDC mics is nice because you'll usually get a more accurate stereo image than with two different mics. I'll use a matched pair of sE Electronics sE8 mics for these demonstrations.

Gibson J-185 True Vintage miked with a pair of sE8 SDC microphones.

Let's hear how this technique sounds with various setups. For each of the following tracks, you'll first hear SDC mic A (panned left), then SDC mic B (panned right), and then both blended together. Remember to experiment with mic placement to see what sounds best for your setup.

TRACK 50: Pair of SDC mics (sE8): strumming

TRACK 51: Pair of SDC mics (sE8): fingerpicking

I particularly love the sound of this setup on a 12-string acoustic. Let's hear how that sounds with a Seagull Walnut 12.

TRACK 52: Pair of SDC mics (sE8): strumming - 12-string

TRACK 53: Pair of SDC mics (sE8): fingerpicking - 12-string

Another common technique with a matched pair of SDC mics is the *ORTF* method, named after the Office de Radiodiffusion Télévision Française, where the technique was developed in 1960. You can read all about it online.

Dual Microphone Technique: SDC and LDC

Another common technique is to place a LDC behind the bridge and a SDC at the neck/body joint. This will usually result in a bit more bass response. Let's hear the WA-14 behind the bridge combined with the sE8 at the neck/body joint. For each of the following tracks, you'll first hear the SDC mic (panned left), then the LDC mic (panned right), and then both blended together.

TRACK 54: SDC (sE8) and LDC (WA-14): strumming

TRACK 55: SDC (sE8) and LDC (WA-14): fingerpicking

TRACK 56: SDC (sE8) and LDC (WA-14): strumming - 12-string

TRACK 57: SDC (sE8) and LDC (WA-14): fingerpicking - 12-string

It should be abundantly clear by now that mic choice and position make a *huge* difference. Don't underestimate the importance of getting the sound right at the source!

Recording Direct

If your guitar is equipped with a pickup system, you have the option of plugging in and recording direct. This generally won't sound quite as full or natural as a microphone (unless you have a *very* nice onboard electronics system, in which case it will likely blend a pickup with a small microphone), but it has its place and can be made to fit in nicely when used appropriately.

TOOLBOX

Recording Procedure

If your guitar has only a passive pickup (i.e., there's no battery), then you'll need to run through a direct box or acoustic preamp of some sort to get the level up to a usable one. This can be something like an LR Baggs Para Acoustic D.I. or a full-fledged acoustic effects processor, such as the Boss AD-8, which models the sounds of different body types and includes onboard effects.

If using the external preamp route, plug your acoustic into the preamp and then run out of the preamp into an XLR jack on your interface. If you have no external preamp, you can try running into your interface's guitar/bass (high impedance) input if it has one, as that will be better than nothing!

If your guitar has an onboard preamp, you could run straight into a line in jack on the interface, but many people still choose to use a preamp or DI box to convert the signal to a balanced one so they can go into the XLR input on their interface. Once you're in the interface, arm the input, assign it to a track, check your levels, and you're ready to go.

LR Baggs Para Acoustic D.I.

My Gibson J-185 True Vintage acoustic features a K&K Pure Mini pickup, which has no onboard preamp. Let's listen to the sound of the guitar plugged directly into the instrument input of my interface. I've added a bit of reverb for some ambience.

TRACK 58: Direct acoustic with reverb: strumming

TRACK 59: Direct acoustic with reverb: fingerpicking

And now let's hear what it sounds like running through an L.R. Baggs Para Acoustic D.I. and then into an XLR input on the interface. I've kept the EQ pretty flat on the Para D.I. so as not to color the sound.

TRACK 60: **Direct acoustic through Para D.I. with reverb: strumming**

TRACK 61: **Direct acoustic through Para D.I. with reverb: fingerpicking**

You won't have mic placement to worry about when recording direct, but you'll most likely want to tweak the EQ a good bit to achieve the best tonal balance for the recording. What the guitar sounds like in the room doesn't matter in this case; it's only what ends up on the recording that matters.

Blending a Mic with a Direct Signal

One other option is to blend a mic (or mics) with a direct signal to form a composite tone. This is essentially done by just combining the two previous methods and using them simultaneously.

TOOLBOX

Recording Procedure

Plug a cable from your guitar's output jack (or run through an external preamp first if necessary) into your interface on channel 1 and run a mic to channel 2. Assign each one to a separate track, arm them, set levels, and go!

Let's check out the sound of the Gibson J-185 with the sE8 mic and the K&K system blended. On the following tracks, you'll first hear the direct signal, then the mic signal, and then finally the combination of the two.

TRACK 62: **Acoustic with SDC (sE8) aimed at neck/body joint and direct signal blended: strumming**

TRACK 63: **Acoustic with SDC (sE8) aimed at neck/body joint and direct signal blended: fingerpicking**

As you can hear, this results in a unique character. You get the very immediate, detailed sound of the pickup with the fullness and rounder tone of the mic.

TOOLBOX

Don't Forget About Phase!

Phasing issues are a concern when you combine two different captures of the same signal. This applies to dual-miking a guitar cab or acoustic and especially combining a DI signal with a mic signal. If you think about it, electricity travels *way* faster than sound, so the direct signal from your pickup is going to reach your converters before the sound from the microphone (which has to travel as sound waves through the air to the mic). If you record the direct and miked signals to different tracks, this is clearly visible in your DAW.

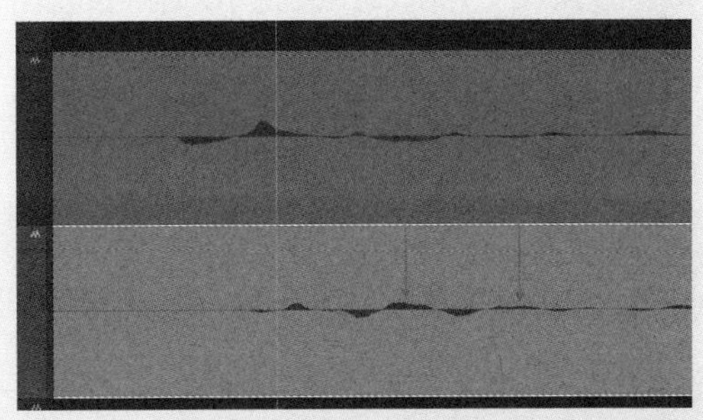

Notice how the DI signal is ahead of the miked signal.

If the crest of one signal is mostly occurring during the trough of the other, you're likely going to end up with a thin, weak sound that's lacking bass. You can correct this by either A) nudging one of the tracks to better align the waveforms, or B) by inverting the phase of one track.

Listen to the following track to hear an example of what phasing issues sound like. The mic is positioned in such a way as to emphasize the out-of-phase sound, which you'll hear at the beginning. Halfway through the track, I'll invert the phase on one of the channels, thereby placing the signals more in phase.

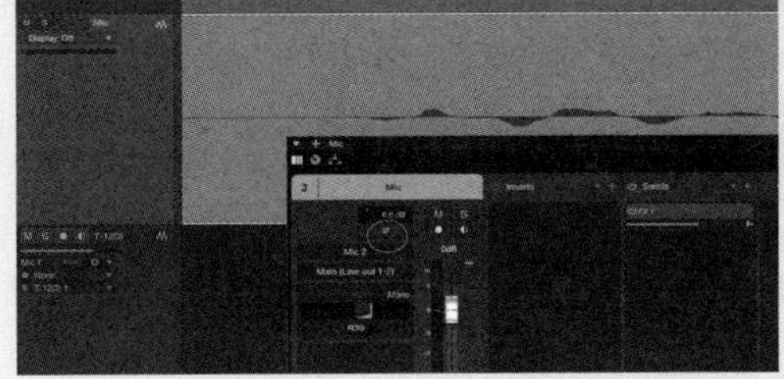

Phase invert button in Studio One

 **TRACK 64:** **Phase demonstration**

Chapter 7:
Recording Bass Guitar

In any style of music, the bass acts as the foundation, so it serves as the harmonic anchor for the song. If it's too thin, the recording will lack body; if it's too boomy, the recording will sound muddy and unclear. In this chapter, we'll take a look at how to get that bottom end happening.

> TOOLBOX
>
> **Remember to Tune Up!**
> Since the bass is often one of the first pitched instruments to get recorded—and the one atop which all the remaining instruments will sit—it's *vitally important* that it's in tune! Again, if you can use the same tuner for all your stringed instruments, this will usually yield the best results.

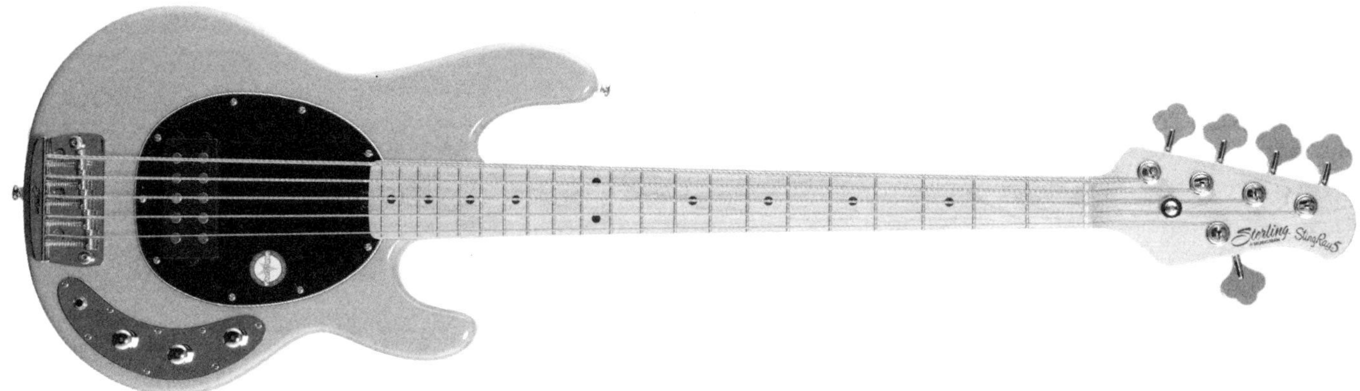

The Sterling by Music Man Stingray Ray25 is an active bass and uses a 9V battery. Active basses feature a higher output signal than passive ones.

We'll look at three different methods for recording bass guitar in this chapter:

- Recording direct
- Miking a bass amp
- Combining a miked amp with a direct signal

As with guitars, it's common to compress bass on the way in. See Chapters 11 and 13 for more on this.

> TOOLBOX
>
> **To Pick or Not to Pick**
> Although fingerstyle is more common on bass, don't forget about the pick! On certain songs, it can be just what the doctor ordered. The list of famous pick players is not exactly a short one and includes none other than Sir Paul McCartney as well as Chris Squire (Yes), session legend Carol Kaye, and, on occasion, John Paul Jones (Led Zeppelin). I'll make use of both techniques for the recordings in this book.

Recording Direct

Recording a bass guitar direct is probably the most commonly used method of all. It usually produces a full, present, and predictable tone with little fuss, which is always a good thing. There are several ways to do this, so let's examine some of the most common.

Plugging Straight In or Using a Direct Box

One option is to simply plug the bass straight into the guitar/bass input of your interface or use a direct box if your interface doesn't have one. It's as simple as it gets.

TOOLBOX

Recording Procedure

Plug your bass into the guitar/bass (high impedance) input of your interface, set the levels, arm the track, and go.

If your interface doesn't have a dedicated instrument input, plug your bass into a direct box and run an XLR cable from the DI box into your interface. Set the levels, arm the track, and go.

Even if your interface has a dedicated instrument input, I'd recommend trying a direct box, as the sound could be noticeably different.

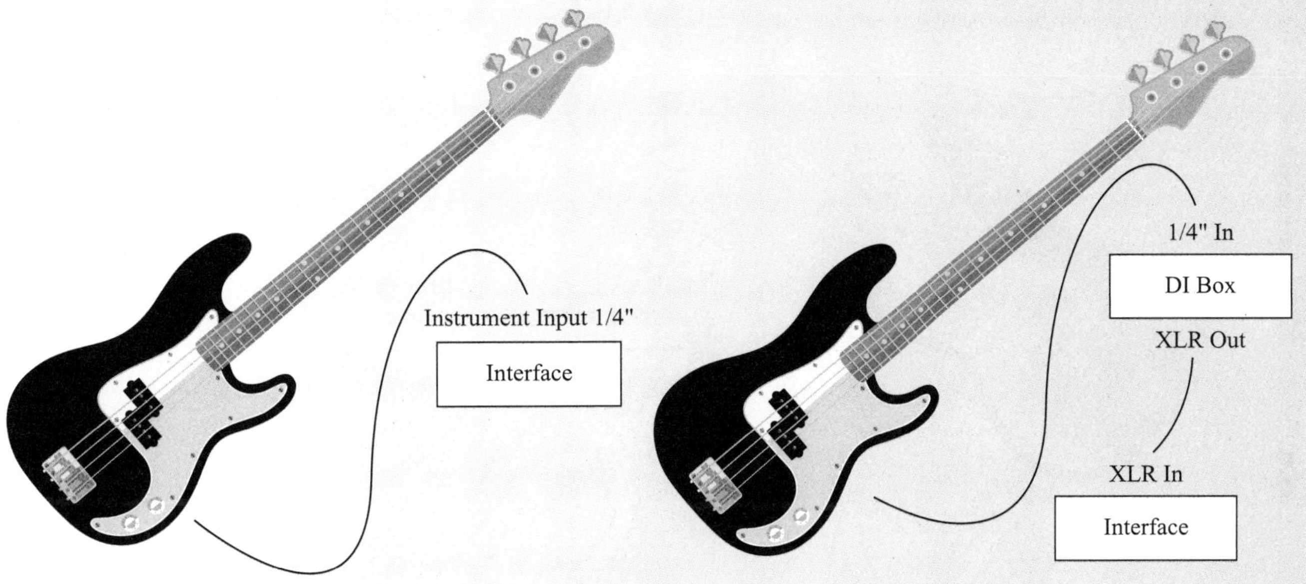

Instrument Input 1/4"
Interface

1/4" In
DI Box
XLR Out
XLR In
Interface

Let's listen to two different basses using the straight-in method: a Sterling by Music Man Ray25 and a Fender P-bass with a mute and flatwound strings. This is the sound of plugging straight into the instrument input of my interface with no processing whatsoever. For the purpose of this demonstration, I'll run all the knobs on the basses (volume and tone) full up (although I will often adjust these when recording).

TRACK 65: Ray25: straight into instrument input

TRACK 66: Ray25 with pick: straight into instrument input

TRACK 67: P-bass: straight into instrument input

TRACK 68: P-bass with pick: straight into instrument input

As you can hear, the choice of bass and playing style makes a huge difference. Depending on the bass, you may want to EQ the signal a bit as well, so don't be afraid to experiment with that.

Using the Direct Output Jack on Your Bass Amp

Another common method for running direct is to simply run a line from your amp's direct output if it has one. This allows you to, depending on the signal path (consult the amp manual), possibly make use of the amp's EQ on the way in for fine-tuning the tone.

TOOLBOX

Recording Procedure

Plug your bass into the amp and run a 1/4-inch cable from the direct output jack into a line input on your interface. Set the levels, assign/arm the track, and go. This is the method we used in Chapter 5 when we recorded our first song.

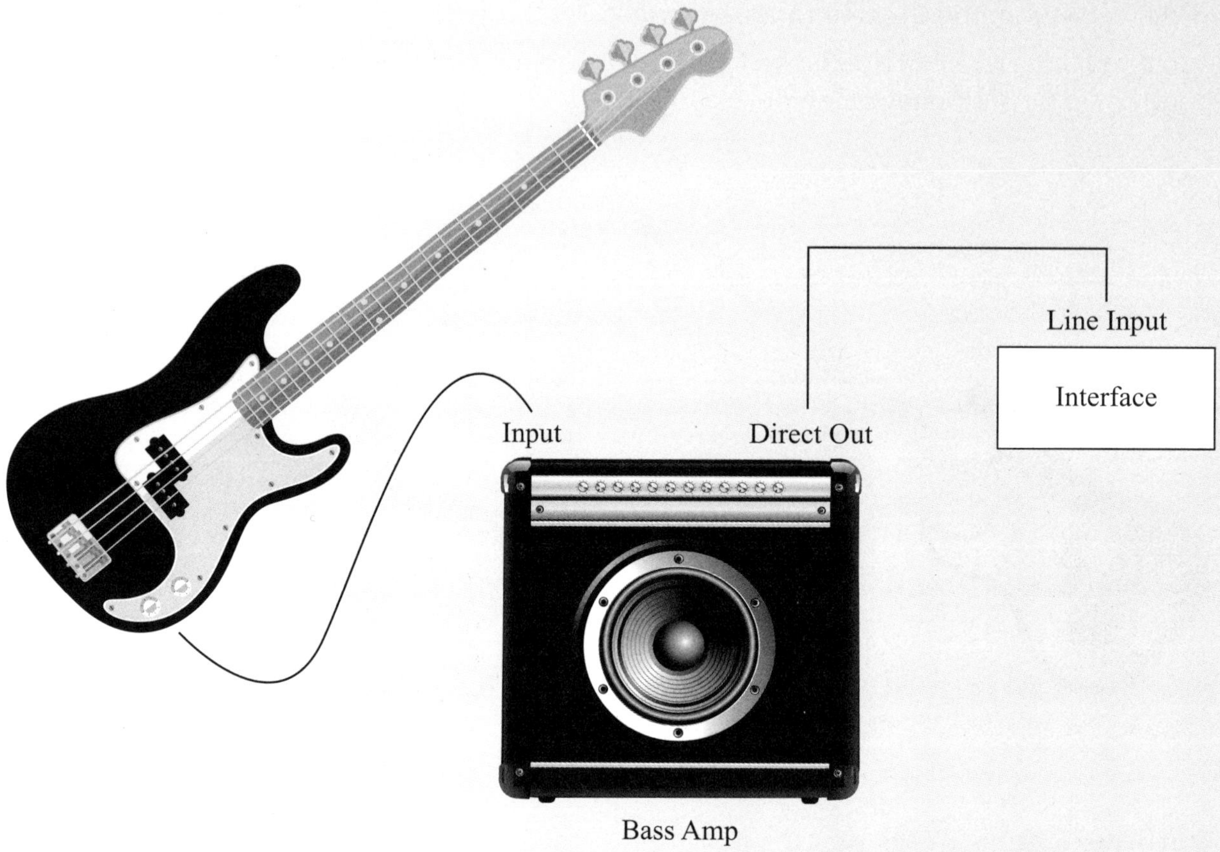

Line Input

Interface

Input

Direct Out

Bass Amp

Let's hear what these basses sound like running through the direct out of an Ampeg Micro-CL bass amp. For the sake of comparison, I'll leave the EQ on the amp flat for these tracks, but of course you can adjust it to your taste when recording.

TRACK 69: Ray25: direct from Ampeg Micro-CL

TRACK 70: Ray25 with pick: direct from Ampeg Micro-CL

TRACK 71: P-bass: direct from Ampeg Micro-CL

TRACK 72: P-bass with pick: direct from Ampeg Micro-CL

Using an Amp Modeler (External or Plug-in)

If you need to gig as a bassist or even rehearse, owning a bass amp makes a lot of sense. But if you only plan on recording bass, an amp modeler can be the perfect ticket. It's also nice even if you own a bass amp, of course, as bass amps are often not back-friendly. If you store your amp in a room other than where you'll be recording, you may not want to move it every time you record.

Just as with guitar, you'll find both hardware (external) and software (plug-in) versions of bass amp modelers, and both can offer excellent results. Check out the Zoom B3n or Tech 21 SansAmp Bass Driver DI for great-sounding, affordable hardware versions. For our purposes, I'll demonstrate some of the bass amp models within IK Multimedia's AmpliTube 4.

Ampeg Micro-CL

Copyright Ampeg, used with permission.

Zoom B3n Bass Multi-Effects Pedal

SansAmp Bass Driver DI

TOOLBOX

Recording Procedure

Plug your bass into the guitar/bass input on your interface or run through a DI box first if your interface doesn't have one. Arm/assign the track and set the levels. Add the plug-in and select the amp model (and effects if desired). Check your level within the plug-in, and you're ready to go.

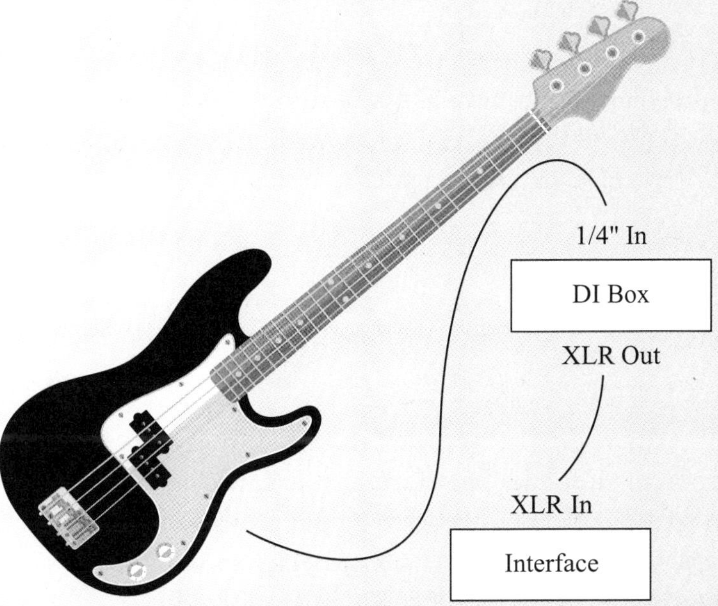

If using an external amp modeler, the process will be the same as with using the direct out on an amp. You'll just be using the amp modeling unit in place of the amp.

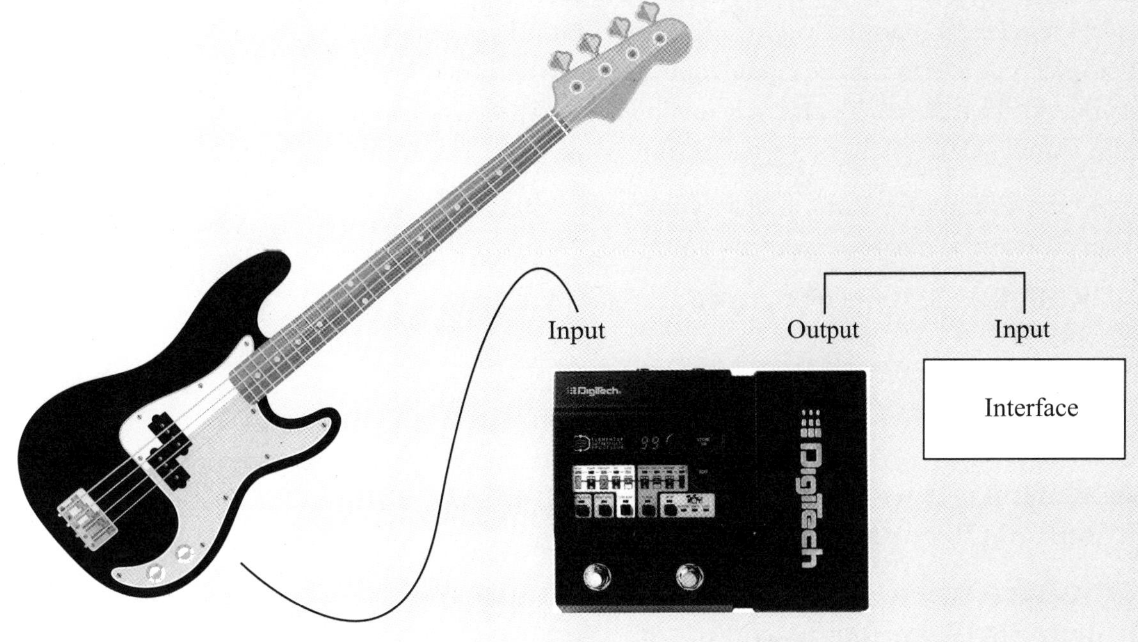

Let's hear what these basses sound like through some different amp models within AmpliTube 4.

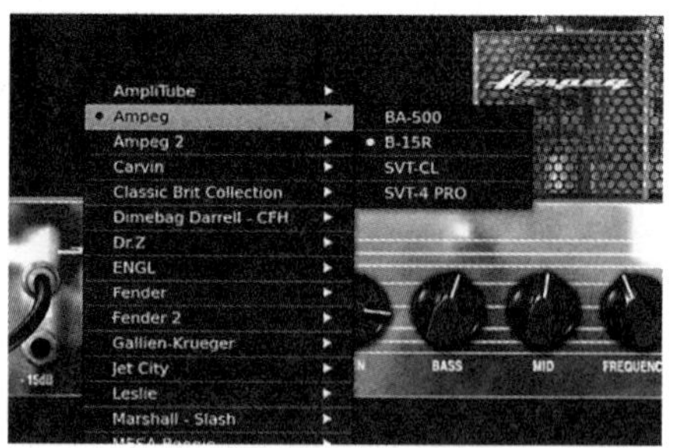

IK Multimedia's AmpliTube 4 has many licensed amp and effects brands available, including several bass amps by Ampeg and Orange.

- **TRACK 73:** Ray25: AmpliTube 4 – Ampeg B15-R
- **TRACK 74:** P-bass: AmpliTube 4 – Ampeg B15-R
- **TRACK 75:** Ray25 with pick: AmpliTube 4 – Ampeg SVT
- **TRACK 76:** P-bass with pick: AmpliTube 4 – Ampeg SVT
- **TRACK 77:** Ray25: AmpliTube 4 – model based on Acoustic 360
- **TRACK 78:** P-bass: AmpliTube 4 – model based on Acoustic 360
- **TRACK 79:** Ray25: AmpliTube 4 – Orange AD 200
- **TRACK 80:** P-bass: AmpliTube 4 – Orange AD 200

It's certainly nice to have a whole arsenal of sounds at your fingertips when you're searching for just the right tone on a song. In this way, amp modelers really are nice to have around. And don't forget that you can manipulate the speaker cabinet (and mics placed on them) as well with most amp modelers, including AmpliTube 4, for more tonal versatility.

Miking a Bass Amp

Miking a bass amp is definitely not as common in home studios, and it's not difficult to guess why. Bass amps are loud, and bass frequencies carry (and carry)! Generally speaking, dynamic mics are usually the most common, but that doesn't mean you can't try a LDC or a ribbon mic.

> **TOOLBOX**
>
> **Recording Procedure**
> Plug your bass into your amp and run a cable from the mic to your interface. Assign/arm the track and check your levels.

Dynamic Mics

Though ambience is common in guitar, keyboard, and drum tracks (at times), you generally want to avoid it on bass tracks. If you have some gobos (see Appendix for how to make your own), you can place several around the amp to cut down on the reflections if you have to record in a reflective space.

Most people will use a close-mic technique similar to that on guitar amps—i.e., a few inches off the grill and positioned somewhere between the cone and edge of the speaker. You normally don't need to crank the bass amp to performance levels in order to achieve a good tone. If your significant other screams at you to turn it down, it's probably too loud. But if they ask you nicely to turn it down, that's probably a good starting point.

Let's listen to the sound of a Shure SM57 dynamic mic placed at two different spots (close and one foot away) on an Ampeg Micro-CL.

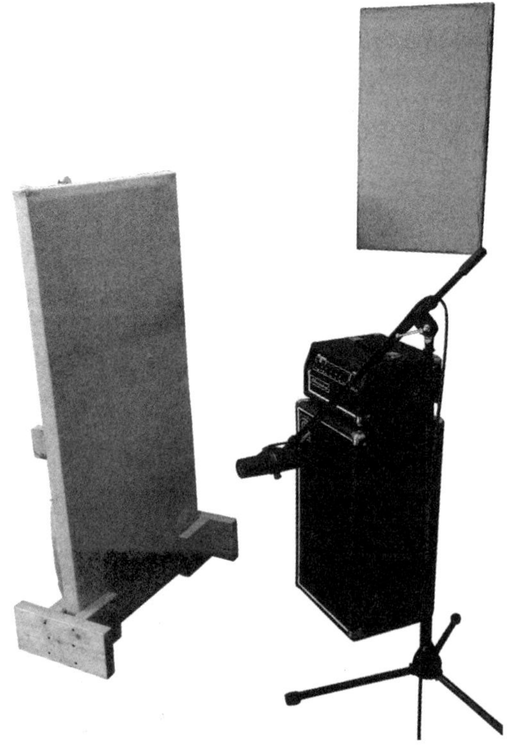

Ampeg Micro-CL bass amp close-miked with a Shure SM7B dynamic microphone. Normally I would enclose the mic with another baffle, but it's been left out to show the mic position.

- **TRACK 81:** Ray25: Ampeg Micro-CL close-miked with Shure SM7B
- **TRACK 82:** P-bass: Ampeg Micro-CL close-miked with Shure SM7B
- **TRACK 83:** Ray25 with pick: Ampeg Micro-CL miked with Shure SM7B one foot away
- **TRACK 84:** P-bass with pick: Ampeg Micro-CL miked with Shure SM7B one foot away

Condenser Mics

As mentioned earlier, there's no reason not to experiment with condenser (or ribbon) mics on a bass amp. If you have your amp turned up loud, you may want to engage the pad (if available) on your condenser mic. For moderate volumes, though, it won't be necessary.

Let's have a listen to how a WA-14 sounds on the Ampeg Micro-CL amp. We'll place the mic about 10 or 12 inches off the grill aimed at the cone. Compare these to tracks 81-82.

TRACK 85: Ray25: Ampeg Micro-CL miked with WA-14

TRACK 86: P-bass: Ampeg Micro-CL miked with WA-14

Of course, you could always blend two different mics—a dynamic and a condenser, for example—together as well to see what you come up with. If you like the definition that one mic provides but don't like its low end very much, you could pair it with a mic that has a better-sounding low end. Experiment!

Combining a Miked Amp with a Direct Signal

This is actually quite a common method in professional studios, and it can be put to good use in home studios as well. You can capture the definition and clarity provided by a DI signal while still retaining the warmth and power of an amp. Of course, you should ideally record each signal to its own track if possible, as you'll then be able to blend/process each to taste.

TOOLBOX

Recording Procedure

First, you'll need to split your bass signal so that you can send it to two different places. For this, you can just use a DI box. A typical DI box will have two 1/4-inch jacks—one is an input and the other a "thru"—and one XLR output. You plug your bass into one of the 1/4-inch jacks—it usually doesn't matter which one—and run a cable from the other 1/4-inch jack to your amp. Then you run an XLR cable from the XLR jack to your interface.

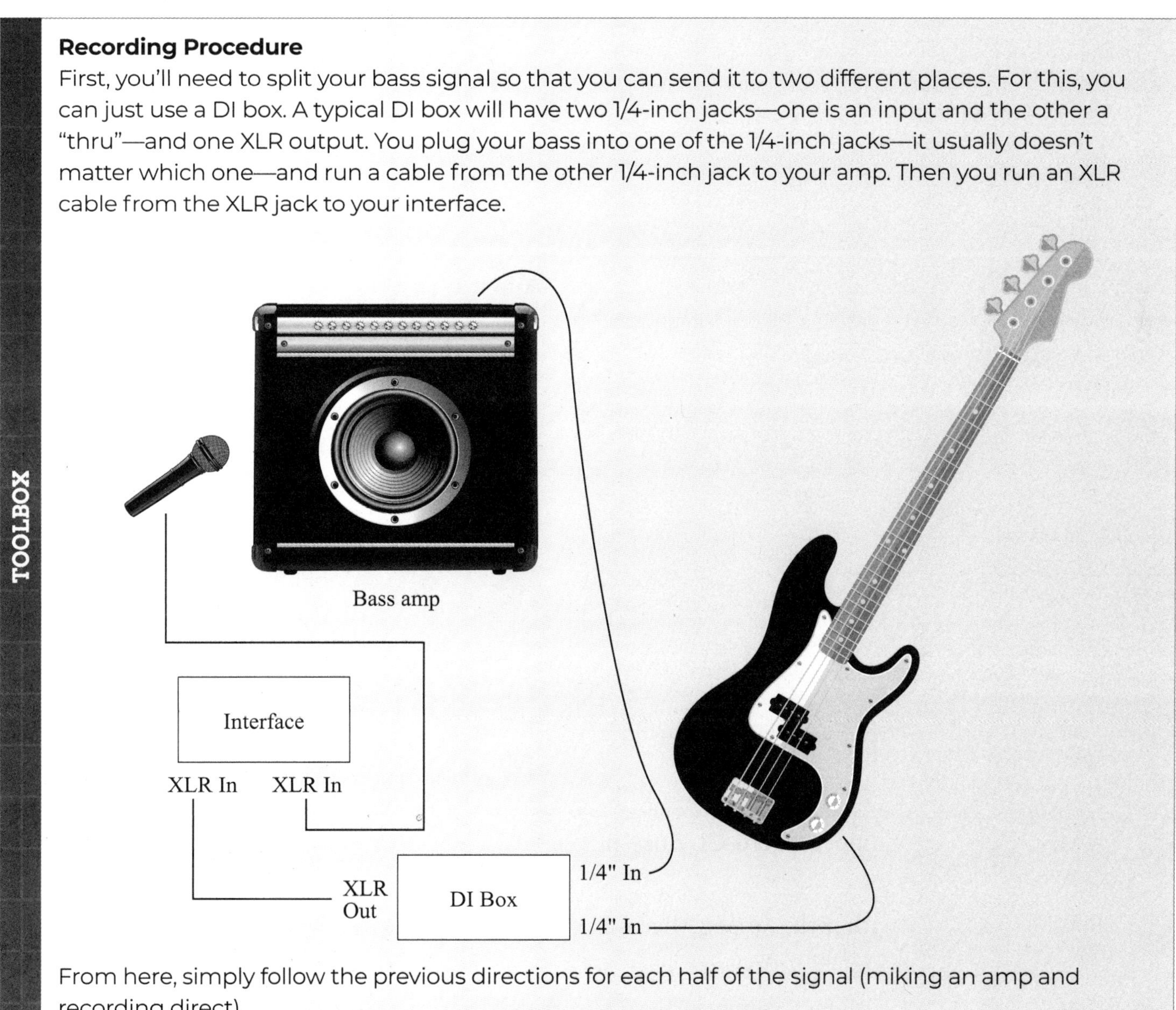

From here, simply follow the previous directions for each half of the signal (miking an amp and recording direct).

TOOLBOX

Remember Phase!
Combining two different signals could result in phasing issues. See page 57 in Chapter 6 for more details on this.

Let's hear this idea in action. We'll mic the bass amp with the Shure SM7B dynamic mic a few inches off the grill, and we'll run into an XLR input on the interface with the direct signal. For each of these tracks, you'll first hear the direct signal, then the amp signal, and then the combination of the two. Compare these to tracks 69–72 and 81–84.

TRACK 87: Ray25: combined direct and amp

TRACK 88: P-bass: combined direct and amp

TRACK 89: Ray25 with pick: combined direct and amp

TRACK 90: P-bass with pick: combined direct and amp

As you can hear, this approach can produce a really well-rounded tone. It's important to remember that, when using this approach, you want the tones to complement each other. So if your direct tone has lots of highs in it, you may want to move the mic farther away from the cone, etc. The trick is to remember that they're supposed to work together.

Chapter 8:
Recording Keyboards and Other MIDI Instruments

Keyboards and MIDI instruments are the not-so-secret weapons of the home recordist. With the explosion of virtual instrument technology, we're now able to flesh out our songs with convincing approximations of everything from vintage electric pianos and analog synths to tubas, pizzicato strings, suitcase organs, and just about any other instrument you can imagine. In this chapter, we'll talk about the myriad of options available and how to employ them.

The Source: MIDI Keyboard Controller or Keyboard with Built-In Sounds

The first thing we need to record keyboards is ... a keyboard. Seems obvious, yes? But as with most things in today's recording world, there's more than one way to skin the cat. There are two main options: a *keyboard with built-in sounds* and a *MIDI keyboard controller*, which is used to control sounds from another source (software or hardware).

Some MIDI controllers (with no built-in sounds at all) can get extremely fancy, offering all kinds of onboard control options that can all be assigned to various parameters for very expressive performance capability. I'd suggest that, at minimum, your controller—whether it's a synthesizer or MIDI controller only—have at least a pitch wheel, a mod (modulation) wheel, and a sustain pedal jack (if you're at all considering recording piano sounds).

The Graphite 49 from Samson Audio is a 49-key USB MIDI controller with numerous features geared toward music production.

TOOLBOX

MIDI vs. Audio

When dealing with virtual instruments (MIDI instruments), just about every part of the performance can be edited even *after* the track has been recorded, including the instrument (sound or *patch*) itself. Think of it as akin to a word processor. You can type a whole paragraph and then go back to change the font, font size, color, delete/add words, etc.

If you're recording the built-in sounds of a keyboard to a track, however, you're not recording MIDI data; you're recording audio. This is similar to what we talked about in Chapter 6 with regard to recording a miked amp signal vs. recording a D.I. guitar signal and adding an amp simulator via plug-in. This is more like using a vintage typewriter. If you make a big mistake or want to change something, you basically have to type it all over again.

Recording the Built-In Sounds from a Keyboard

Let's start with this method, because it's the least complicated. All you need is a keyboard with some onboard sounds that you like and a 1/4-inch instrument cable.

TOOLBOX

Recording Procedure
Run a cable from your keyboard to a line input on your interface. If recording a stereo patch, run two cables—one from each L and R jack—to two inputs on your interface. Assign/arm the track(s) and check your levels. (Pan the two left and right if recording in stereo.)

It's pretty much the same procedure as recording a bass or a guitar direct. The thing to remember is that you're "printing" the sound (and any effects you may have added to it) to the track. This means you can't change it later the way you can when using softsynths (virtual instruments), so you've got to get the performance right from the source.

Recording with a MIDI Controller

A MIDI keyboard controller is sort of like the typing keyboard on your desktop computer. By itself, it does nothing. But if you plug it into the computer and use the right software, all of a sudden, the buttons can produce letters in all shapes, sizes, colors, etc. So it is with a MIDI keyboard controller. You just need to connect it to a sound source. There are two ways to do this: *external sound modules/synths* (hardware), or *virtual instrument plug-ins* (software).

External Sound Modules/Synths

Although the "romplers" of the 90s aren't quite as common these days, analog synths have made a huge comeback. Many analog synths don't have built-in keyboards; they only have knobs, buttons, and other ways to manipulate sound. In order to play melodies on them in a conventional way, you need to use a MIDI controller or a sequencer (which is included in your DAW).

TOOLBOX

Monophonic or Polyphonic?
You may have heard this term before and not known what it meant. This simply refers to the ability of a synthesizer or instrument to play more than one note simultaneously. If it can only play one note at a time, it's *monophonic*. This is common in some older Moog synths that are meant for lead or bass sounds. An instrument that can play more than one note is *polyphonic*. This is common in synths that emulate string sounds, for example.

Using a MIDI Controller to Play in Real Time

It's important to remember here that, even though we're using a MIDI cable, we're not *recording* the MIDI. The MIDI controller is controlling the sound module, and we're recording the sound module (audio signal).

TOOLBOX

Recording Procedure
Run a MIDI cable from the MIDI OUT jack of your controller to the MIDI IN jack of the external sound module/synth. Then run an instrument cable from your sound module/synth to a line input on your interface. Assign/arm the track and check levels.

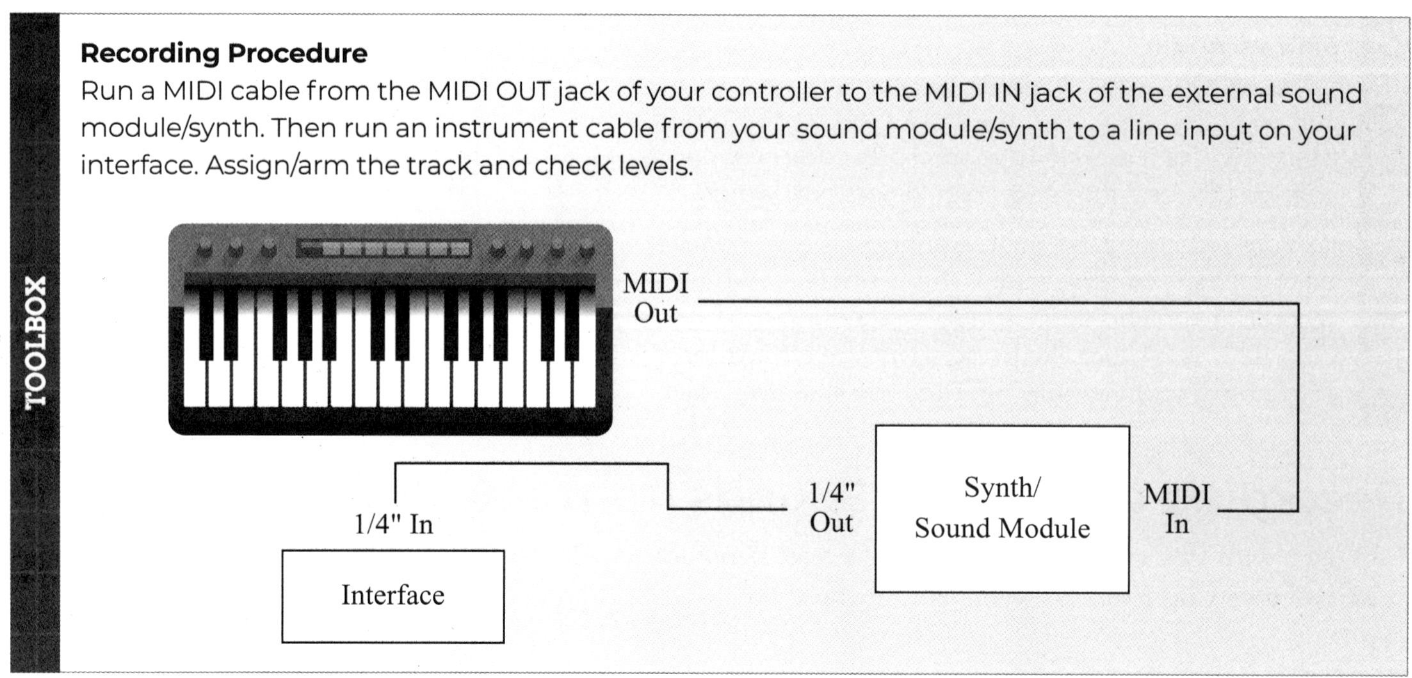

TOOLBOX

All MIDI Controllers Have MIDI Jacks, Right?

Actually, no! Since computers—and particularly USB cables—infiltrated the recording world, many USB MIDI controllers actually *don't have MIDI ports.* Instead, they feature only USB outputs and, as such, are designed primarily to plug straight into a computer for use with virtual instruments. Other MIDI controllers contain only MIDI ports and no USB ports. These can also be used to play virtual instruments on your computer if your interface has MIDI ports. (If not, you can get USB MIDI adapters to make this work.)

The MicroKey 25 from Korg is a compact 25-key MIDI controller with a USB output only.

Then there are many units that contain both MIDI and USB ports, so you have the best of both worlds. Depending on your specific needs, make sure you check these features on a controller before you make a purchase!

Controlling a Hardware Synth with a Sequencer

A sequencer is essentially an automated MIDI controller. Instead of playing notes with the keyboard to directly control the synth, you just enter that data into the sequencer (by various means) and then have the sequencer "play" the synth. This frees up both of your hands to twist knobs on the synth. How do you enter the data into the sequencer? There are three main ways:

- Play in real-time with a MIDI controller and record the sequence.
- Enter the notes by hand (with your mouse or other method)—known as "step recording."
- Import a MIDI file.

In this case, you'd then have your sequencer (which is normally in your DAW, though there are external sequencers too) control your hardware synth and route the audio output of the synth back into your interface.

TOOLBOX

Recording Procedure

This is a bit more complicated than some of our other setups. First, run a MIDI cable from the MIDI OUT jack of your controller to the MIDI IN jack of your interface Alternatively, if you're using a USB-equipped controller, then simply plug it into your computer via USB. (You may need to consult your DAW's manual to help make sure it's recognized in the software.)

Run a MIDI cable from the MIDI OUT jack of your interface to the MIDI IN jack of your hardware synth. Then run a 1/4-inch audio cable from the output of your hardware synth to an available input on your interface.

You'll then need to add a MIDI track in your DAW and direct its output to the MIDI OUT jack. (Consult your manual on how to do this.) Arm the MIDI track and make sure its input channel (1-16) is the same as your MIDI controller's transmit channel.

This will send the incoming MIDI signals (from your controller) out the MIDI OUT jack of your interface and to the hardware synth. Then add an audio track in the DAW and arm/assign it to the input you used for the cable coming from your synth. You should then be able to hear your synth when you play the MIDI controller.

Note: If you want to enter the notes via step recording mode, you don't need a MIDI controller at all. You just draw the notes into the MIDI track by hand.

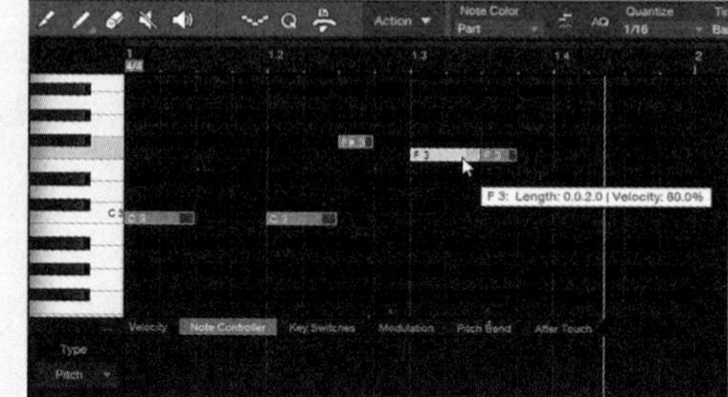

If you don't have a MIDI keyboard, you can simply draw notes in by hand, although it's much more time-consuming.

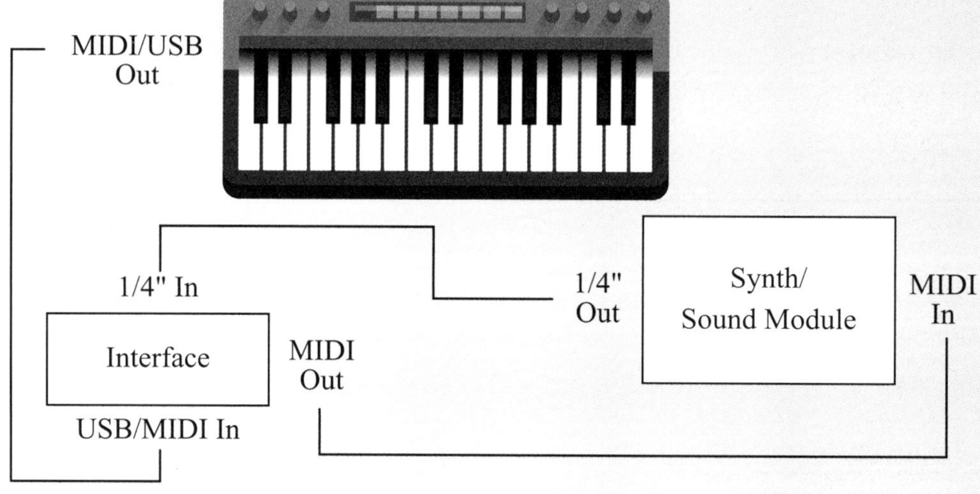

In this instance, you *will* be recording MIDI. So, once you have your MIDI sequence recorded, you can simply press play and then adjust your hardware synth to achieve the sounds you want.

Working with analog synths can be a lot of fun; there's nothing like twisting actual knobs to create different sounds. Here's an example with a Behringer Model D analog synth, which is monophonic. All the variations you hear are created by twisting knobs on the synth while playing a sequence from Studio One.

TRACK 91: Behringer Model D played with Sequencer

Using Virtual Instruments

When using virtual instruments for the first time, you'll likely feel like a child who's walked into a candy store. You can just about play *anything* with your little MIDI controller. Pianos, organs, electric pianos? Of course. But how about congas, flute, cello, sitar, toy piano, theremin, slap bass, or tympani? No problem!

TOOLBOX

Recording Procedure

If using a MIDI cable, run it from the MIDI OUT jack of your controller to the MIDI IN jack of your interface (or USB MIDI adapter). Create a track on your DAW, select "MIDI" for the input, and open the effects window.

If using a USB cable, run the cable from your controller to a USB port on your computer. (Follow the instructions for installing the necessary drivers, if necessary.)

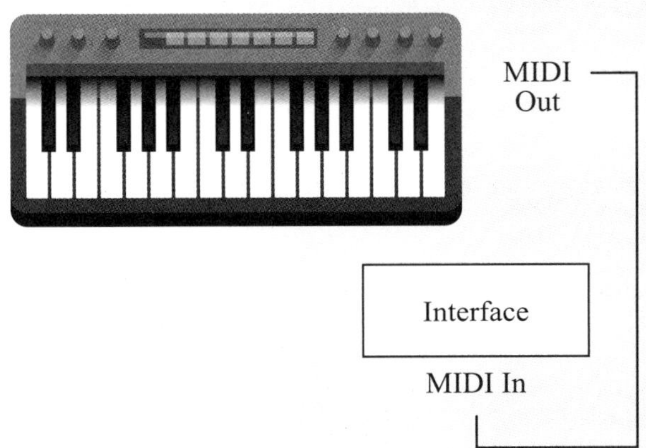

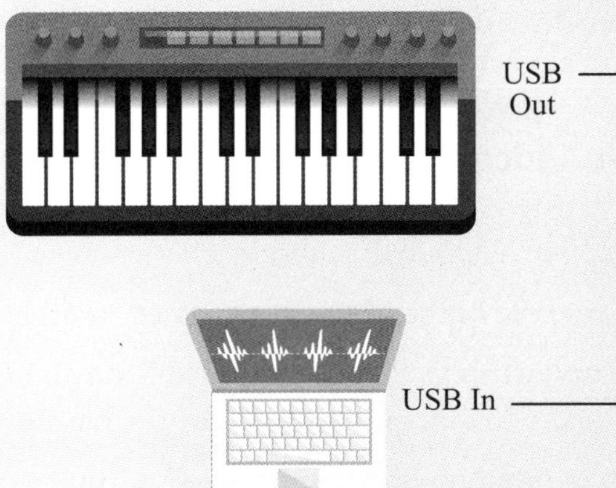

Note: In some DAW programs, you may have to enable your MIDI controller after plugging it in for the first time.

Open a track, insert the virtual instrument plug-in, and select MIDI input. Assign/arm the track and check levels.

Selecting a virtual instrument in Studio One.

Let's listen to a few examples of these virtual instruments.

Applied Acoustics Systems Lounge Lizard Session features classic electric piano sounds.

- **TRACK 92:** Applied Acoustics Systems Lounge Lizard Session: Mellow Rhodes
- **TRACK 93:** Applied Acoustics Systems Lounge Lizard Session: Rhodes with gentle growl and tremolo
- **TRACK 94:** Applied Acoustics Systems Lounge Lizard Session: Wurlitzer Dry
- **TRACK 95:** Toontrack EZKeys 2: Session Grand
- **TRACK 96:** Toontrack EZKeys 2: Mellotoon (Flutes)
- **TRACK 97:** Toontrack EZKeys 2: Electric R-MK I
- **TRACK 98:** Presonus Classic Orchestra: Vibraphone and Strings
- **TRACK 99:** Arturia Analog Lab V: Combo Organ
- **TRACK 100:** Garritan World: Native American Flute
- **TRACK 101:** Garritan World: Indian Ensemble

TOOLBOX

What's Up with the Waveform?
After recording a MIDI track, you'll most likely notice that it doesn't look like normal audio tracks. Instead, the media window will (usually) show little rectangular blocks instead of a waveform. This indicates that it's a MIDI track and not audio.

If you were to disable (bypass) your effects on that track now, you'd hear nothing from the track when you pressed play. This is because, again, MIDI data is not audio. It's simply instructions telling the sound generator (virtual instrument) what to do.

A MIDI track recorded in Studio One looks different than an audio track.

Tips for Added Realism

If you're trying to use a virtual instrument as a convincing stand-in for a real one, there are a few things to keep in mind that will help sell the illusion:

- **Observe the range of the instrument**: In other words, don't use a flute sound to play a bass line.
- **Don't play things that are impossible on an instrument**: If you're playing with an acoustic piano sound, for example, you don't want to use the pitch bend wheel.
- **Keep in mind physical limitations**: Wind instruments—such as woodwinds, brass, reeds, etc.—require breathing; therefore, don't hold their notes eternally.
- **Read the manual**: Be sure to at least thoroughly skim through the manual for the virtual instrument you're using. There are often many more options "under the hood" that you may not discover without it.

TOOLBOX

Bundle Up!
Many times companies will sell several products together as a bundle for a hefty discount, so think before you buy. For example, if a company offers several different instruments for $80 each, you may find a bundle of three for $150, resulting in a savings of $90!

Chapter 9:
Drum Samples and Loops

The budget-minded home recordist has really lucked out on the drum department. Recording good drum sounds at home is notoriously difficult. Not only does the kit need to sound good and be tuned well (which isn't quite as easy as tuning a guitar), but the room also plays a big role in the sound.

So, what's the good news? Well, we don't really *have* to record live drums anymore. Virtual drums have gotten so good at this point that it's not only possible for you to fool people into thinking they're real drums, it's been happening for years!

There are basically three overarching categories with regards to electronic drums: external drum machines, drum loops/samples, and virtual drum plug-ins.

External Drum Machines

The *external drum machine* was the tool of choice throughout most of the 80s, and it's continued to be used to some extent today—especially in hip hop and R&B styles. Analog drum machines are especially popular in this regard.

Along with analog synths, analog drum machines, such as the very affordable Korg Volca Beats, have experienced quite a resurgence.

Most drum machines nowadays come with only stereo L/R output jacks, which means you must make all drumkit mixing decisions (volume, panning, etc.) within the box. (There are workarounds to this: see "Need More Control?" on page 73.) If the machine does have extra outputs, you can usually send some drums (the kick and snare are common) to their own output, which allows you to process them individually. You could add a different amount of compression on the snare, for example, or you could EQ them separately, etc.

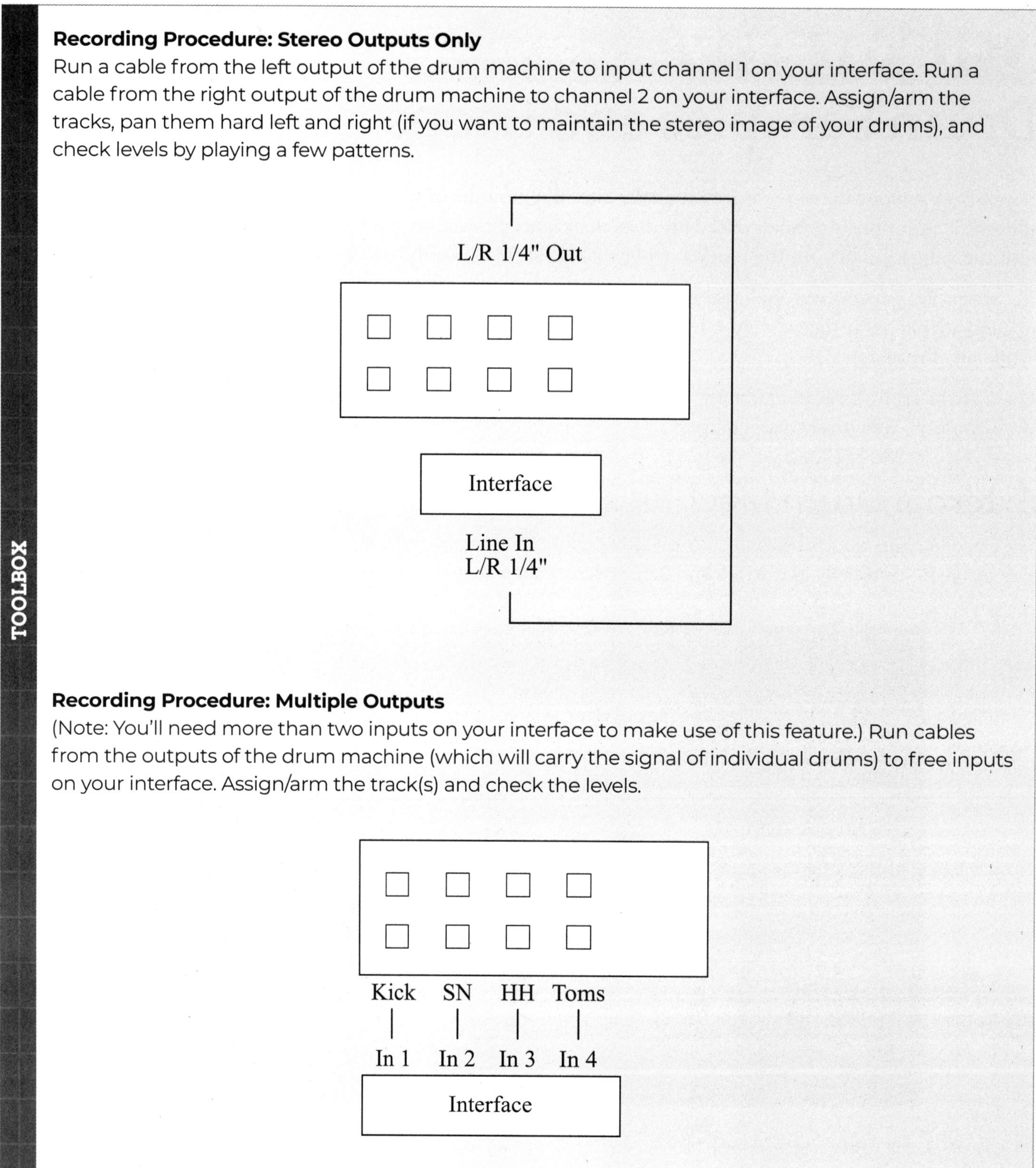

Recording Procedure: Stereo Outputs Only

Run a cable from the left output of the drum machine to input channel 1 on your interface. Run a cable from the right output of the drum machine to channel 2 on your interface. Assign/arm the tracks, pan them hard left and right (if you want to maintain the stereo image of your drums), and check levels by playing a few patterns.

Recording Procedure: Multiple Outputs

(Note: You'll need more than two inputs on your interface to make use of this feature.) Run cables from the outputs of the drum machine (which will carry the signal of individual drums) to free inputs on your interface. Assign/arm the track(s) and check the levels.

You can either program the song's parts on the drum machine itself (if it has a sequencer), or you can program them in your DAW using MIDI. (This would be the same process as explained in "Controlling a Hardware Synth with a Sequencer" from Chapter 8. See page 67 for details.)

TOOLBOX

Need More Control?

If your drum machine is limited by its number of outputs, or if it's mono instead of stereo (such as the Korg Volca Beats), you're not out of luck. There's still a way you can process and/or pan each drum individually. Here's what you do:

1. Set up the routing described on page 67 under "Controlling a Hardware Synth with a Sequencer."
2. Create a drum sequence on the MIDI track (Track 1) using either a MIDI controller or via step recording. You may need to set your MIDI controller to MIDI channel 10. (Your drum machine should default to this channel, as it's the standard drum/percussion MIDI channel.) And you may have to hunt a bit on your MIDI controller to find the drum notes. (The kick drum is usually assigned to the note C1, with the other drums close by.)
3. Once you have your sequence written, disarm the MIDI track. As long as your audio track (Track 2) is still armed, you should hear the drum machine play the sequence when you hit play on your DAW.
4. Next, make several copies of the audio track—one for each individual drum sound you need. The input assignment should transfer with the copied track, but just in case it didn't, make sure the input is set to the same for each track. Disarm all tracks but the original audio track (Track 2).
5. Go into the drum sequence on the MIDI track and mute all the notes except the bass drum. This way, when you play the sequence, you should only hear the bass drum.
6. Name Track 2 "Bass drum." Hit record on your DAW. Your bass drum should be recorded (as an audio file) onto Track 2.
7. Disarm Track 2, arm Track 3, and name it "Snare Drum." In the MIDI sequence, mute everything but the snare drum notes. Hit record on your DAW. Your snare drum should be recorded (as an audio file) onto Track 3.
8. Repeat this process with the remaining drum sounds.

You'll end up with audio tracks for each individual drum. From here, you can pan and process them each on their own to your heart's content!

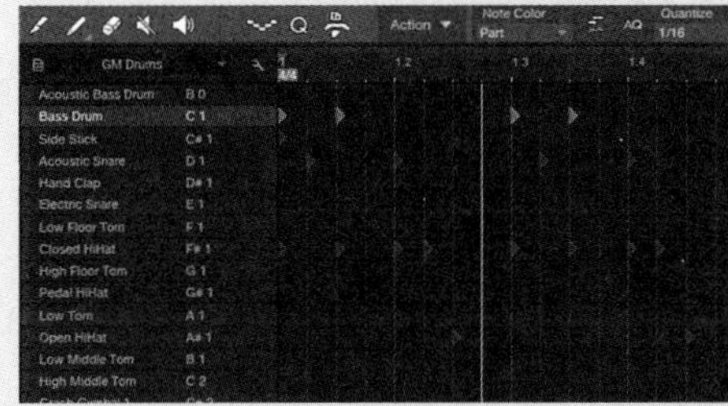

With everything muted but the bass drum, you'll only be recording it to the current track.

After performing this trick, you'll no longer be bound by an analog drum machine with only one or two outputs!

Samples and Loops

Drum loops and samples are another common home studio tool. Some software only contains short stereo files of recorded drum loops; in other words, it's just a collection of audio files. Your DAW software will likely come with a collection of loops as well. And then there are other loop programs that are more like beat-making factories. They also allow you to manipulate the tempo, tuning, etc. for more versatility.

There really is no "recording procedure" for using samples and loops because you're not really *recording* anything. You're simply importing them into your project to assemble a drum track piece by piece. You can usually just grab an audio file and drag it into your DAW project. If you're using a click track in your song, make sure you have the "snap to grid" setting engaged so that the loop with perfectly align with the beat you want.

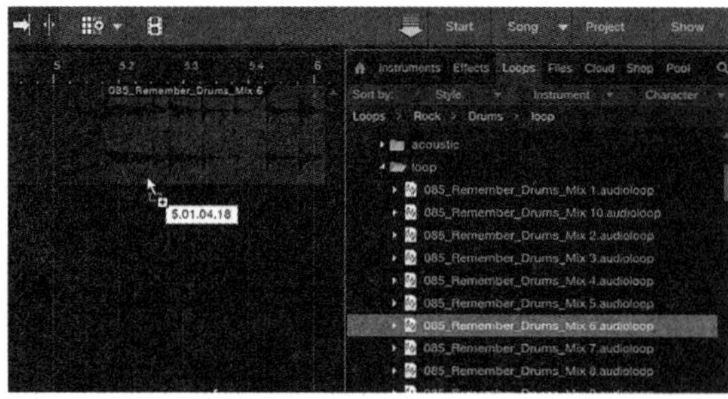

Pulling a drum loop into a Studio One project.

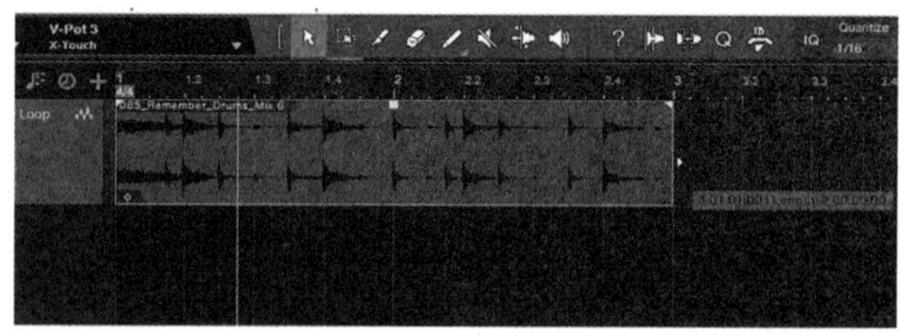

Once the loop is in the DAW project, it's an easy matter to extend it for however many bars you'd like.

TOOLBOX

Time Stretching
Although all loops were originally recorded at a specific tempo, they can be *time-stretched* a good bit faster or slower and still be useable. If your song is at 90 bpm, and the loop says 96 bpm, then it can easily be time-stretched and still be usable. (Your DAW may do this automatically by default. Consult the manual as necessary.)

Virtual Drum Plug-ins

Virtual drum plug-ins are collections of professionally recorded drumsets, playable via MIDI controllers, with each drum individually controllable in many ways. You can usually mix the kit however you'd like (i.e. make the snare louder, pan it to the right, etc.) and apply your own effects to the individual drums. Toontrack's Superior Drummer 2.0 and EZDrummer 3 are brilliant in this category, the latter being one of my favorite bang-for-the-buck items in the world of home recording. Other popular titles include those from XLN Audio (Addictive Drums line), Steven Slate Drums, and Sonic Reality.

Toontrack EZDrummer 3

TOOLBOX

Recording Procedure
Run a MIDI cable from the MIDI OUT jack of your controller to the MIDI IN jack of your interface or plug your USB-equipped MIDI controller into your computer. Create a track, select "MIDI" for the input, and add the drum plug-in. Assign/arm the track and check levels.

As stated earlier, while you can certainly program drums with a MIDI keyboard, you may find it much more intuitive with other controllers that feature pads (for ease of hitting—with fingers or sticks). Many keyboard MIDI controllers include several pads for this purpose.

IK Multimedia's iRig Keys I/O 25 is a compact MIDI controller that includes eight velocity-sensitive pads.

After you've got the plug-in set up in your DAW, you're ready to get started.

Step 1: Choose Your Kit

Most virtual drum plug-ins will come with several drum kits from which to choose, so the first step is to choose which kit you want to use for your recording. I'm going to use EZDrummer 3's Vintage kit for this demonstration.

TRACK 102: EZDrummer 3: Vintage kit sounds

Step 2: Decide Whether You Want to Start from Scratch or Use Patterns

Most virtual drum plug-ins will contain many built-in patterns and fills that you can use to create your drum track if you prefer. Some prefer to finalize the drum track first, while others prefer to simply lay down a basic beat and track the instruments on top of that, coming back to create the "real" drum track afterward.

Using Patterns

EZDrummer 3 makes it incredibly easy to find a suitable pattern for your song, thanks to its smart search feature. For example, you can tap a kick rhythm, and it will show you all the patterns available that contain that rhythm on the kick.

 **TRACK 103:** EZDrummer 3: Pattern selected

Searching for a pattern in EZDrummer 3 based on the kick rhythm.

After you find the pattern you like, you can simply drag and drop it into your DAW program. And just as with audio drum loops, you can copy and paste the MIDI pattern for as long as you'd like.

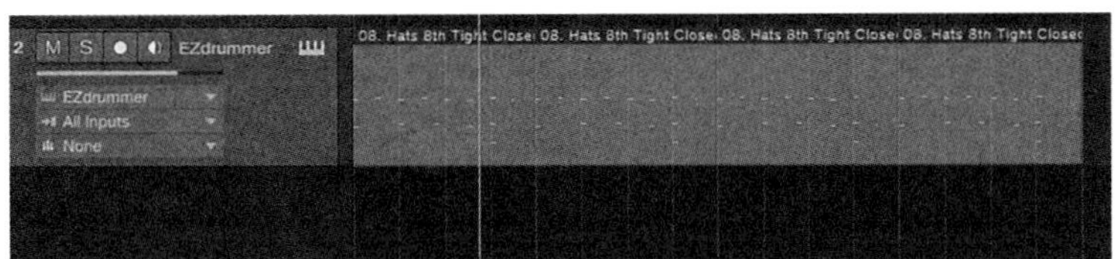

After selecting a drum pattern, you can copy and paste it as many times as you want.

Recording Your Own Track from Scratch

If you're dealing with a very specific type of song that doesn't conform to a standard feel or beat, then you'll most likely need to create your own drum track from scratch. Again, you can use a MDI keyboard or MIDI drum controller (see Chapter 3) to record the parts.

It may be necessary to record the drum track in stages, depending on the complexity of it. You can specify in your DAW whether you want a MIDI track recording to replace an existing one or overdub onto it. This way, you can record the kick and snare on the first pass, let's say, and then come back and overdub the hi-hat, for example.

The kick and snare have been recorded in the first pass.

 **TRACK 104:** EZDrummer 3: Kick and snare recorded

 **TRACK 105:** EZDrummer 3: Hi-hat part added to kick and snare

Typically, you may record a four-bar pattern and then copy and paste it if applicable. If you have the chops for it, though, feel free to play through the entire track. You can always leave holes where you'd like the fills to go or just come back and add the fills after the fact by switching to the "replace" mode instead of "overdub."

On a second pass, the hi-hat part has been added using the "overdub" setting.

Step 3: Edit (if Necessary)

After you've recorded the entire drum track, it's a good idea to listen to the whole thing to make sure nothing sticks out. You should also check to make sure that you don't have any extra measures anywhere, which can happen on occasion if you're doing a lot of copying and pasting.

Quantization

When you *quantize* a MIDI performance, you correct rhythmic imperfections by moving notes to the closest specified rhythm. If you choose to quantize to the nearest 16th note, for example, it will move every note forward or backward to the nearest 16th note in the measure.

If you set the quantization factor to 100%, it's going to make every note metronomically perfect, which will sound like a machine. But if you're going for a natural sound, you can choose the specific quantization percentage. If you choose 75%, for example, it'll only move each note 75% of the distance to the nearest rhythm point.

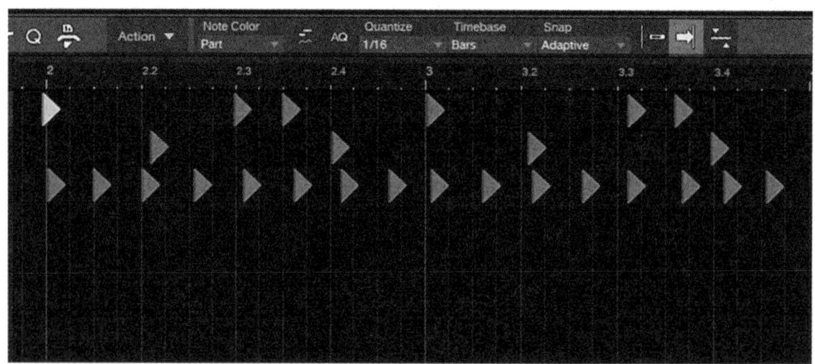

A sloppy drum performance before any quantization.

As you can hear, this beat is a little on the sloppy side.

TRACK 106: Recorded drum groove without any quantization

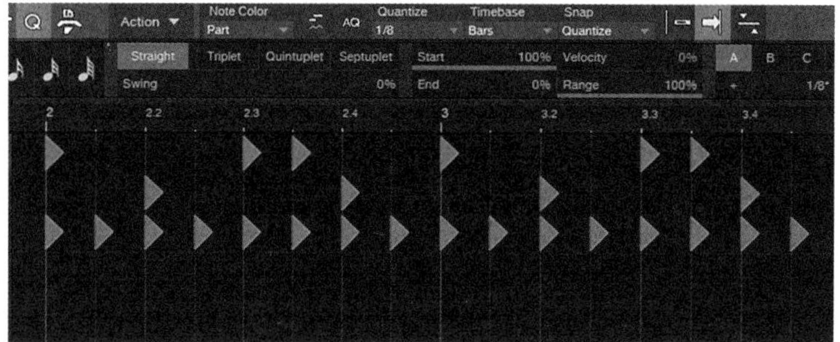

The same drum performance after 100% quantization to 16th note: notice how each note now perfectly aligns with the grid.

Now it sounds totally mechanical.

TRACK 107: EZDrummer 3: Previous drum groove quantized with 100% setting

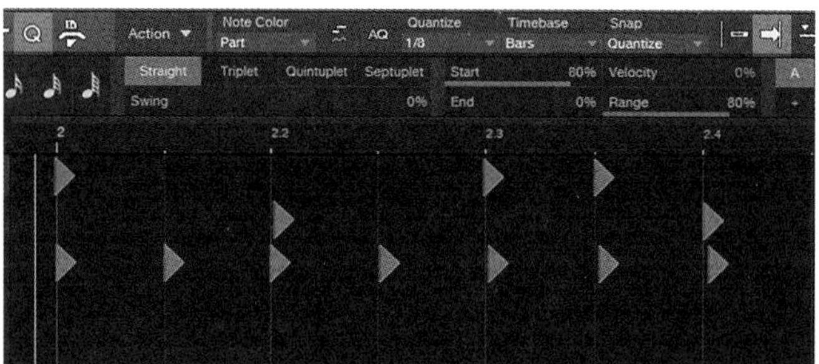

The same drum performance after 80% quantization: each note is pulled closer to the grid but not all the way.

This is a nice compromise. It sounds in time now, but it still sounds human.

TRACK 108: EZDrummer 3: Previous drum groove quantized with 80% setting

It should be mentioned that the quantization will usually only affect the currently selected MIDI events (pattern, fill, etc.). So if you have 20 events or so in your total drum track and you want to quantize the whole thing to the same setting, then you should glue (or merge) them together first so that they become one event. In Studio One, this is accomplished by selecting all the events and selecting "merge."

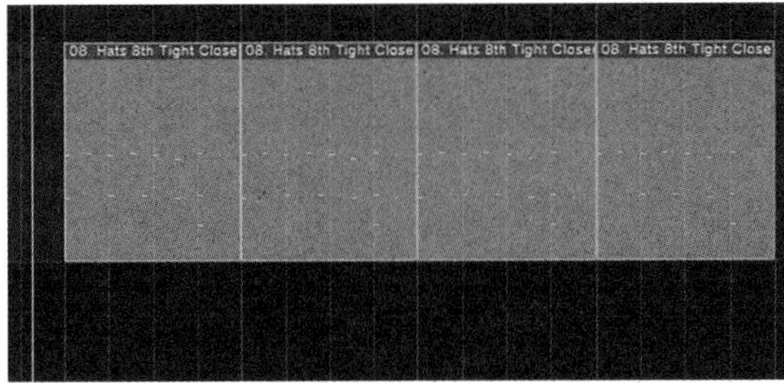

This drum track consists of many separate events. If you apply quantization to one of them, it won't affect the rest.

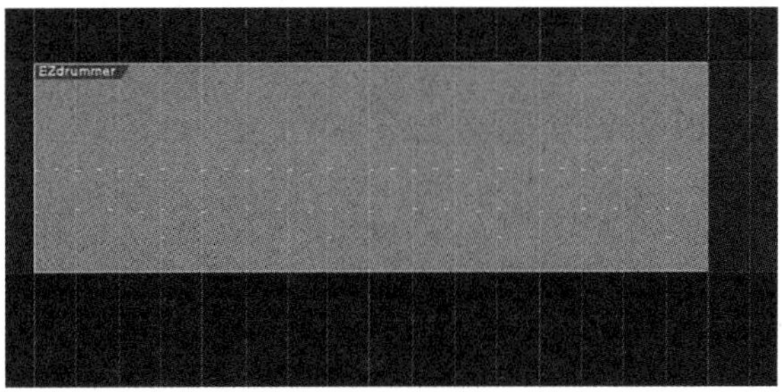

After gluing the items together, they become one. Now you can quantize the whole track at once.

Tips for Realistic Drum Tracks

If you're going for the robotic 80s drum machine sound, then that's pretty easy to get. But just as with other MIDI instruments, there are many things to keep in mind when programming a drum track if you want it to sound totally convincing.

- **Don't program impossible parts**: A drummer only has four limbs, so don't play five drums/cymbals at once. Also, don't program impossibly fast parts.
- **Don't over-quantize**: The more human feel you can retain in your track, the better. If you have to quantize a recorded part severely for it to sound acceptable, then you should probably re-record it and get a cleaner take.
- **Listen to real drum tracks and notice the subtleties**: Spend a good amount of time listening closely (with headphones) to recordings that feature drum parts you like. What happens to the kick or hat when they play a fill? What happens when they come back in after a fill? Subtle though the difference may be to the untrained ear, a drummer would spot these types of things right away.
- **Try to use a MIDI drum controller if at all possible**: Playing with sticks in your hand really does help you mimic the feel better. Even a four-pad controller is preferable to pecking it out on a keyboard in my humble opinion.
- **Don't forget flams, double stops, rolls, drags, and other subtle touches**: Drummers will mix it up often in real performances, especially when it comes to fills, so listen to the way they do this on recordings and add a few of these techniques into your programmed tracks.

Chapter 10:
Recording Vocals

Compared to other instruments, recording vocals can seem deceptively simple on the surface. After all, you just sing into the mic, right? However, considering the fact that the vocals are usually *the centerpiece* of the song (if it contains vocals), they need to be handled with care. In this chapter, we'll look at the equipment of choice and some tips on getting the best performances out of the vocalist (whether it's you or someone else).

TOOLBOX

Don't Delay!
Since the vocals are usually the most important element in a song, many people end up recording them last. However, it's always a good idea to record at least a scratch vocal track early in the process. Why? You can spend a great deal of time layering on the ear candy and creating the perfect backing track, only to discover later that one (or more) of the parts totally conflicts with the lead vocal. (Ask me how I know this!)

The Recording Space

Vocals are usually recorded in a dry environment so that they have clarity and presence. Any ambience, such as reverb or delay, etc., is usually applied electronically via effects after the fact. This is why the "vocal booth"—a fairly small room that's acoustically "dead" (for the most part)—is so common.

Most home studios don't have the benefit of a custom-built vocal booth. However, there are alternatives that are leagues better than an untreated bedroom. For example, a carpeted closet filled with lots of hanging clothes can make a pretty decent vocal booth. There are also several products available that can serve as temporary vocal booths. The Samson RC10 Reflection Mic Filter is one such product.

Samson Audio RC10 Reflection Mic Filter

It's also possible to build your own portable vocal booths for a very reasonable amount (see Appendix), and you can achieve excellent results! If your room is not too reflective, you may be able to get away without it.

Large Diaphragm Condenser Microphones

By and large, the prototypical microphone used for vocals is the large diaphragm condenser. However, everyone's voice is completely unique, and therefore vocal microphone choices can be much less standardized than mics used for other instruments.

There are favorite classic vocal mics, such as a Neumann (U67 or U87) or AKG C12, but these cost thousands and therefore don't make many appearances in the home studio. When choosing a vocal mic, it's best to try it out in person—if at all possible—with *your* voice (if you're going to be recording your vocals, that is) before you buy it. If that's not possible, read up as much as you can, as this will help you at least get basic feedback about a mic (if it's darker/brighter, etc.).

The WA-14 microphone, from Warm Audio, is a fabulous-sounding, affordable LDC.

TOOLBOX

Back It Up!

When singing into a condenser microphone, you don't "eat the mic" the way you often do when singing live (usually with a dynamic mic). You'll generally be singing between six to eight inches away from the mic and usually with a *pop filter* to help prevent plosive sounds—such as those created with "b" and "p" words—from disrupting the mic's diaphragm and creating brief "pops" in the vocal track.

The pop filter clamps onto the microphone stand and prevents air bursts from disrupting the mic's diaphragm.

TOOLBOX

Recording Procedure

Plug the mic into your interface and set the levels. (Remember to make any mic cord connections with phantom power off!) Assign/arm the track, and that's all there is to it! (Note: Recording vocals with compression on the way in is very popular as well. See Chapters 11 and 13 for details on this.)

Let's have a listen to the WA-14 LDC from Warm Audio. This mic costs $400, yet it sounds as though it should cost five times that. While we're demoing the sound of this mic, we'll also demonstrate the effect of my homemade vocal booth. (See Appendix for information on how to build your own.)

TRACK 109: WA-14 Male rock vocal in bedroom

TRACK 110: WA-14 Female rock vocal in bedroom

TRACK 111: WA-14 Male rock vocal in bedroom with portable vocal booth

TRACK 112: WA-14 Female rock vocal in bedroom with portable vocal booth

TRACK 113: WA-14 Male intimate vocal in bedroom

TRACK 114: WA-14 Female intimate vocal in bedroom

TRACK 115: WA-14 Male intimate vocal in bedroom with portable vocal booth

TRACK 116: WA-14 Female intimate vocal in bedroom with portable vocal booth

As you can hear, the portable booth makes a noticeable difference in the sound of the vocal. It's more present and focused sounding, which will definitely make a difference in the final mix.

TOOLBOX

Proximity Effect

The *proximity effect* is the increase in bass frequency buildup that happens when you get closer to the microphone. The science behind why this happens is a bit complicated, but the effects are quite noticeable. Check out the following track to hear it in action.

 **TRACK 117:** Proximity effect

For such a small action (moving a few inches in), the difference is more than subtle. If a person's voice is on the smaller-sounding end, it can add apparent weight to the vocal. However, it sometimes results in a bit of muddiness and should therefore be implemented cautiously.

Tube Microphones

While technically an LCD, the tube microphone works differently and therefore is often singled out. Many people refer to tube mics as adding a pleasing warmth to the signal, which is often welcome in the digital recording domain. The tube mic I'm using here is a WA-47 by Warm Audio, which is a beautiful-sounding mic available for about $900 new. We'll hear the same previous phrases sung through it here.

TRACK 118: WA-47 Male rock vocal

TRACK 119: WA-47 Female rock vocal

TRACK 120: WA-47 Male intimate vocal

TRACK 121: WA-47 Female intimate vocal

Compare these tracks with the previous ones to hear the difference in tone.

Warm Audio WA-47 Large-diaphragm Tube Condenser microphone

Samson G-Track Pro Professional USB microphone

USB Microphones

Yet another classification within the LDC umbrella is the USB microphone. This is a mic with a USB jack that allows you to simply plug straight into the computer's USB port. In other words, you don't even need an audio interface to record with one (it's built into the mic)! They're especially handy when you want to take a laptop on the road and don't want to have to lug around a bunch of gear. For this reason, they're especially popular with podcasters.

Dynamic Microphones

Generally speaking, dynamic mics are often employed in louder, more rock-oriented vocal tracks, but there are many exceptions to this. Thom Yorke of Radiohead prefers an Electro-Voice RE20 dynamic mic for nearly all of his vocals. Another very common dynamic vocal mic in the studio is the Shure SM7B, which is used by Sheryl Crow and Wilco's Jeff Tweedy. Oh, and you may have heard of a little album by Michael Jackson called *Thriller*, yes? Yep—the King of Pop recorded his vocals with the SM7B.

Let's hear the same rock and intimate phrases through the Shure SM7B. We'll be singing much closer to the mic on this track than with an LDC, which is generally in keeping with dynamic mic technique.

TRACK 122: Shure SM7B Male rock vocal

TRACK 123: Shure SM7B Female rock vocal

TRACK 124: Shure SM7B Male intimate vocal

TRACK 125: Shure SM7B Female intimate vocal

Tips for Better Vocal Tracks

Recording vocals can be a very rewarding or very frustrating experience, depending on a number of factors. But there are several things can help make the process go as smoothly as possible:

- **Choose a quiet time**: Since you're most likely not going to have a soundproof vocal booth, you need to make sure that the neighbor's dog isn't going to be barking a duet with you.
- **Have a lyric sheet in place**: Even if the singer knows the song cold, it can't hurt, and it usually makes communication smoother.
- **Make sure nothing is jingling, crinkling, or rattling on the singer**: Leave the loud jewelry out of the vocal booth.

- **Give the vocalist exactly what they want in their headphone mix**: Everybody is different in this regard. Some people like their vocal loud and proud; others want it barely audible.
- **Try to learn their preferred method of working**: Some singers like to only sing entire takes of the song, while others don't mind punching in line-by-line if necessary.
- **Try to be positive and specific with any comments or criticism**: Rather than saying "That sucks; let's go again," try to give them something they can use. Instead, you could say something like, "Ok, it's getting better, but I know you've still got a better take in you."
- **Set the mood**: If it's a slow, intimate vocal, maybe try turning the lights down and lighting some candles or firing up the lava lamps.
- **Be mindful of fatigue**: If you can tell their voice is starting to go, don't push it (unless they want a strained, tired sound for effect). This can only lead to increased vocal strain that could possibly result in an extended recovery time.

TOOLBOX

The Headphone Dilemma

Singing with headphones can be notoriously difficult. This explains the many interesting things you often see when singers are recording with them. Many times, one headphone will be off the ear, or you may see them holding the headphones against one ear, etc. This isn't because the headphones are about to fall off their head. It's simply the singer's way of trying to get comfortable while singing with them on. It's a different feeling than hearing your voice in the room.

Some singers prefer not to fight this battle at all. Peter Gabriel, among others, is a proponent of singing *without headphones*. He simply sings along with the monitors in the room. And yes, that means there will be *some* bleed into his vocal mic. However, this isn't the end of the world. If you face the mic opposite the speakers (in cardioid mode) and keep the monitors to a dull roar, the bleed is normally negligible and isn't heard at all within the context of the entire mix. (It didn't seem to give Pete any trouble.) Give it a try!

Chapter 11: Outboard Gear

In today's world, where we have plug-ins to emulate everything, one might wonder why we'd ever need to break "out of the box" at all. There are actually several reasons you might want to consider some outboard gear, which we'll discuss in this chapter. The good news is that there's never been a better time to do so, as the variety and quality of outboard equipment available to the home recordist is awe-inspiring.

What Is Outboard Gear?

So, what do we mean by *outboard gear*? This term generally refers to any sound-processing equipment used outside of your DAW and audio interface. Commonly used pieces of outboard equipment—in pro and home studios alike—include:

- External microphone preamps
- Compressors/limiters
- Equalizers
- Effects processors

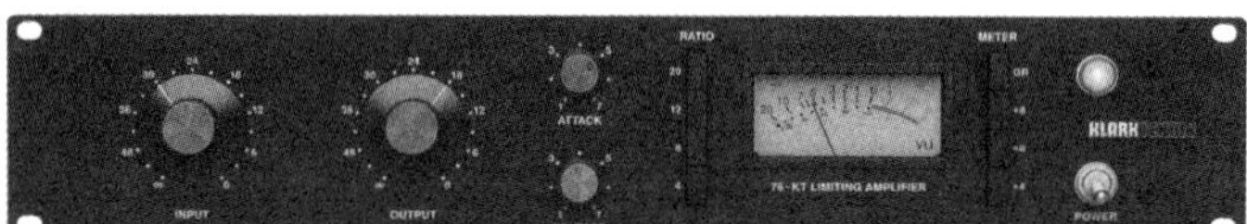

Klark Teknik 76-KT "1176-style" compressor

Most of this equipment is *rack-mountable*, which means it's built to a standard width and height so that it can be mounted in a rack. The height of a unit is measured in "spaces," which is abbreviated with "U." So a unit that requires two rack spaces would be a 2U unit. Most outboard gear is 1U or 2U. You can buy separate rack cabinets that sit on the floor and have casters, which are good for moving around easily if you need to.

The On-Stage WSR7500 Workstation Rack Cabinet has a 12U capacity and optional casters for easy transport.

Author's hand-made studio desk.

Lots of studio desks also have racks built-in to them. If you're handy with power tools, you can make your own studio desk. Here's the studio desk I built from my father's old bedframe from the 50s—nice solid maple! Between the floor and desktop racks, it has a 40U capacity, and with the free wood (which was nice, of course!), this cost me about $20 in hardware to build. A comparable studio desk from a store would cost hundreds or thousands!

There's been a definite resurgence in the use of outboard gear in home studios over the past decade. I see it as somewhat analogous to guitar amps. Although tube guitar amps managed to survive the solid state revolution of the 70s and 80s, many people swore that their days were numbered when digital modeling amps showed up in the 90s. Yet, here we are 20+ years later, and tube amps are still the preferred choice for many working guitarists out there.

Just as with modeling guitar amps, the flexibility, price, and convenience of plug-ins is extremely attractive and useful; there's no doubt about that. However, there's still something to be said for good ol' analog equipment. Whether it's the sound, the tactile interface, or simply the inspiring vibe it brings to your studio, I don't think analog is going anywhere anytime soon.

The Power of One (or Two)

If you've been to a truly pro studio before, you've no doubt been blown away by the sheer amount of gear. But realize that they need to be able to record a *lot* of tracks simultaneously with top-notch equipment. As home recordists, we usually don't need that redundancy.

This is why many people will put together one or two channels of nice outboard gear, which can then be used throughout the tracking and overdubbing processes. For example, you might get a really nice external preamp, a nice outboard compressor (or two), and a nice tube EQ. This way, for those one or two channels, you can rival the pro studios.

Again, the good news is that several companies are making fantastic-sounding outboard recreations of many classic sought-after units—such as Neve-style mic preamps, LA-2A- or 1176-style compressors, and Pultec-style EQs—for a fraction of what the original units go for. Two bang-for-the-buck names in this regard are Warm Audio and Klark Teknik.

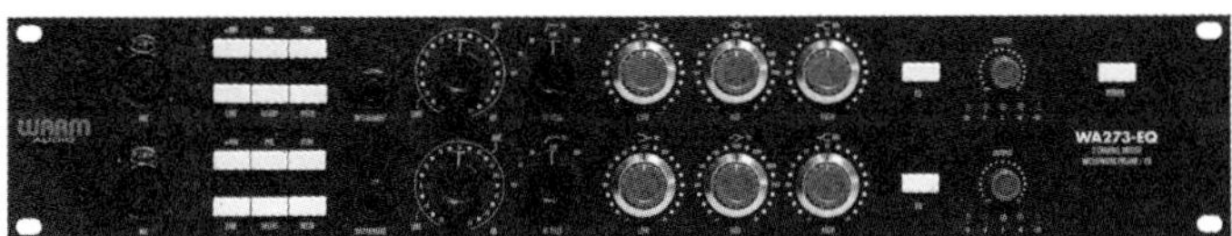

The Warm Audio WA273-EQ is an incredible-sounding two-channel Neve-style mic preamp with a three-band EQ and a high pass filter on each channel.

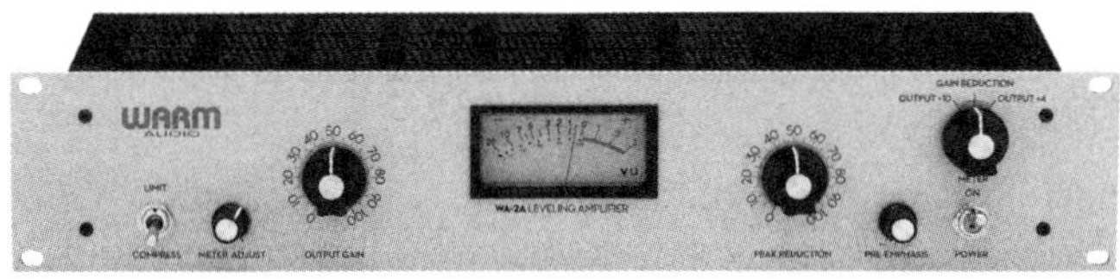

The Warm Audio WA-2A is an optical tube compressor modeled after the famous LA-2A. With minimal controls, it's easy to dial in classic compression on numerous sources.

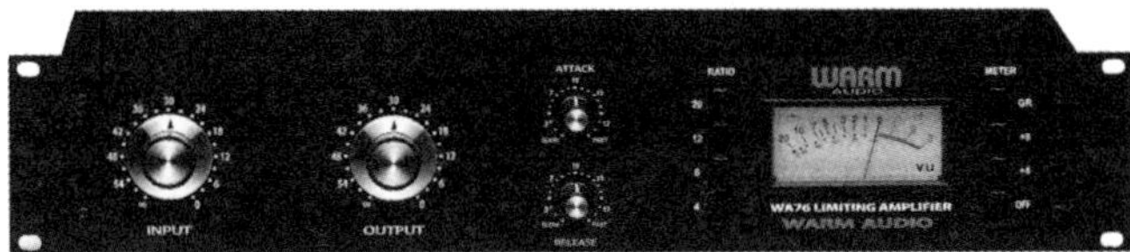

The Warm Audio WA76 is an FET-type discrete compressor that faithfully reproduces the circuitry of the 1176 compressor—quite probably the most widely-used compressor of all time.

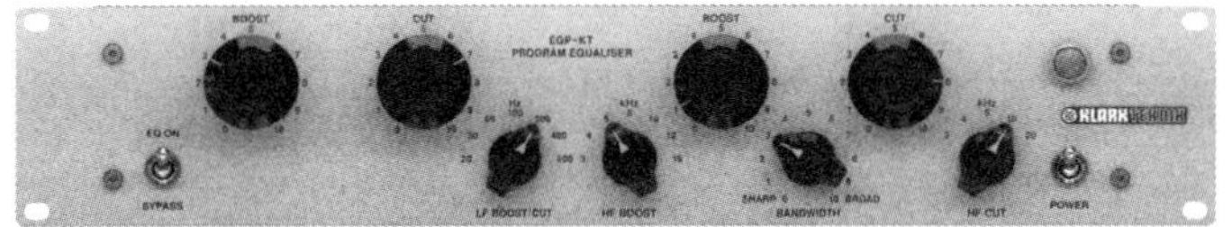

The EQP-KT by Klark Teknik is a tube EQ modeled after the holy grail of all EQs: the Pultec EQP-1A. Literally just about anything you put through this thing sounds better!

I make use of all of these outboard units on the accompanying audio tracks for this book. With the affordable prices of these units, you can grab a stereo pair of Pultec-style EQs and compressors (LA-2A or 1176 style) for a fraction of the price you'd pay for one vintage unit!

Typical Uses

There are two common ways most people implement these outboard units in their recordings: printing the effect, or as an insert effect.

Printing the Effect

When printing an effect, we run through a unit on the way to the interface. This means that the sound will be processed and recorded that way. For instance, a very common practice when recording vocals is to run through a preamp followed by a compressor (or two) on the way to the interface.

Typical Vocal Chain

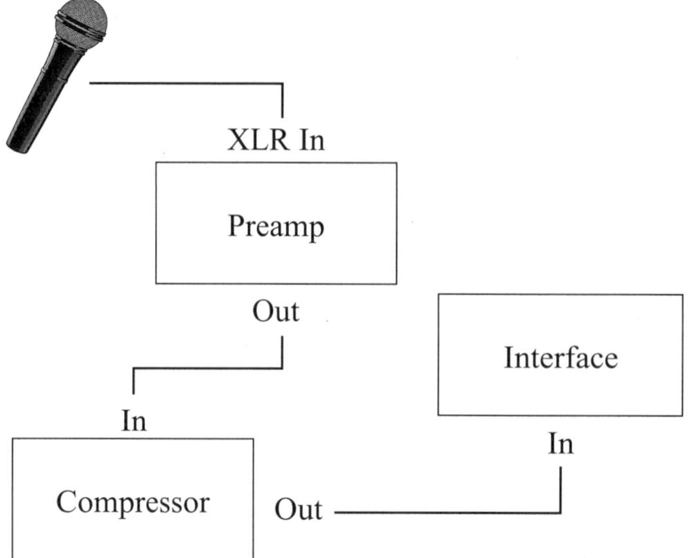

This type of setup is also commonly used for miked instruments as well, such as drums, guitars, etc. Of course, anything you do will be printed on the track and cannot be undone. Therefore, you need to make sure you get the preamp gain and/or compression correct. This takes a bit of practice at first, but it will soon become second nature. (We'll talk more about compression settings, etc. in Chapter 13.)

Using as an Insert Effect

Another way to use outboard gear is as an *insert effect*. In this scenario, you're applying the effect to a track that's already been recorded. Note that you will need an interface with more than two outputs for this. The idea is to send a track out one of your interface's extra outputs—channel 3, let's say—through the outboard unit and back into an input on your interface. You then record the processed signal on a new track in your DAW.

Inserting an Outboard Compressor

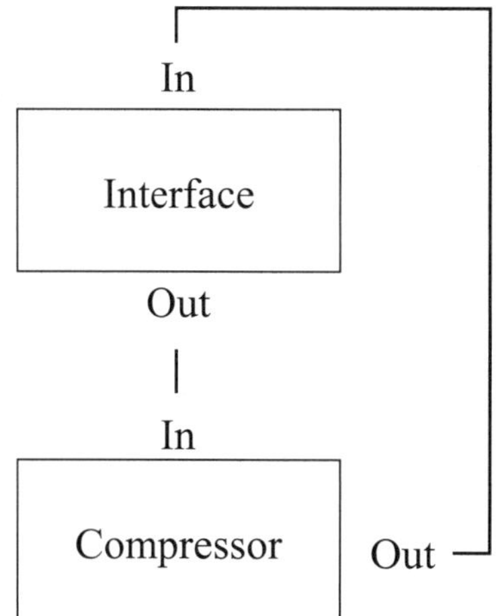

With this method, if you add too much compression the first time, you can simply undo that track and do it again. This method also allows you to use the same outboard processor on as many different tracks as you want. The more outputs you have on your interface, the more insert effects you can apply at the same time.

Chapter 12: Editing

After you've recorded all your tracks, the final step before mixing is usually *editing*. This step can vary greatly from person to person. Whereas some may not even choose to edit anything at all (a stereo live-in-the-studio recording, perhaps), others may spend the bulk of their time here, building the song up brick by brick.

We're going to cover some common editing techniques that apply to most at one point or another. In this chapter, we'll generally assume that you've recorded a multi-track song and you still have a bit of tidying up, rearranging, tweaking, or fine-tuning before you're ready to begin the mixdown process.

Common Reasons for Editing

Before we get into specifics, let's look at a few of the most common reasons that you'd need to edit in the first place.

- **Song Arrangement:** This is one of the broadest editing strokes you can make. What if, after recording the song, you decide that you really want the chorus to repeat at the end of the song? Well, if you recorded to a click, it's usually a fairly simple procedure of copying and pasting.
- **Timing Issues:** This is a very commonly used technique. If upon listening back, you discover that the bass is rushed on a few beats, and you'd rather not punch in or re-track the part, it's a simple task to move a few notes forward or backward in time to align better with the beat.
- **"Comping" Takes:** *Comping* (short for "compiling") involves choosing different parts of several different takes for the same instrument and patching them together into one finished track. The most common application of this technique is usually vocals.
- **Level Adjustments:** Just as with timing concerns, if a few notes of the guitar solo are sticking out like a sore thumb, it's an easy matter to adjust the volume of those notes.
- **Getting Rid of Noises or Unwanted Notes, Etc.:** A great deal of the editing process simply involves cleaning up noises when nothing is happening on the track.
- **Pitch Correction:** Again, most commonly used for vocals, pitch correction has completely changed the recording industry, for better or worse. Energy was great, but that high note that's just a little flat? No problem; just run it through a vocal tuning plug-in, and all is right.

> TOOLBOX
>
> **The Magic of Undo**
> It's important to realize—if you didn't already know—that just about all of these editing techniques are *non-destructive*. In other words, regardless of what you do to a media item, the original file is still intact on your hard drive and can be accessed if necessary. To get back to the way it was before the edit, you just hit undo.

Let's take a closer look at each editing procedure and see what's involved. These are in no particular order, but I usually start with the "big picture" jobs first.

Editing the Arrangement of the Song

This seems like the first editing step to me because it has the capacity to affect things by the greatest amount. It largely involves the move, copy, and paste tools. In the following example, we're going copy the intro of a song and insert it after the first A section to serve as an interlude. If you haven't already thus far, this is a good time to place *markers* in your song, as this can make finding the location of specific phrases quicker and easier.

Here's how our guitar riff looks originally. Notice that the B section immediately follows the A section.

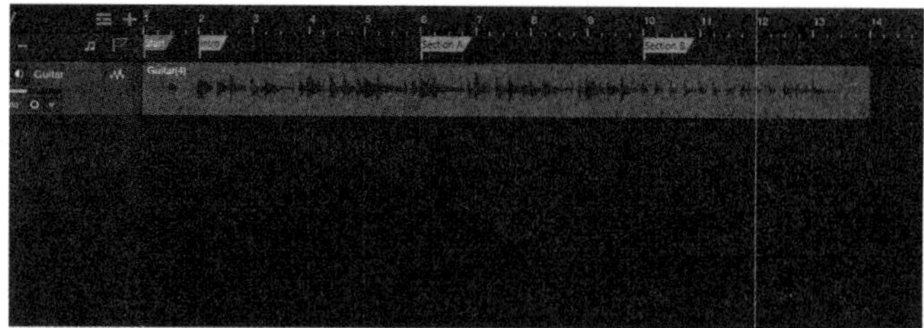

Originally, section B immediately follows section A.

The first thing we need to do, if it's not already done, is split the media item at the end of the A section. Again, if you recorded to a click, these types of operations are much easier. You'll want to have the "snap to grid" feature enabled at this point. It's not impossible if you didn't use a click, but it's usually a bit more time-consuming. (If you didn't use a click, "snap to grid" should be *disabled*.)

We'll select the media item after the split (the beginning of section B) and move it forward to allow room for the added section. In this case, that's four measures.

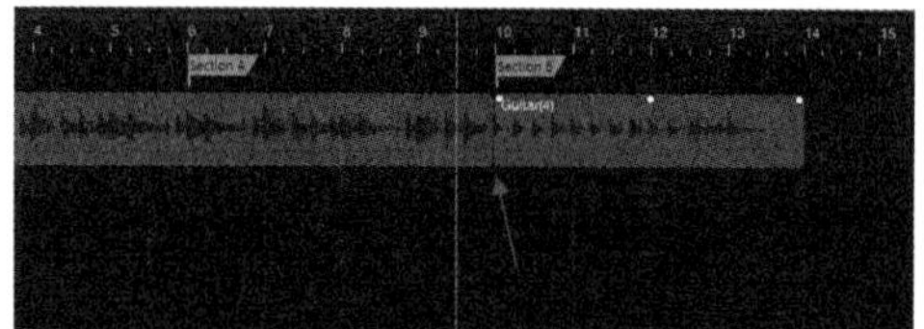

The media item is split at the end of section A.

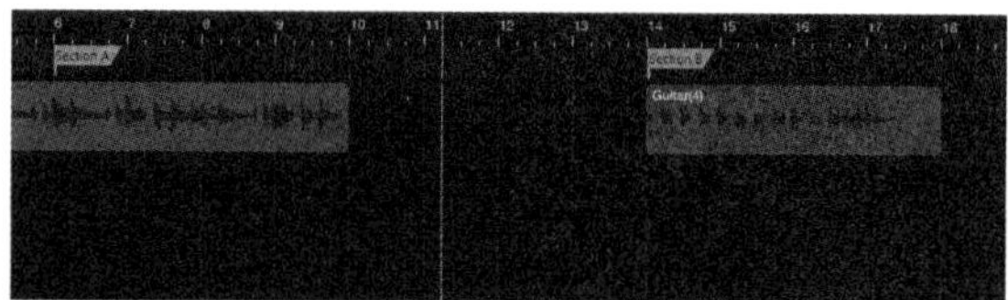

The media item is moved forward four measures.

Next, we need to make sure the intro is sectioned off by splitting the item at its end if necessary. Then we simply select the four measures of the intro, copy them, and then paste them in place. To paste them, move the cursor to the beginning of the space and use the paste command. (Note: If you were doing this with multiple tracks, you want to make sure you have the first of those tracks selected when you go to paste them. In other words, if you copied tracks 1–4 and want to paste them later, be sure you have track 1 selected when you paste them.)

Here's how our new arrangement looks:

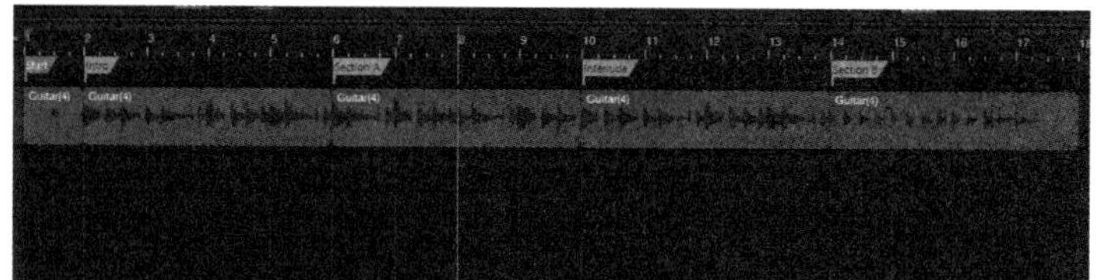

The four-measure intro has now been inserted as an interlude between sections A and B.

Regarding most editing processes, there are usually several ways to accomplish the same thing. Depending on the situation, you'll find that one method may work better than the other. If any of the instruments aren't smoothly transitioning through the edit, you may need to tweak them individually at the edit point using the tools described in the topics that follow.

Cleaning Up Noises and Miscellaneous Sounds

This is always a satisfying step—especially for the anal retentive among us. You have the ability to make any part of a track that doesn't contain music absolutely silent. The method I normally use involves splitting items and deleting the unwanted sections. For example, let's look at the beginning of a tune that involves several tracks: drums, bass, and two guitars.

The drums are virtual MIDI drums, so they aren't a problem. However, the bass track has a slight buzz that's audible, as does one of the guitars. The other guitarist has a case of "can't shut up"—all too common—and is noodling all over the place before the song starts.

 **TRACK 126:** A noisy pre-song intro

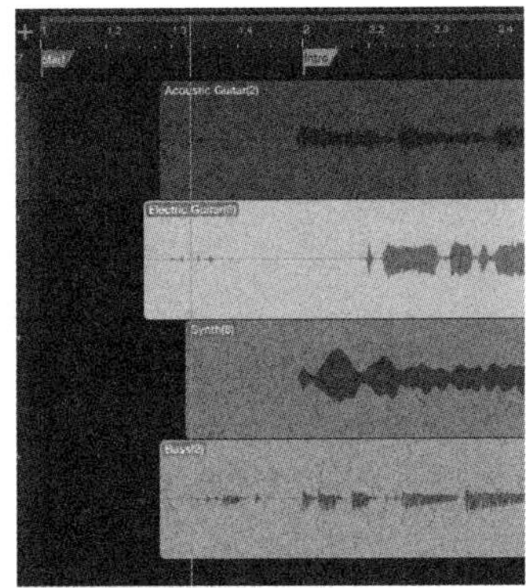

This song includes all kinds of unwanted noise before the downbeat.

No problem. These are all easy fixes. Simply split an item right before the first note starts, select the unwanted portion and delete!

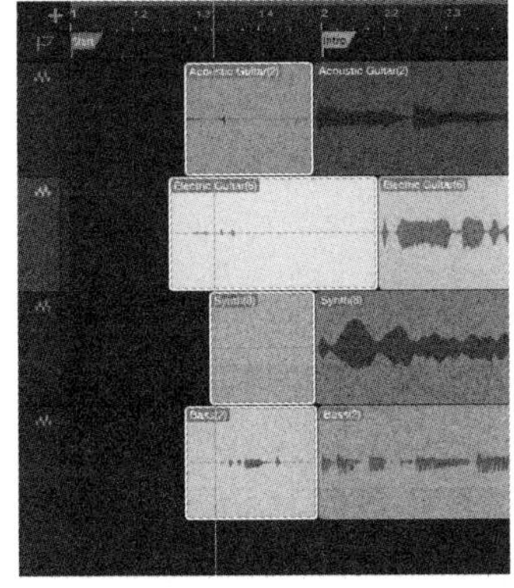

The items have been split, and the unwanted portions have been selected.

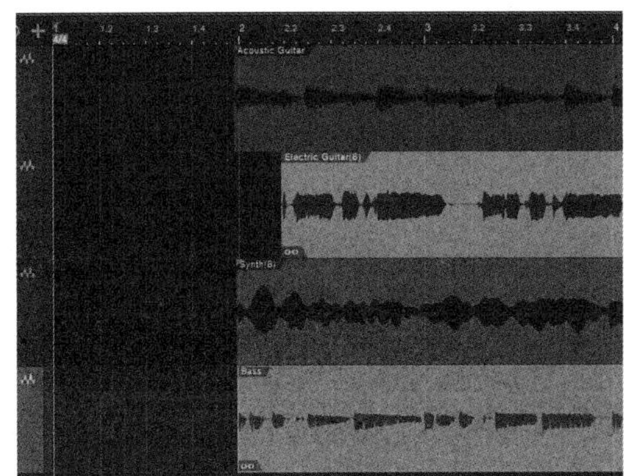

Delete! Ahhh ... So satisfying! That's better.

TRACK 127: Clean intro with no noise before the downbeat

Fixing a Timing Error

This is a common edit for when someone just rushed or dragged a bit during a certain phrase. Let's check out an example in which the guitarist rushed a few chords during a riff. Here's the original phrase along with a drum pattern, which establishes the tempo.

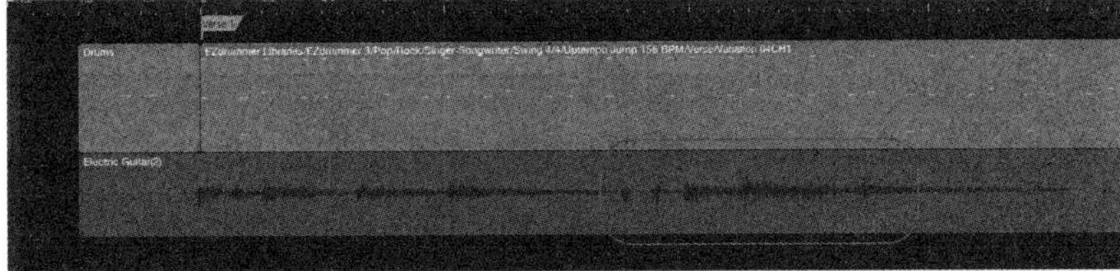

You can see how the guitar is ahead of the beat on a few chords here.

TRACK 128: Guitar part is rushed on a few chords

For this type of editing, we'll want to turn the snap setting off, because we'll need to have more precise placement capabilities. The first step is to split the item before and after each offending chord. If necessary, we can trim the ends of the media items to prevent overlapping. Consult your DAW's manual if necessary to see how this is done.

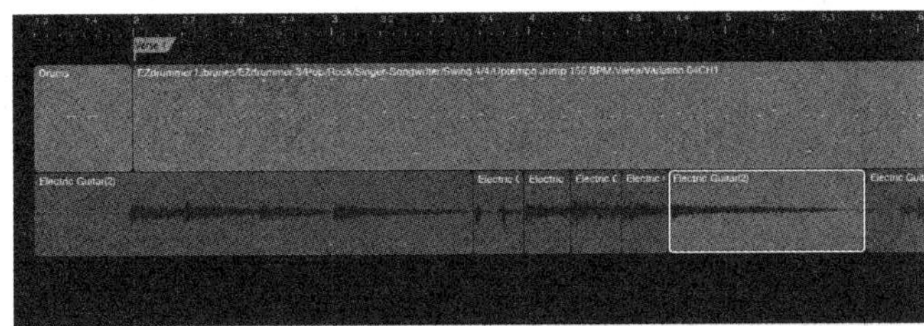

The offending chords are all moveable on their own now.

We can now move these individual chords and place them on the beat.

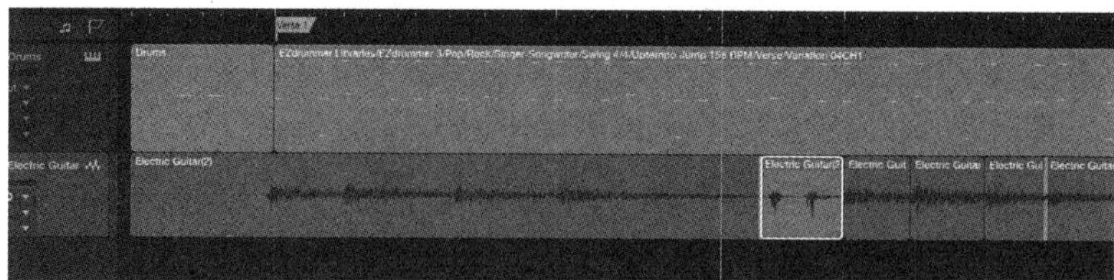

The offending chords have been moved, and the guitar part now sounds in time.

TRACK 129: Guitar part's timing is corrected

Adjusting the Level (Volume) of a Phrase or Note

There are several ways to do this, and I employ different ones depending on the situation. If it's just a few notes here and there, I'll usually split the items to single out the notes and then manually adjust the volume of the individual item. (See "Clip Gain" Toolbox.)

For example, here's a phrase from a guitar solo in which two notes are just inappropriately loud and stick out a bit too much.

TRACK 130: Guitar phrase with a couple of notes that are too loud

So, after splitting the item to isolate those two notes, we can adjust the volume up or down.

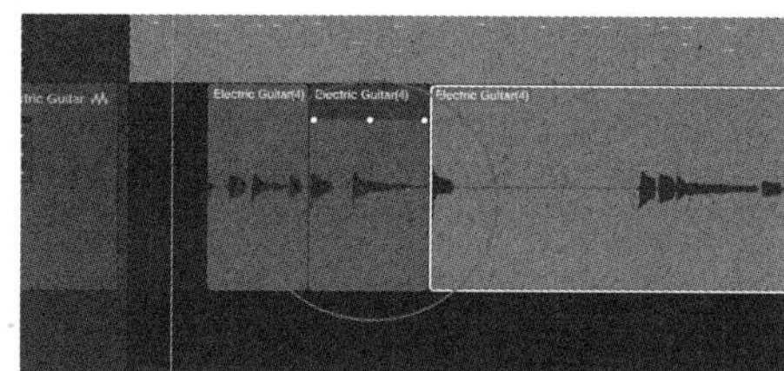

In Studio One, you can grab the top of a media item and drag its volume level up or down.

Now it sounds much smoother.

TRACK 131: Guitar phrase with loud notes attenuated

If the volume of an instrument is more erratic and would require extensive slicing and dicing to make it sound smooth (even with a compressor), then I may use some automation. You'll have to refer to your DAW's manual on how to do this, but most programs will allow you to record automation and/or draw it in manually.

Here's an example of how this type of automation curve looks on Studio One. Again, this can be accomplished by either playing the song (or a section of it) and "recording" the fader movement on the track, or you can begin with a straight volume envelope and draw in points by hand.

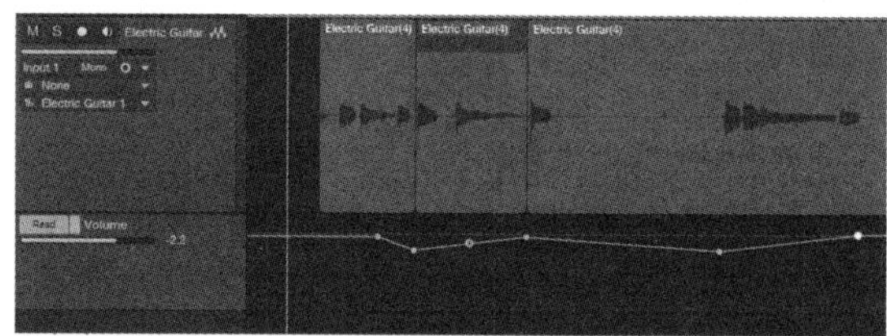

Studio One allows you to create automation of volume (or pan, effects, etc.) by recording fader movements or drawing in envelope curves by hand.

Note that if this track has (or will have) level-dependent effects on it (such as compression), I will automate with clip gain (see below) instead of track automation, leaving the latter for the mixing process.

TOOLBOX

Clip Gain

The term *clip gain* refers to another form of volume automation. The name is derived from the fact that, in Pro Tools, individual media items are called "clips" (instead of "events" or "items"). So, this term simply refers to the practice of adjusting the volume envelope of one specific item instead of the whole track. It has nothing to do with clipping or signal distortion.

In Studio One, this is called a *Gain Envelope*. You can see in the screenshot that the volume envelope doesn't extend past the event. This is how you can tell it's clip gain instead of a standard volume envelope (which affects the whole track).

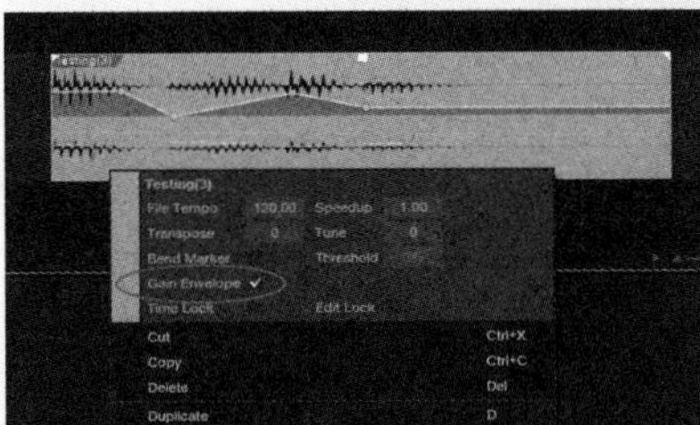

In Studio One, the Gain Envelope feature allows you to adjust the volume envelope of individual events.

What's the difference between clip gain and a standard track automation volume envelope? It's where it happens in the signal flow. Clip gain is happening *pre-send* and *pre-effects*, whereas track automation is happening *post-send* and *post-effects*. In other words, clip gain is at the very beginning of the signal path, and track automation is at the very end of it.

What this means is that adjusting the clip gain *will* affect the level you're sending to your effect plug-ins, whereas track automation won't. This is easy to verify, too. Try the following experiment:

1. Add a compressor plug-in to a track and adjust it so that you're seeing a good deal of gain reduction (GR), such as 10 dB or more.
2. Create a playback loop lasting a measure or so, turn on looping, and press play.
3. Now, watch the compressor plug-in while you turn down the track's fader. You'll notice that the amount of GR doesn't change.
4. Bring the fader back to 0 and then use the volume handle on the media event/item to lower the volume. (This is the same thing as adjusting the clip gain; it's just not automated.) Notice how the GR is affected.

So, what does this mean? Well, the short story is that it means clip gain is usually best for the editing stage, whereas track volume automation is best for the mixing stage. This is because, with clip gain, you can get a nice, balanced level *before* ever hitting your processors. With track volume automation, you can adjust the level of the affected signal without changing the way it's interacting with any effects.

Comping Takes

"Comping" takes refers to the practice of cherry-picking the best parts of several performances of the same material and assembling them into one final performance. Again, there are several ways to do this as well, and it partly depends on how the performances were recorded. For this example, we'll use a bass track.

Each Take Recorded to a Separate Track

If you recorded each take to a separate track, and you're not short at all on CPU power, then you could simply split the items to section off phrases as needed and mute or delete all but the saved take. For example, here we see two different bass takes, each on their own track. We've sectioned off the phrases by splitting the items as necessary and then muted the unwanted portions.

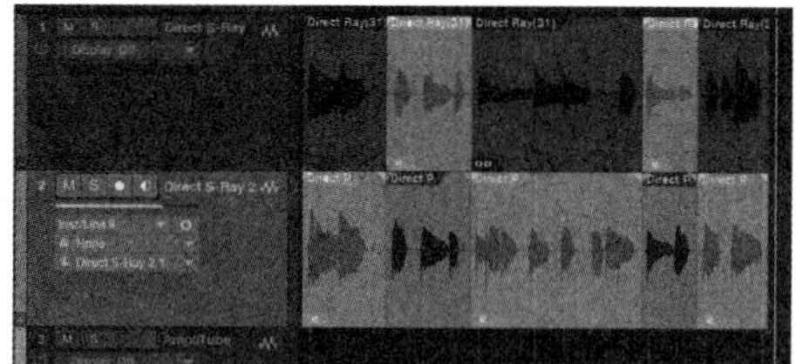

Two bass takes, each on their own track, are sectioned off phrase by phrase and muted as necessary to leave one final take remaining.

Each Take Recorded on the Same Track

If you record each take on the same track, they will usually be stacked on top of each other. You can set your DAW up to handle this in different ways, but in this example, Studio One has been set to display each take in a separate lane. This option is called "Takes to Layers" in Studio One.

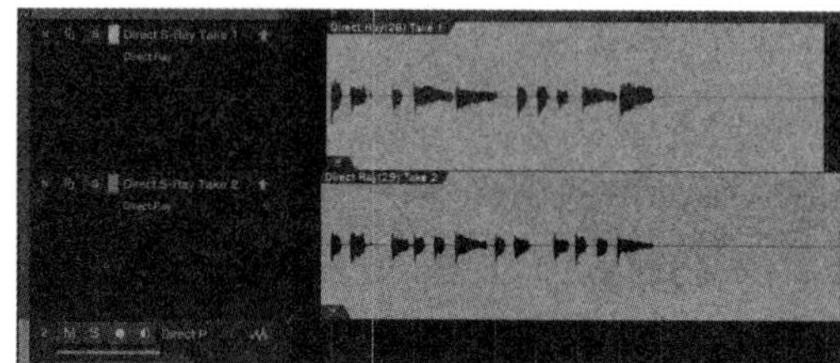

Two bass takes have been recorded on the same track. This is shown in Studio One as two stacked lanes.

From here, you can use basically the same idea, sectioning off the vocal into phrases and picking the best one. With this method, however, you only need to select the best take; the muting of the other two will be done in the process.

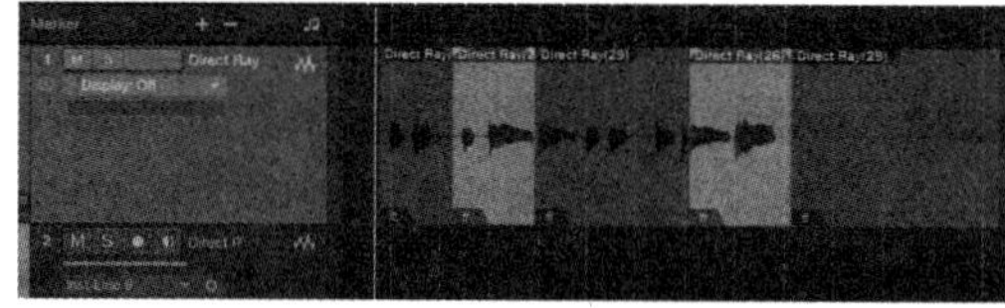

The phrases have been sectioned off, and the winning take has been selected for each.

TOOLBOX

Comping Tips!

- **Listen through headphones**: I prefer to listen to all edits through headphones, because you'll usually hear details that may escape you with speakers. It's very easy to accidentally slice a breath in half when comping takes vocal takes, for example.
- **When comping vocals, split the item after the breath**: This may seem a bit counterintuitive, but I've found that you're actually less likely to create a bad inhale edit if you split the item *after* the inhale and just before the singing begins.
- **Be sure to listen through the entire section or track when you're done**: You can get tunnel vision and lose sense of the big picture when comping takes, so it's important to make sure that the final take you've created sounds consistent and uniform throughout.

Pitch Correction

This is certainly most commonly used on vocals, and it's really changed the way in which vocals are recorded. No longer is it necessary to have both the feel *and* the pitch be there on a vocal take. A note (or a few notes) can be a bit flat or sharp in an otherwise great phrase, and that's good enough, as the software can fix it for you.

Although you can do this manually (similar to adjusting the volume of one or more notes), it's most commonly done with a software plug-in of some sort. Auto-Tune (by Antares) and Melodyne (by Celemony) are the two biggest names in this regard.

Much like quantizing in the MIDI world, several parameters can be adjusted, allowing you to produce natural-sounding correction, total robot vocals, and everything in between.

Let's have a listen to a vocal with several tuning problems throughout.

TRACK 132: Vocal phrase with numerous tuning problems

I'll be using Melodyne here, so you'll need to consult your software's manual if necessary to accomplish the same thing. By specifying the key of the song and instructing the program to correct the pitch by the desired amount, the vocal is transformed instantly into a new take.

TRACK 133: Vocal phrase after tuning with Melodyne

In Melodyne, you can adjust the timing/duration of notes as well, among other things, in many cases making it a one-stop track editor in its own right.

MIDI Editing

As we talked about briefly in Chapters 8 and 9, we have pretty much complete editing control over a MIDI recording even after it's been recorded. Quantizing is only a small part of what we can do. Among other things, we can control:

- Pitches (or the octave or key of the notes)
- Duration
- Volume, a.k.a. velocity (individually and/or by drawing/recording volume curves)
- Rhythmic timing (individually and/or via quantization)
- Adding or subtracting notes
- MIDI channel
- The instrument (sound) itself
- Copying and pasting of notes
- Looping phrases or patterns
- Add/change MIDI control change messages—i.e., pitch bend, modulation, etc.

And this list is hardly comprehensive. We'll demonstrate some of the most commonly employed MIDI editing tools here. For this example, we're going to look at a keyboard phrase and various things we can do to it after it's been recorded.

TRACK 134: Rhodes keyboard phrase in C minor

And here's how the phrase looks in Studio One's MIDI editor using the piano roll view.

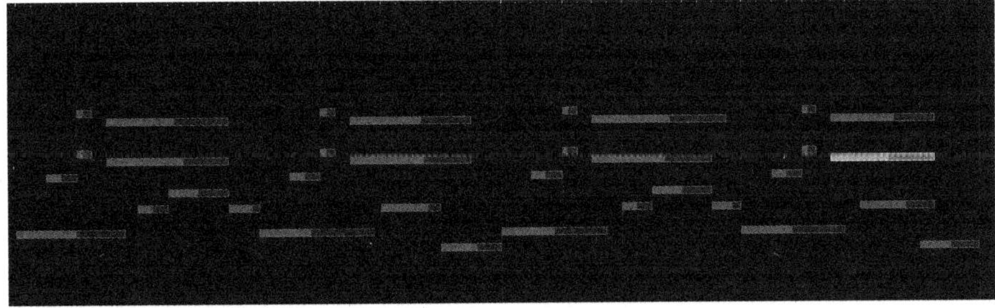

Studio One's MIDI editor displaying the keyboard phrase in piano roll format.

First let's just change a few of the bass notes. It's as easy as clicking and dragging them.

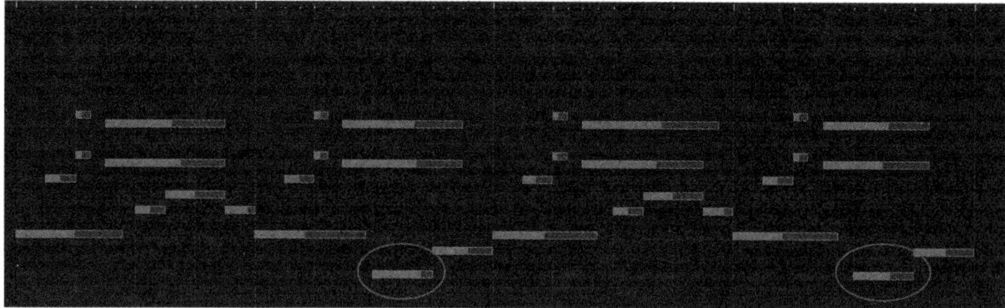

To move a note (or notes) in Studio One's MIDI editor, you simply click and drag them.

TRACK 135: Rhodes keyboard phrase in C minor with bass notes changed

Now let's say we want to bring down the bass line a bit to make the chords stand out. We just select some bass notes and reduce their volume.

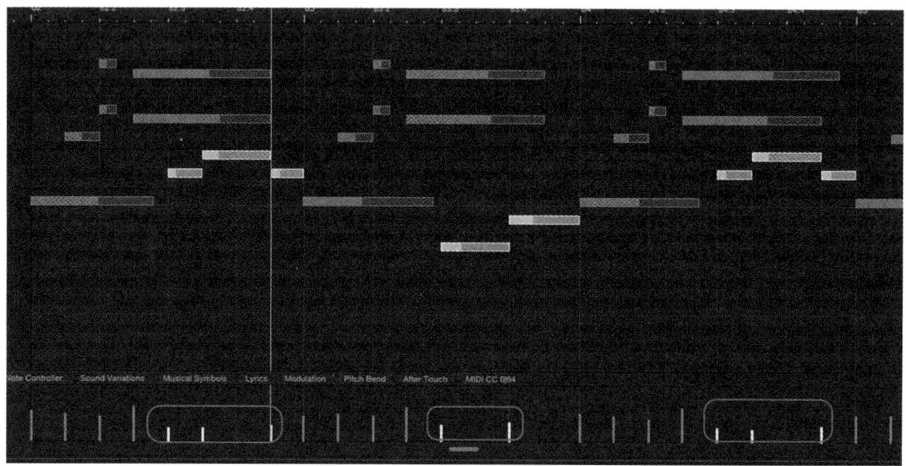

The appropriate bass notes have been selected in the MIDI editor.

TRACK 136: Rhodes keyboard phrase in C minor with quieter bass notes

How about we add a grace note to one of the higher notes? In Studio One, you can simply double-click to draw in a note. And let's say we also want to thin out the phrase so it's not so busy. We just group select the notes we want to get rid of and hit the DELETE key.

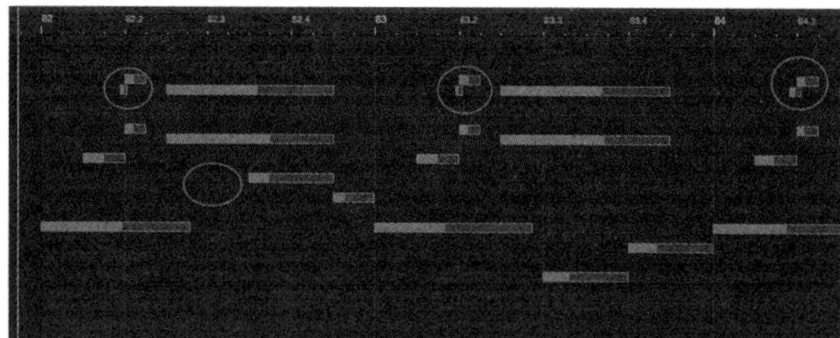

In Studio One, adding a new note is as simple as double-clicking. To remove a note, just select it and hit DELETE.

TRACK 137: Rhodes keyboard phrase in C minor with some notes deleted and a grace note added

Finally, let's say we want to go with a different virtual instrument altogether. No problem. We just delete the Lounge Lizard Session plug-in we were using and add the new one. Here we've replaced it with a Rhodes sound from Toontrack's EZkeys plug-in.

TRACK 138: Rhodes keyboard phrase with new virtual instrument

Again, you can go much deeper than this with MIDI. If you're running a fully-electronic studio, you'll most likely want to educate yourself more thoroughly on the MIDI subject overall.

Chapter 13: The Mixing Process

Once you have all the tracks recorded and have made any necessary edits, it's time to mix the song down. When we mix the song, we make final decisions with regard to track volume, panning, effects, equalization, etc., and then solidify those decisions into a stereo file (MP3, WAV, AIFF, etc.) that can be played anywhere.

At the end of this chapter, you'll find audio tracks of two original songs, demonstrating the concepts discussed. The individual track files for these songs can be downloaded (see the code on page 1 of this book) for personal mixing practice. I greatly encourage you to take advantage of this opportunity, as it's great practice to mix someone else's music. Since you don't have the same emotional attachment (baggage?) that you do when it's your song, you can be truly objective about your decisions and think only of the sound and message you're trying to convey with the mix.

As with most aspects of recording, there is no one way to mix. Some start with the drums and work out from there, while others start with the lead vocal and add everything else around it. Some mix very quickly, while others like to spend several days (or more) on one song. Therefore, it's not my intent to tell you how to mix a song. But I'll discuss some common concepts that are usually considered in the process.

> TOOLBOX
>
> **A Slight Digression**
> It should be mentioned that a song's production plays a big role in mixing. For example, if you have four separate guitar riffs, and they're all taking place in the same low register of the instrument, it's going to be difficult for each to be clearly heard within the mix. In contrast, a song in which each track is occupying its own sonic register can almost seem to mix itself, comparatively speaking.
>
> In this regard, you may find that you need to delete some parts all together—or at least remove them from a certain section—if they're doing more harm than good. A mix can be like its own performance this way, and it's a very subjective thing. You can make as many mixes as you like, so feel free to experiment!

Giving Each Instrument Its Own "Space"

One common goal in mixing is for each instrument to be heard clearly (unless you're going for a specific effect), and this usually gets more difficult with every track you add. There are several tools at our disposal that can help us do this, and we'll discuss them here.

Panning

This is one of the most obvious tools we have for keeping instruments out of each other's way. If you have two instruments that are playing similar parts with similar sounds, for example, you can pan them on opposite sides of the spectrum. Here's an example in which two guitars are both playing in the lower-to-mid register. The track will begin with both of them panned down the center; then they'll be moved out to the sides—around 3 o'clock and 9 o'clock.

These two guitar tracks have been panned to opposite sides of the stereo spectrum.

TRACK 139: Panning of two similar guitar parts for separation

Of course, there are no rules in this regard, so panning can be used as an effect as well. Most of the Beatles' recordings are panned with the vocals all on one side and the instruments on the other. You can also automate the panning of one instrument so you hear it move around in the stereo spectrum. Listen to some old Jimi Hendrix recordings to hear an example of this.

Equalization

One of the primary and most useful mixing tools of all is the *equalizer*, or *EQ*. This is a device that boosts or cuts (i.e., raises or lowers in volume) specific frequencies, thereby changing the character of an instrument's sound. If a vocal sounds too boomy or muddy, for example, you may cut some of the low frequencies with EQ.

TOOLBOX

An EQ will generally have several different "bands," or a selectable group of frequencies that are handled differently depending on the type of EQ used. The most common types of EQs are as follows:

- **Sweepable**: A *sweepable* EQ usually involves two knobs per band—one to select the center frequency (in Hz) and one to select the amount of boost or cut (in dB).
- **Parametric**: The *parametric* EQ is like a sweepable, but it adds another knob per band called the "Q." This knob adjusts the bandwidth, allowing you to focus in on a very narrow or broad range of frequencies surrounding the center frequency.
- **High Pass Filter**: A *high pass filter* allows all frequencies above a certain point to pass through unaffected while cutting all those below it. The name is a bit confusing, but a high-pass filter then cuts *low frequencies*.
- **Low Pass Filter**: The opposite of the high pass filter, the *low pass filter* allows frequencies below a certain point to pass through, so it cuts high frequencies.
- **Shelving**: *Shelving* (high and low) is similar to the high/low pass filter, but a shelving EQ will allow you to select a cutoff frequency and allow you to specify a boost *or* cut at that point.
- **Graphic EQ**: Much more common in outboard form than in plug-ins, a *graphic EQ* consists of many bands (usually between 10 and 30 or so), any of which can be boosted or cut by the desired amount. The frequency points and the bandwidth are both fixed on a graphic EQ.

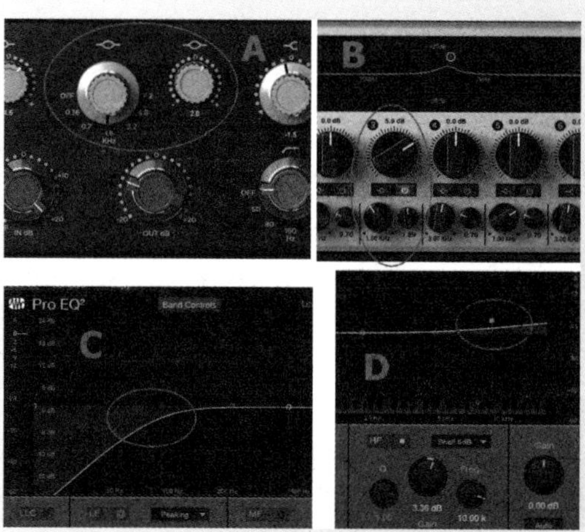

Different types of EQ frequency curves: A) Sweepable at 1.6 KHz (with preset bandwidth), B) Parametric at 1KHz (with a high Q setting), C) High Pass Filter at 100Hz, D) High Shelving at 10KHz.

Most DAWs will come with at least one EQ plug-in—usually a parametric type—but you can, of course, purchase other plug-ins, many of which are designed to model classic hardware EQs.

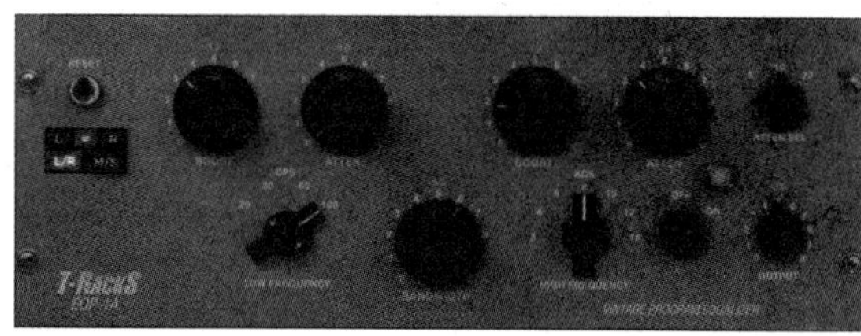

The EQP-1A from IK Multimedia's T-RackS series is modeled after a famous Pultec tube EQ.

And, of course, you can make use of outboard EQs as well, which many people swear by, such as this Pultec clone from Warm Audio. (See Chapter 11 for more info.)

The EQP-WA from Warm Audio is a hardware replica of the classic Pultec tube EQ.

When mixing, EQ can help to provide a musical space for instruments to sit in. For example, if you have two different instruments that both contain a lot of content in the same frequency spectrum, they're going to have a tendency to mask each other a bit, which will obscure their clarity. Common culprits in this regard are rhythm guitar and bass, as each instrument contains a good amount of content in the lower-mid range area.

EQ Examples

As an example, let's listen to a phrase of bass and rhythm guitar.

TRACK 140: Bass and rhythm guitar

You may have noticed that there wasn't a lot of clarity between the two instruments. Let's take a look at a spectral analysis of both tracks using a spectral analyzer plug-in. This is a free program called SPAN by Voxengo.

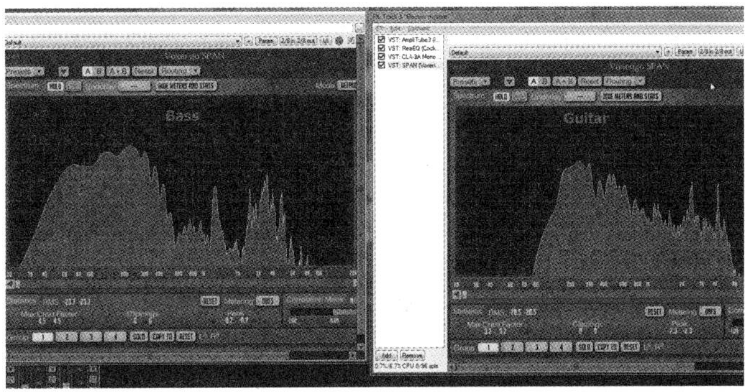

A frequency spectrum analyzer will show you the frequency content of a certain track.

You can see that there's a good deal of content on both instruments in similar frequency ranges. If there weren't a bass guitar, then the guitars could possibly use some of that low-end. But since we have a bass in the mix, it just tends to muddy things up a bit. So listen to what happens when we simply add a hi-pass filter on the guitar at around 100 Hz.

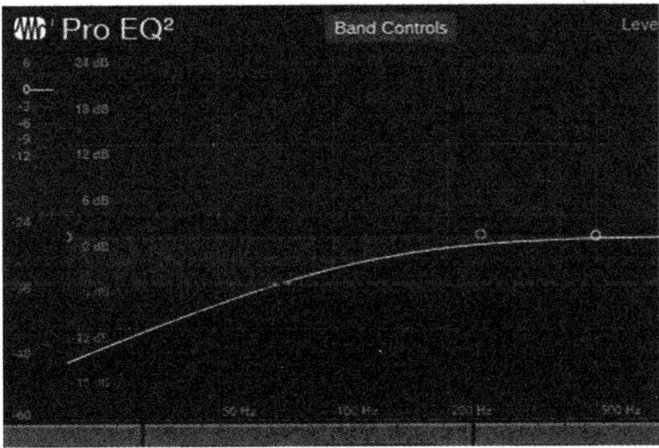

By simply adding a hi-pass filter (or a low cut) on the guitar, we can get rid of much of the muddiness between the instruments.

TRACK 141: Bass and rhythm guitar with hi-pass filter on guitar

While spectrum analyzers are nice tools to help learn about frequencies, the most important thing is to use your ears. There is no substitute for just taking the time and experimenting with EQ to learn what it does and how it affects the sound of one instrument, a group of instruments, or the entire mix.

TOOLBOX

Beware of the Solo Button!

Oftentimes, an inexperienced mixer will solo each instrument one at a time and EQ it until it sounds the best. The problem with this is that the song isn't going to be heard that way; you're going to hear everything together at once. So, even though that electric guitar sounds *amazing* when you solo it, what really matters is how it sounds along with *everything else*.

The solo function is nice when you're trying to identify a problem area on a certain track, for example, but never forget that the most important thing is how an instrument sounds *within the mix*. If that means it needs to be thinned out a bunch, then so be it! What's best for the song wins!

TOOLBOX

EQ Cheat Sheet

Every song and track is different, so there are no one-size-fits-all EQ treatments. With that said, here are some rough guidelines that can help you get close most of the time when you're hearing something you don't like.

Frequency Range	Instruments	Descriptive Terms
15K	Cymbals, breath (vocal)	Air, separation
10K	Vocals, acoustic guitar, cymbals, piano	Brightness, sibilance
7K	Toms/snare (stick sound), finger noise (guitar/bass), piano, guitars	Sibilance, sharpness
5K	Vocals, attack on guitars/piano/toms	Presence, attack
3K	Bass plucking, kick drum (top end), guitars, vocal clarity	Excitement, punch
1K	Snare drum, piano, bass (clarity), guitars	Bang
500 Hz	Vocals (body), guitar leads, bass (clarity)	Warmth
250 Hz	Vocals (warmth), guitars (fullness), cymbals (gong sound)	Warmth, muddiness
50 - 100 Hz	Bottom end (guitars, snare, piano, horns), bass/kick (fundamental)	Thump, boominess, fullness

And here are a few other general EQ tips to keep in mind:

- **Cutting is *generally* preferable to boosting**: There are plenty of exceptions to this rule, but more often than not, you'll probably find that cuts tend to sound more natural than boosts.
- **Cut narrow bandwidths, boost broader ones**: Again, this is merely a guideline, but generally it'll sound better to cut a narrow range (higher Q settings) of frequencies and gently boost (lower Q setting or a shelving EQ) a broader range of frequencies.
- **Just because you have it, you don't have to use it**: If a track sounds fine with no EQ, all the better!
- **Boosts will make the track louder, but don't get tricked into thinking that's "better"**: It's a physiological fact that louder tends to sound better to us. So don't equate a boost as better simply because it makes the track slightly louder!
- **It's always easier to get a great-sounding track at the beginning rather than fixing a poorly recorded track with tons of EQ**: The track that was recorded well from the start will usually sound more natural, and the extra few minutes you spent on mic placement or tone selection will usually pale in comparison to the time spent EQ-ing it.

- **Sweep a boost through the frequencies to find an annoying frequency**: If a guitar track sounds harsh, for example, set up a band with a narrow Q and a generous boost. Then sweep through the frequencies until you hear the annoying frequency really jump out at you. Once you've found it, you can apply the needed cut there.
- **Regularly bypass the EQ to make sure you're improving**: The longer you spend working on a track, the more fatigued your ears will become. Bypassing the EQ can assure you that you are indeed making an improvement!

Mixing in Mono

While we're on the subject of EQ, let's talk about the idea of *mixing in mono*. Some people like to begin their mix by using no panning at all—effectively mixing in mono. Why would you do this? Well, think about it this way: if you can get the instruments to sound distinct and clear with everything in mono, imagine how much more spacious it will sound when you pan things out to the side!

As an example, we'll take a look at a song with the following instrumentation:

- Drums
- Bass
- Acoustic guitar
- Synth
- Electric guitar
- Lead vocal

Here's what it sounds like with all the faders up in a rough level mix. There has been no reverb or any other effects added.

TRACK 142: First rough, dry mix in mono

As you can hear, things aren't quite as distinct as we'd like them to be. So let's go through and add some hi-pass filters to the guitars to help get them out of the way of the bass a bit to start off with. We'll set them around 80 Hz. Here's the result after doing that.

TRACK 143: Rough, dry mix with hi-pass filters added to guitars

Now let's concentrate on the kick/bass drum relationship. Generally speaking, a close-miked kick drum (or sample of one) will often benefit from a hi-pass filter place at around 20 dB or so, as anything below that will usually only produce undesirable results. The same usually applies to the bass guitar.

With those basic moves out of the way, I'll usually solo the bass track and begin to sweep the lower frequencies (from about 80 up to around 250 Hz) to find the frequency that really defines the instrument. This will be different for each track, so you'll have to use your ears. Set up a parametric band with a fairly low Q setting and a moderate boost (6 dB) and slowly sweep through the frequencies to identify the key bass frequency.

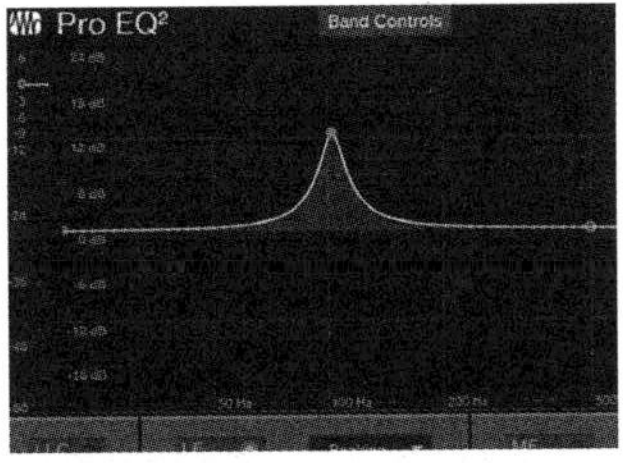

Sweeping the bass frequencies to find where the fundamental bass character frequency lies.

In our instance, this ended up being about 100 Hz. So I may add a gentle boost there—around 3 dB max, usually. Then I'll usually take a look at the low-mids of the bass (between about 200Hz to 500Hz) and see if it's muddying things up a bit. If so, I'll find that frequency and apply a cut there. Next, I'll usually try to determine where the smack of the kick beater lies and apply a similar boost there. This is usually somewhere in the 1K to 3K range. And here's the result so far.

TRACK 144: Rough, dry mix with filters, cuts and boosts on bass and kick

Now it's starting to get cleaned up a bit down there.

The vocal tends to share the same range as the acoustic guitar, so I may try to carve out a little space in the acoustic, if necessary, for the vocal to sit. This just takes practice. You normally don't have to make drastic cuts (although that can work if needed, or if the track was recorded in a less-than-ideal way). But every mix is different so you'll just need to experiment to see what's needed.

And now let's listen to the result of all this work. It's made quite a difference in the overall clarity of the mix, yet everything is still panned straight down the middle. Compare this to the first rough mix (Track 142) to hear the difference.

TRACK 145: Rough, dry mix with preliminary EQ settings on all instruments

> **TOOLBOX**
>
> **Standing on the Shoulders of the Pros: Referencing**
> One common practice when learning to mix is to reference your tracks against other pro recordings that are in a similar style. This isn't entirely fair, because your mix won't be professionally mastered like theirs will be, but it's good for getting a handle on overall colors. Ear fatigue can set in fairly quickly when listening to the same material over and over again, and referencing another recording can be a good reality check. It's important that you do this while seated in your mix position, so you're hearing a pro mix on the same speakers as you'll be hearing your mix!
>
> It's also advised that you take breaks periodically to keep your ears fresh. This can be every hour or two, or even as short as every 30 minutes, depending on your preference. Get up, stretch your legs, walk around the block, etc. Just be sure it's something non-musical so that your ears can reset!

Reverb and Other Spatial Effects

These effects can also contribute to helping instruments find their own space in the mix. We'll cover this idea in more detail later in this chapter. (See "Using Effects" on page 104.)

Compression

The main goal of compression is to tame the peaks (loudest part of the signal) of a track, which will help it sound more consistent. You can think of a compressor as an automatic volume control. It's like your own little personal minion that constantly rides the fader so you don't have to, turning down the really loud parts and bringing up the quieter parts so that the whole track level is more consistent. They can affect a signal in other ways as well, and we can use their signal-shaping capabilities to great effect when shaping a sound.

On a typical compressor, there are usually several settings. Let's look at the basics.

Threshold

This is a volume level (in dB) that specifies at what point the compressor should take action. Any signal that doesn't breach this threshold (i.e., one that's not loud enough) will pass through the compressor unaffected. Not all compressors—the 1176 and LA-2A are two examples—feature this control, instead using an "input" knob to essentially set the threshold level.

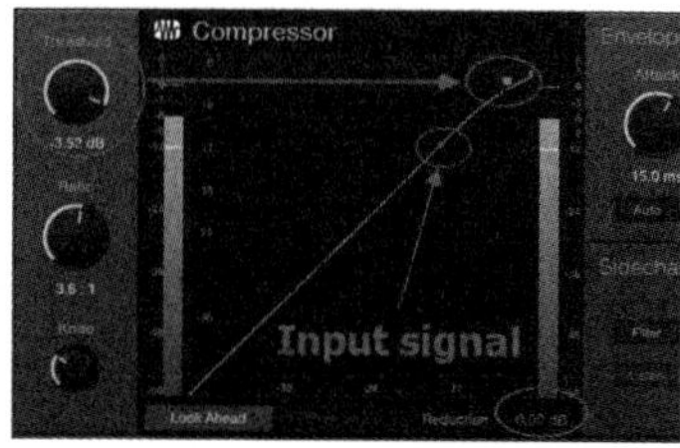

Signals that fall below the threshold will not be compressed at all.

Ratio

This setting, expressed by ratios such as 2:1 (read "2 to 1") or 4:1 ("four to one"), tells the compressor how much to attenuate (turn down) the signal once it breaches the threshold. A setting of 2:1 indicates that, for every 2 dB that crosses the threshold, only 1 dB will be able to pass. Said another way, the compressor would attenuate any signal over the threshold by 50%. In an 8:1 setting, the compressor would only allow 1 dB to pass through for every 8 dB that's over. In other words, a 2:1 ratio will politely ask the signal to keep it down a bit, whereas an 8:1 ratio would just start swinging.

When the ratio is infinite—i.e., the signal is not allowed to breach the threshold at all—you have what's called *brick wall limiting*. This is commonly expressed as ∞:1, and it's often used during the mastering process (or in live sound) to prevent any digital clipping.

Attack and Release

These controls tell the compressor how fast to start and stop what it's doing. With an attack time of 10 ms, for example, the compressor will wait 10 ms after the signal crosses the threshold before it clamps down on the volume (by the amount set in the ratio). The release specifies how long the compressor waits to let go of (i.e., stop attenuating) the signal after it falls back below the threshold.

1176-style compressors are famous for their incredibly fast attack times—as low as 20 ***microseconds****! Turning the knobs clockwise actually results in* ***faster*** *attack and release times—the exact opposite of most compressors.*

The attack and release settings will have a crucial impact on the sound, as they dictate the way the compressor reacts to the signal over time. Slower attack times will let more *transients* through (the very beginning of a signal—the smack of a snare drum, for instance), whereas a fast attack time will squish them more. Release times are often tempo-dependent. In other words, you'll often want to make sure the compressor releases before the next attack. A properly set release time can add sustain to a note (on a bass, for example), whereas fast release times can add more excitement and aggression to a track (on drums, for example).

It's a delicate balance, though, because if you're not careful, you can create some (usually) unwanted artifacts like *pumping* or *breathing*, in which case you can hear the compressor working in an unnatural way. (This type of effect is common in EDM styles, however.) Experimentation is key in learning to achieve the results you want.

Output or Make-up Gain

Since a compressor only attenuates (turns down) a signal, it makes sense that, if it's working at all, the average level of the signal is going to be *lower* than before. The output/make-up gain allows you to boost the entire level of the signal to get that lost volume back. It's just that now the softer parts are sounding louder, while the louder parts aren't sticking out as much.

Knee

This setting affects the threshold and, indirectly, the attack time. A "hard knee" compressor is kind of the default. In other words, it does exactly what the instructions tell it to: it waits for the signal to cross the threshold and then applies the full amount of compression (ratio) immediately as soon as the attack time is reached. It's like just hanging 50 pounds around the neck of a runner 10 ms after they start going above the speed limit (if the attack time is set to 10 ms). The heavier the weight (higher the ratio), the more he'll slow down. A "soft knee" setting isn't so abrupt. It's like running alongside the runner as they approach the speed limit and gradually adding weight bit by bit until the full weight is added.

TOOLBOX

A Picture Is Worth 1,000 Words

It's sometimes easier to visualize what a compressor does by looking at some graphs—just like in high school Algebra class. Here we see two graphs depicting compression: hard-knee and soft-knee.

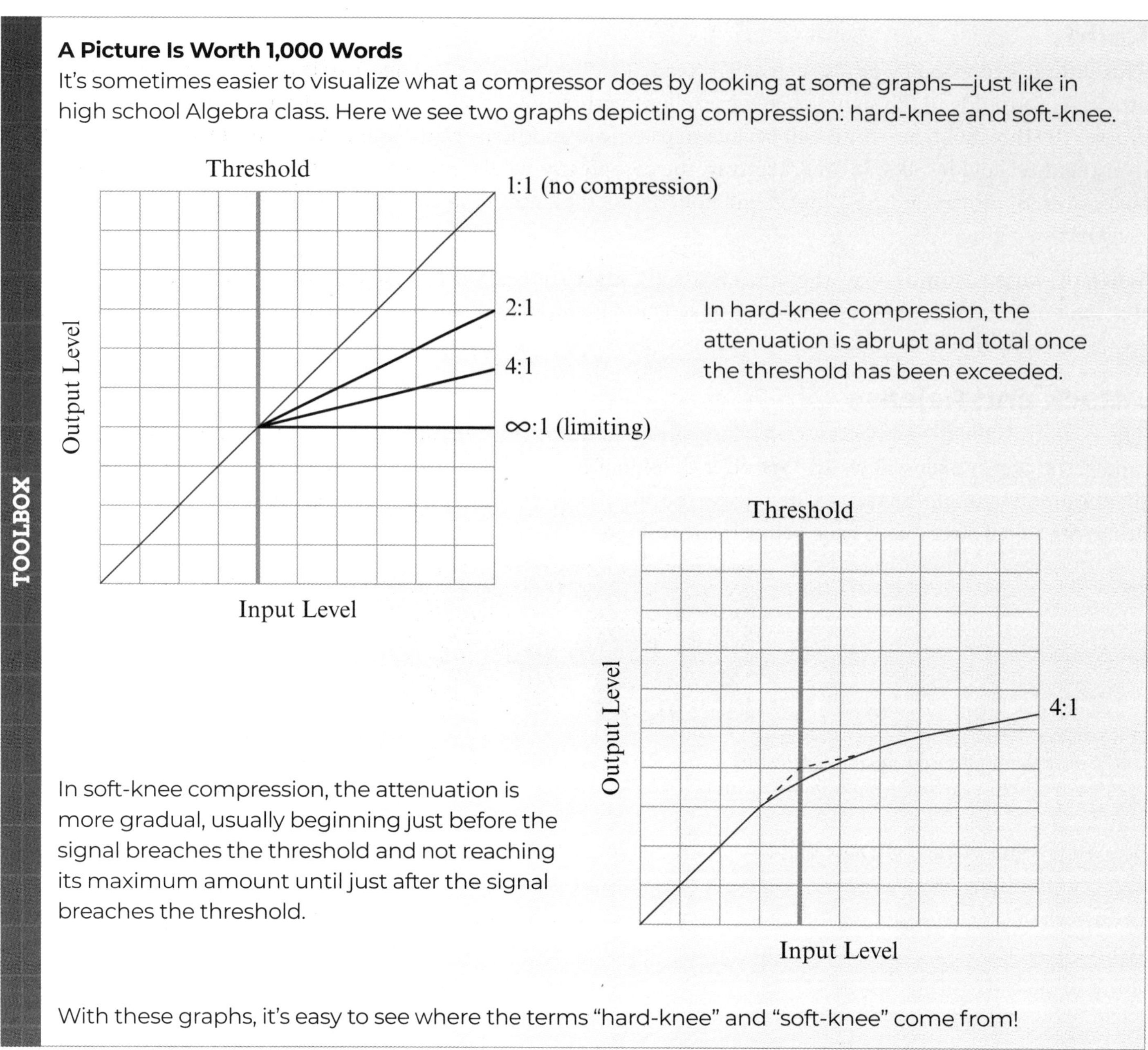

In hard-knee compression, the attenuation is abrupt and total once the threshold has been exceeded.

In soft-knee compression, the attenuation is more gradual, usually beginning just before the signal breaches the threshold and not reaching its maximum amount until just after the signal breaches the threshold.

With these graphs, it's easy to see where the terms "hard-knee" and "soft-knee" come from!

Compression Examples

Let's have a listen to some examples of compression in various settings so we can hear how it affects the sound. We'll also compare some plug-ins with outboard gear to hear the difference. All of the recommended settings here should be considered starting points. As every mix is different, you should adjust them as necessary until you achieve the desired sound.

Snare Drum

With a snare drum, you can increase punchiness a bit with a slower attack time (around 1 ms or so), a quicker release (about 50 ms), and a good amount of *gain reduction* (about 5 to 10 dB). Let's hear the IK Multimedia T-RackS Black 76 plug-in with these settings at an 8:1 ratio with about 6 dB of gain reduction. For each track, we'll hear the snare mic isolated and then with the rest of the kit.

TRACK 146: Snare drum with no compression

TRACK 147: Snare drum with IK Multimedia T-RackS Black 76 compressor plug-in

By adjusting the attack/release times, you can greatly shape the sound—increase/decrease sustain, accentuate/attenuate the "crack," etc. To illustrate the importance that attack and release times have, let's listen to the same snare track while only adjusting these two controls on the T-Racks Black 76 compressor. We'll keep all other settings the same.

TRACK 148: Snare drum with T-RackS Black 76: Slowest attack/fastest release, Mid attack/fastest release, Fastest attack/fastest release

TRACK 149: Snare drum with T-RackS Black 76: Slowest attack/mid release, Mid attack/mid release, Fastest attack/mid release

TRACK 150: Snare drum with T-RackS Black 76: Slowest attack/slowest release, Mid attack/slowest release, Fastest attack/slowest release

Acoustic Guitar

On acoustic strumming, it's common to use a slower attack time and a quick-to-moderate release. This will let the pick sound (transient) through but still control the dynamics so that it sits better in the mix. Let's hear the sound of the IK Multimedia T-RackS White 2A, which is based on the Teletronix LA-2A.

The LA-2A compressor doesn't have adjustable attack and release times. Instead, it's "program dependent," which means it changes slightly depending on the signal. The average times are about 10 ms for the attack and anywhere from 60 ms to a full 5 seconds for release. We'll aim for about 4 dB of gain reduction here. A nice, affordable hardware version is the Klark Teknik KT-2A.

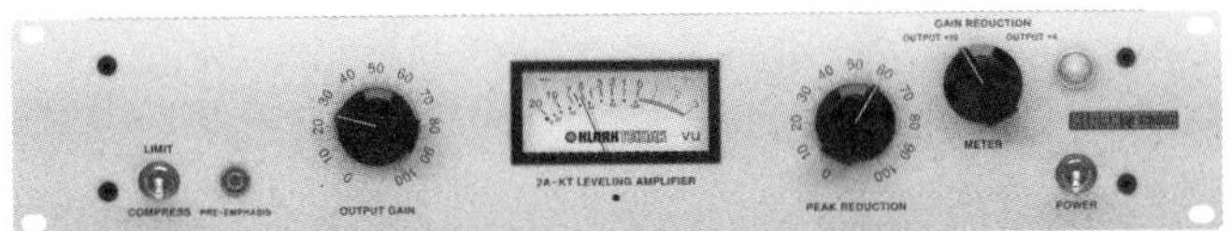

The Klark Teknik KT-2A is modeled after the Teletronix LA-2A, one of the most legendary tube compressors of all.

TRACK 151: Acoustic guitar with no compression

TRACK 152: Acoustic guitar with T-Racks White 2A compressor plug-in

Bass Guitar

Bass is certainly no stranger to compression, and for good reason; it helps provide a solid foundation in the low end. Again, a slower attack will give a punchier tone, while a faster attack will provide a duller, more controlled sound. A common trick used on bass guitar (and other sources as well) is called *serial compression*. This involves running through two (sometimes more) compressors in a row, with each one set for only a few dBs of GR, as opposed to one compressor set for 6 or 8 dBs of GR. This tends to result in fewer artifacts on the tone.

Let's hear how this works with the T-RackS Black 76 plug. After hearing the bypassed track, we'll use one plug-in to achieve about 6 or 7 dB of GR. Then we'll use three instances of this plug—one after the other—with the same settings for each (slower attack and faster release), aiming for about 2 dB of GR on each one.

TRACK 153: Bass guitar with no compression

TRACK 154: Bass guitar with standard compression (one plug-in): 6-7 dB of GR

TRACK 155: Bass guitar with serial compression (three plug-ins): about 2 dB of GR on each

You can try this technique on other sources as well. Note that this is not to be confused with *parallel compression*, which we'll talk about in a bit.

Vocals

Vocals are another element that rarely go uncompressed throughout a recording. The dynamics of a vocal can be extremely erratic, and in order to make sure that each word can be clearly heard, many people go to great lengths, including adjusting the clip gain (as mentioned in Chapter 12) before even applying compression.

It's also very common to apply serial compression to vocals as well. A particularly common chain is an 1176-style compressor followed by an LA-2A-style compressor. Usually, the 1176 is set to catch the spikes with about 4 to 8 dB of GR, whereas the LA-2A is providing a gentler smoothing of levels with about 3 dB of GR. Again, the attack and release times on the 1176 can be adjusted to achieve the desired tone.

Let's hear this chain in plug-in form with the IK Multimedia T-RackS plugs.

TRACK 156: Vocal with no compression

TRACK 157: Vocal with series compression using plug-ins

Parallel Compression

Another handy trick is called *parallel compression*, which involves blending an uncompressed track with a compressed version of the same thing. You can use it on any source, but it's especially popular on a stereo drum bus. (Note that this is separate from any other compressors you may be using on the individual drum tracks or on a stereo bus, etc.)

Some compressor plug-ins have a mix setting that lets you choose from 0% (no signal is passing though the compressor) to 100% (all of the signal is passing through the compressor). This is the easiest way to set up parallel compression. For instance, you can set the mix to 50%, and you'll hear 50% of the signal dry and 50% of it compressed.

To set it up when using a compressor without a mix control, you'll first need to add a stereo track—you can name it "parallel drum bus"—and add a compressor to the track. We'll use the T-RackS Black 76 plug-in from IK Multimedia, as an 1176-style compressor is quite common for parallel compression duties. Specifically, we'll use the "all buttons in" mode (aka "British mode"), which means all four ratio buttons are pushed down.

The parallel drum bus track has been added with the compressor plug-in applied to it.

Next, we need to add sends from our drum tracks to the parallel drum bus track. (Make sure the tracks are sent to the main mix *and* the parallel drum bus track.) You can choose which ones you want to send or send them all. The kick, snare, and toms are almost always included, but the cymbals and hi-hat may or may not be. Make sure the sends are *pre-fader*, so that the send levels won't be affected by the fader.

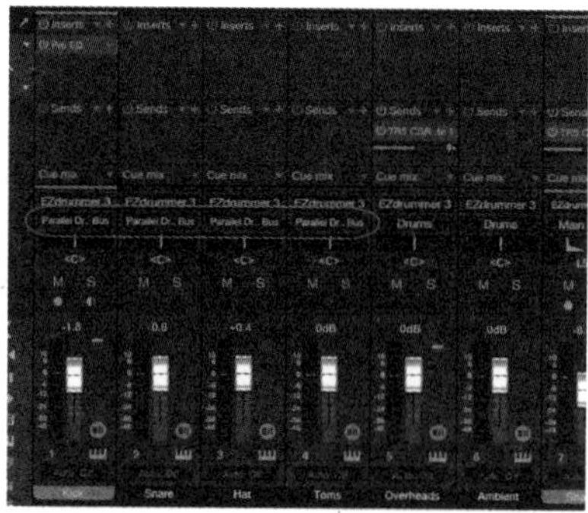

The kick, snare, and toms are sent to the parallel drum bus track.

Next, adjust the compressor to get the desired amount of compression. We're going to use a slow attack and fast release and smash the hell out of them to get about 15 dB of GR. You can adjust the send levels on the drum tracks as needed to get the proper mix. Then you just adjust the fader on the parallel drum bus track to taste.

So, here's what the drums sound like on their own without the parallel compression.

 **TRACK 158:** Drums with no parallel compression

Here's what the parallel bus track sounds like when it's soloed.

TRACK 159: **Parallel compression soloed**

And now let's blend it in with the normal drums. You'll hear three different settings for the parallel drum bus:

1. Subtle
2. Medium
3. Not subtle

TRACK 160: **Parallel compression blended behind normal drums**

As mentioned, this trick can be used on any source; vocals and bass are two other common choices.

Compression on the Master Bus

Another common practice—and one that is greatly debated—involves placing a stereo compressor across the master bus. In other words, you're compressing the entire mix. Proponents of this idea usually speak of a "gluing" effect, which helps make everything sound a bit more cohesive. Some choose to add it from the very beginning, while others wait until they're nearly finished with the mix.

Regardless of when you do it, most people go for a very subtle effect, with a low ratio (1:2 or 1:3) and only 1 or 2 dB of gain reduction (3 dB at the most). The attack and release times will be dependent on the groove/tempo of the song, but longer times are generally the norm—say 100 to 400 ms for the attack and maybe 250 to 800 ms for the release. Improper attack and release times can end up creating a "pumping" effect, in which the sound will duck down slightly after each kick drum hit, for example, and produce an unnatural feel. You'll need to experiment with those suggested settings to tailor it for the particular song.

One of the most popular bus compressors of all is the SSL stereo bus compressor, which is found on the SSL G Series console. Again, there are numerous plug-in and outboard recreations of this legendary compressor available, including the Warm Audio Bus-Comp (outboard), the Waves SSL G-Master Buss Compressor (plug-in), and the IK Multimedia T-RackS Bus Compressor (plug-in).

The Bus-Comp from Warm Audio emulates the famous SSL G-Series stereo bus compressor.

Let's have a listen to a mix to hear bus compression at work.

TRACK 161: **Mix with no bus compression**

TRACK 162: **Mix with bus compression: T-RackS Bus Compressor**

It should be mentioned that the SSL-style compressors can sound fabulous on other sources as well, but they especially shine on program material (i.e., mixes).

Dynamic Elements in the Mix

Another common idea often neglected by beginners is that of dynamic movement in the mix. While this can work well in more natural settings, it usually sounds more exciting to create some sense of motion in the mix when you're dealing with pop or rock styles. Granted, too much can tend to sound gimmicky and get old, but when tastefully done, it can add another dimension to a static mix.

There are a few different ways to do this. We can change the panning, level, or EQ of instruments. We can also add and remove effects or do the same with whole instruments themselves. So let's examine a few common techniques used to create a dynamic mix.

Adding or Removing Instruments Throughout the Song

Often, people are so happy with all the great sounds they've recorded, they want to include them throughout the whole song. This can lose your listener's interest, however, as they're only listening in a linear fashion for interesting things to happen.

Sometimes, though, you may want to omit a few things at certain times to keep things interesting. Omission can often make a bigger statement than addition in this regard.

Adjusting Levels or Panning

Another method of creating movement in the mix is by varying the levels and/or panning of certain instruments throughout the song. There are some instruments (kick, snare, bass, vocal, etc.) that are customarily panned down the middle, and so they're not toyed with as much with regard to panning (although there are no rules). But the tracks that act more as "ear candy"—such as melodic fills, auxiliary percussion, etc.—are ripe for the picking in ideas like this.

Let's check out an intro containing drums, bass, keys, rhythm guitar, and a melodic guitar. In this first mix, everything will remain static.

TRACK 163: Mix 1 of Intro: Each track remains static throughout

And now let's have a little fun with the lead guitar during the intro, letting it wander about the stereo field a bit before it settles into the middle.

TRACK 164: Mix 2 of Intro: Lead guitar is panned back and forth

These types of adjustments are exactly the kind of thing for which you'd use automation.

Using Effects

Effects are kind of like musical toys; they're very fun to play with. Often, they help us reconcile the unnatural method in which we record instruments (i.e., using close-mic techniques etc.) by creating a more natural sound with reverb, ambience, etc. But they can also help you apply a unique sonic stamp to a song when used creatively. Let's look at some strategies for using them during mixdown.

Reverb

Reverbs are often used to help create the illusion that several instruments were recorded in the same space, be it a large room, a church cathedral, or anything in between. Generally speaking, the more reverb you add to a track, the farther away it will appear to sound. So you can create a sense of depth in your mix by varying the amounts of reverb you use on different tracks.

Let's check out an example here. This first mix will be completely dry, with most of the instruments sounding very much "in your face."

TRACK 165: Mix 1: All instruments are completely dry

And now let's use a reverb plug-in called Valhalla Room—an amazing sounding yet very affordable plug-in—to add different levels of the same reverb to each instrument. We'll do this by adding the plug-in to its own track and then adding sends for each track to the reverb track. (See Chapter 5 for more on this process.) Leave the mix control on the plug-in 100% wet for this. The amount of reverb for each instrument should be adjusted at the send level.

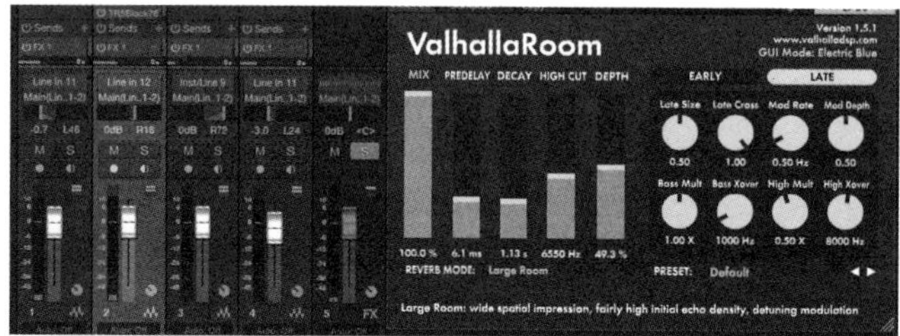

Reverb has been added to each instrument (in varying amounts) by using a send.

TRACK 166: Mix 2: Reverb has been added to each instrument in different amounts

It feels completely different now, right? There's no right or wrong here; it's mainly a matter of personal taste, so feel free to experiment. Also listen closely to recordings you like and pay attention to the level of reverb (if any) that's being applied to different instruments. You can even try to recreate certain recordings or sounds as an exercise to get familiar with various aspects of the process.

That said, here are some general conventions and/or suggestions with regards to setting reverb levels:

- For a "natural" sound, add just enough reverb so that you can hear it clearly and then back it off a bit.
- For faster-paced songs, you'll generally want to use reverbs with shorter decay times so they don't obscure the beat. Conversely, ballads will generally sound nicer with longer decay times.
- When adding reverb to a vocal, using a bit of *pre-delay* can help provide clarity while still adding a bit of depth (see below for more information on this).
- You don't have to use the same reverb for every instrument, although this is a nice way of making everything sound as though it was played together if you're going for a very natural sound.
- Adding reverb to low-pitched instruments, such as bass guitar, kick drum, etc., can tend to produce muddiness in the mix. For this reason, many engineers don't add any reverb at all (or very little) to such instruments.
- It's very common to place a hi-pass filter (which cuts all frequencies below the chosen frequency point) on reverbs, especially in denser mixes, as it helps avoid muddiness. The filter frequency can be anywhere from 150 or 200 Hz up to 1K or higher. Experiment to see what sounds best for the given situation.

TOOLBOX

Adding Pre-delay to Reverb

A dry vocal will often sound very unnatural and stick out like a sore thumb, so it's usually treated with reverb or delay. However, adding reverb to a vocal can sometimes make it less intelligible. Using a *pre-delay* will often help. This is the amount of time it takes for the reverb to kick in after it receives a signal. So, you'll get a fraction of a second of dry vocal before the reverb begins.

It's a common practice to time this setting to a rhythmic value of the song, such as a quarter note, eighth note, sixteenth note, etc. Generally, the faster the song's tempo, the longer the pre-delay can be. A simple way of determining these values in milliseconds (which is used for the pre-delay time) is to divide 60,000 by the tempo of the song in beats per minute. This will give you the length of a quarter note. Let's say we have a song that's 120 bpm:

60,000 / 120 = 500 ms (quarter note)

From there, we just divide that number by 2 to get an eighth note, again for a sixteenth note, and so on.

250 ms (eighth note)

125 ms (sixteenth note)

Let's hear the difference between a reverb with and without a pre-delay on the lead vocal.

TRACK 167: No pre-delay on lead vocal reverb

TRACK 168: Sixteenth-note pre-delay on lead vocal reverb

It's a subtle thing, but you can hear that it does make a difference. Again, experiment with the pre-delay time to find what works for the song.

Delay

Delay is another very common effect on vocals and other instruments. Assuming it's timed to some sort of logical rhythm with regard to the song, it can add depth with less clutter than reverb. Common rhythmic timings are eighth note, dotted eighth note, quarter note, and quarter-note triplet. The level of the delay and the feedback are usually set fairly low when you're just wanting some ambience.

Let's check out the same vocal as the previous one with delay instead of reverb on it.

TRACK 169: Eighth-note delay on lead vocal

TRACK 170: Dotted eighth delay on lead vocal

To determine the quarter-note triplet time, you can simply divide the quarter-note millisecond time by 3. That would give you an eighth-note triplet time. Double that, and you have a quarter-note triplet.

120 bpm
500 ms = quarter note
500 / 3 = 167 ms (eighth-note triplet)
167 x 2 = 334 ms (quarter-note triplet)

Another common use for delay is a "stinger"—a delay placed on only one specific note of a vocal or instrument. For example, this may occur on the last note of a melody that coincides with the first beat of a new section. Quarter notes and eighth notes are popular rhythmic values for this type of thing. Here's an example of that kind of idea.

TRACK 171: Delay placed on final note of phrase only

TOOLBOX

Running Low on CPU? Rendering Is Your Friend!

Plug-ins all eat up CPU resources. The more complex they are, the more RAM they use. If your CPU starts running in the 70% region or higher, you may start to experience glitches during playback. This can really be a nuisance and can make it very difficult to record new tracks as well.

If upgrading your system isn't an option, there is a workaround. You can *freeze* or *render* a track to help free up CPU resources. Basically, when you freeze a track, the program makes a copy of the track and prints all the effects to it, and any CPU resources normally being used by the effects are freed up. Of course, you can always revert to the original track, make adjustments, and re-freeze it again as necessary. In Studio One, this is called Track Transform.

This guitar track has several effects on it, which are eating CPU resources.

After freezing the track, all of the effects are printed on the track. Of course, you can always revert back to the unfrozen track and make adjustments if necessary.

Another use for delay, especially in more retro styles, is *slapback*. This is a single, loud delay with a short time (less than 100 ms) and one repeat. It's very common for that rocakabilly guitar sound of the 50s and 60s, but it's also used on vocals (think "Watching the Wheels" by John Lennon), piano, drums, and more.

TRACK 172: Slapback delay on guitar: 100 ms

TRACK 173: Slapback delay on vocals: 96 ms

Modulation Effects

Aside from the common reverb and delay effects, anything else is up for grabs. For example, you could try running background vocals through a phaser or flanger and see what you get. Let's check that out!

TRACK 174: Background vocals processed with phaser

Other effects to try include tremolo, chorus, and vibrato. These are commonly used on guitars and keyboards, but there's no rule that says you can't try them on something else.

Tape Saturation Emulation

Another common plug-in effect is, somewhat ironically, analog tape simulation. These plug-ins are designed to give your recordings a bit of the warmth and non-linear artifacts that are present with analog tape.

This effect is commonly used on the master bus and/or individual tracks—especially drums, guitars, and bass. I'm using the IK Multimedia T-RackS Tape Machine 440 plug-in here on drums and then a master bus. The effect is usually pretty subtle, but it can be adjusted with various parameters. On each recording, you'll first hear the tracks without the effect and then again with.

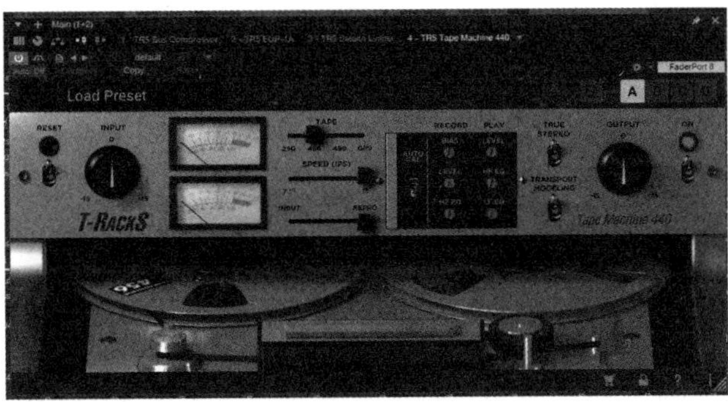

IK Multimedia T-RackS Tape Machine 440 plug-in

On each of the following, you'll hear the track first unprocessed and then again with the plug-in engaged.

TRACK 175: Tape emulation on drums

TRACK 176: Tape emulation on master bus – subtle

TRACK 177: Tape emulation on master bus – more pronounced

Final Rendering

Once you've gotten your mix sounding just the way you want it, it's time to create the stereo file that will be playable on normal music players. This may be called rendering, exporting, or mixing down (or something similar) depending on your DAW.

When you open the mixdown window, you'll have numerous options, including things like:

- **File location**: where the file will be saved.
- **Bit depth**: 24-bit has been the standard for a while now and provides more than enough dynamic range for the vast majority.
- **File type**: WAV, etc.
- **Boundaries of the rendering**: Entire project, time selection, selected tracks only, etc.
- **Stereo/mono**
- **Sample rate**: 44.1 kHz, etc.

Until you learn more specifically about all the options, it's usually fine to just go with the default settings. Just make sure you take note of where the file will be saved so you know where to find it!

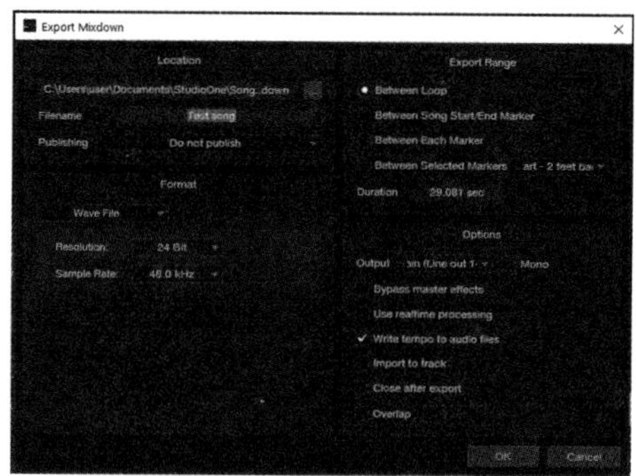

Studio One's export window provides numerous options for the final two-track stereo file.

That's it! Now you can take the mix and listen to it on every system (car, earbuds/headphones, smart speaker, etc.) so you can to hear how it sounds. You'll most likely find that you want to make a few revisions because you'll still be getting used to how your monitors sound in your control room. Again, ideally, the mixes will translate everywhere perfectly, but mixing in a bedroom isn't an ideal situation; it's a "make the best of what we have" situation. But even pro mixing engineers make revisions, so don't feel bad!

To bring this all home, here are my final mixes of two original songs of mine.

TRACK 178: "Something in the Woods"

TRACK 179: "Shade Fails"

TOOLBOX

A Quick Note on Mastering

The subject of *mastering* is well beyond the scope of this book and could easily fill one of its own. It's basically the process of taking a mixed song, or album of mixed songs, and preparing them for the final medium. This includes trivial tasks, such as possibly adding fades, placing the songs in the correct order, etc. But it also includes the process of making the tracks sound like a cohesive unit and other audio sweetening in the form of EQ, compression, limiting, stereo enhancement, and other tools. A mastered song generally has more "punch" than a non-mastered one and will generally be considerably louder as well so as to compete with other professional tracks when played on the radio, etc.

Mastering engineers normally work in very specialized rooms with expensive tools and have specific experience in the field. It's very common for an artist to have an album professionally mastered even if they mixed it themselves. This can cost anywhere from a few hundred dollars for an album to several thousand or much more (for world-class engineers), but a ballpark figure for non-famous mastering engineers would be somewhere around $100 to $300 per song. It's an art unto itself.

If you'd like to give it a go yourself (after all, every mastering engineer has to start somewhere), there are numerous "mastering suite" plug-ins available that feature common tools of the trade, including multi-band compressors, EQs, limiters, etc. There are also plenty of online tutorials on the subject (check out www.groove3.com), which can help you get your feet wet. It is possible to do more harm than good, however, so if you're serious about your music sounding as professional as possible, you'll probably want to have a pro handle it (if you can afford it) until you begin to get a good feel for it.

Final Thoughts

Well, we've covered a lot of ground, and there's still plenty more ahead if you choose to explore it. Recording is a life-long hobby for many, and you never stop learning or improving. Now that you have an idea of what's involved in the process, apply your newfound listening skills any time you can to expand your knowledge. Dissect your favorite recordings to see if you can identify types of reverb, guitars, effects, etc. How is space used? Does the mix change or remain the same throughout the song? Do some instruments sound nearer or farther than others?

This is a big book, so in closing, I'd just like to reiterate a few things that are paramount in my opinion, and so I don't want them slipping by the wayside.

- **Experiment**: There is no greater teacher than hands-on experimentation. Start with a preset on an effect and then tweak one parameter to see what it does. Put that one back where it was and then tweak another, etc.
- **Read the manual(!)**: Did I already say this? I just can't stress it enough. This applies to your DAW program, plug-ins, etc. I don't know how many times I've learned something *really* helpful after cracking open the manual while looking for something completely unrelated.
- **Listen, listen, listen**: And when I say listen, I mean listen *with your ears*—not your eyes! Many people will spend hours nudging every single note of every single instrument until it's all perfectly aligned without even once actually *listening* to the dang thing! I personally don't care what it looks like as long as it sounds good. For this reason, I made a computer monitor cover (actually from the box the monitor came in) that I'll slip over the screen when listening at times so I'm not tempted to look at the music. It really helps me focus on the most important thing: the *sound*. Also, listen to some of your favorite commercial recordings in your mix position with your monitors! This helps you learn what a good, balanced mix should sound like on your system.
- **There are no rules—only conventions**: A lot of people like to tell you that you can't or shouldn't do certain things. The simple fact is that there are no rules when it comes to music or recording. *Any* method you use for recording music is a viable one if it accomplishes what you want. There are certainly conventions, but seriously, if it sounds good to you to pan the entire drumset hard left, then by all means do it! The Pan Police aren't going to bust down your door and haul you off. Remember that many concepts or techniques we take for granted as acceptable nowadays were once the crazy idiosyncrasies of rule-breakers and innovators, including close-miking, guitar distortion, the cassette "Portastudio," and even multi-track recording itself!

It's been a joy to share this information with you, and I sincerely hope you've found it useful and inspiring. Feel free to contact me at chadjohnsonguitar@gmail.com with any questions or comments. I wish you the best of luck in your recording adventures and remember to experiment and have fun!

– Chad Johnson, 2025

Appendix

Welcome to the Appendix; stay a while! Here you'll find some fun, money-saving projects should you be so inclined to take them on. There's also an extensive glossary that you can use as a reference throughout your recording adventures. Enjoy!

The DIY Corner

In the spirit of home studios, I felt it incumbent upon me to share some DIY ideas that can help you stretch your dollars and increase the quality of recordings at the same time. None of these are terribly difficult, although they may require a few requisite skills—or at least a bit of practice obtaining those skills—before you can complete them.

1. Absorptive Sound Panels

These panels are the ones that you can hang in your control room at the reflective points (see Chapter 2 for details). The first one may take an hour or two, but once you get the hang of it, you can knock these out assembly line-style in no time.

Materials Needed (for one panel):

- (2) 2x4x8 boards
- (8) L brackets and wood screws
- Burlap fabric – at least 2 ½ x 4 ½ feet
- Miscellaneous fabric (for back side) – at least 2 ½ x 4 ½ feet
- 2x4 sheet of mineral wool*
- Staple gun with staples (I use a $30 gun with 3/8-inch staples)
- Electric drill

*Mineral wool is usually available in sheets of 2x4 feet in thicknesses of one, two, or four inches. For bass traps, I'd recommend a minimum of four inches. For all other reflective points, I'd recommend two inches.

1. Cut one 2x4 at the middle to create two pieces approximately four feet long (they will be slightly shorter than this because of the thickness of your saw blade).
2. Cut the other 2x4 into four equal lengths of approximately two feet each (again, they'll be slightly shorter than this).
3. Assemble a frame with two 4-foot pieces and two 2-foot pieces using the L brackets and screws (see illustration).
4. Cover the back side of the panel with your miscellaneous fabric by stapling it around the edges (I use old bed sheets a lot of times). Trim as necessary so there is no overlap hanging over the edges.
5. Stuff the mineral wool inside the frame. Cut the excess off and save it for later use.
6. Cover the front top and sides with the burlap, wrapping it around and stapling it to the back side.

Note: If you're making a two-inch panel, you can rip the 2x4x8 boards down their length to create 2x2x8 boards (approximately) for the frame and make twice as many.

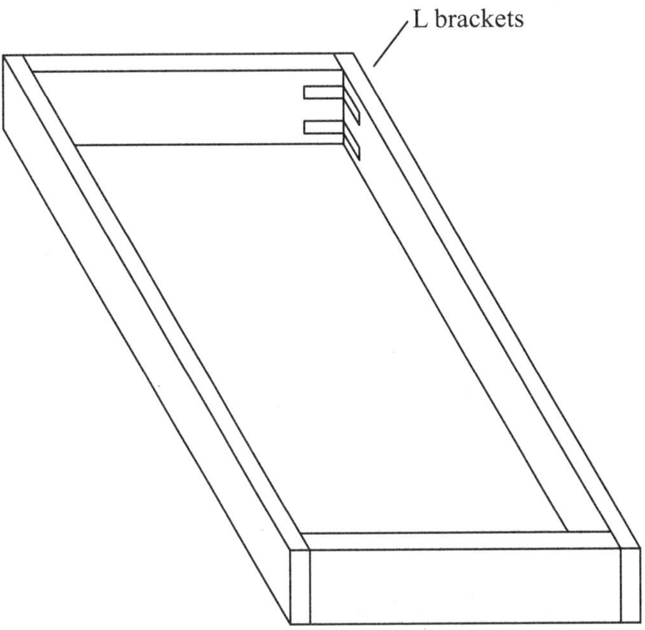

These panels may not look fancy, but they're cheap, easy to make, and work well.

Alternative Method:

To make them a bit more attractive, do this:

1. After you build the frame, stain it with a stain of your choice.
2. Cover the back with fabric and then stuff the mineral wool inside.
3. Cover the front only with burlap, just as you did the back (with no material overlapping the edges of the frame).
4. Then rip some 1x4x8 boards down the middle to create some 1x2x8 boards. Stain these boards with the same used for the frame.
5. These 1x2 boards can then be attached to the front via screws (use a counter-sink bit) to form a border.

With just a little more effort, you can make the panels much more attractive by adding a front border and staining the wood.

2. Gobos

This is the quickest and easiest way I know to make gobos that work well and are easy to set up and tear down. You can make these two or four inches thick for extra absorption.

Materials needed (for one gobo): See material list for Absorptive Sound Panels and add:

- 2x6x8 board

1. Make a burlap covered panel, as shown in project #1.
2. Use the 2x6 board and some long wood screws to create two feet to stand up the gobo (see illustration).
3. If you desire a live side and dead side, you can add a thin reflective surface to one side of the panel, such as pegboard, etc. (If you do this, make sure to account for any extra thickness when building the feet from the 2x6 boards.)

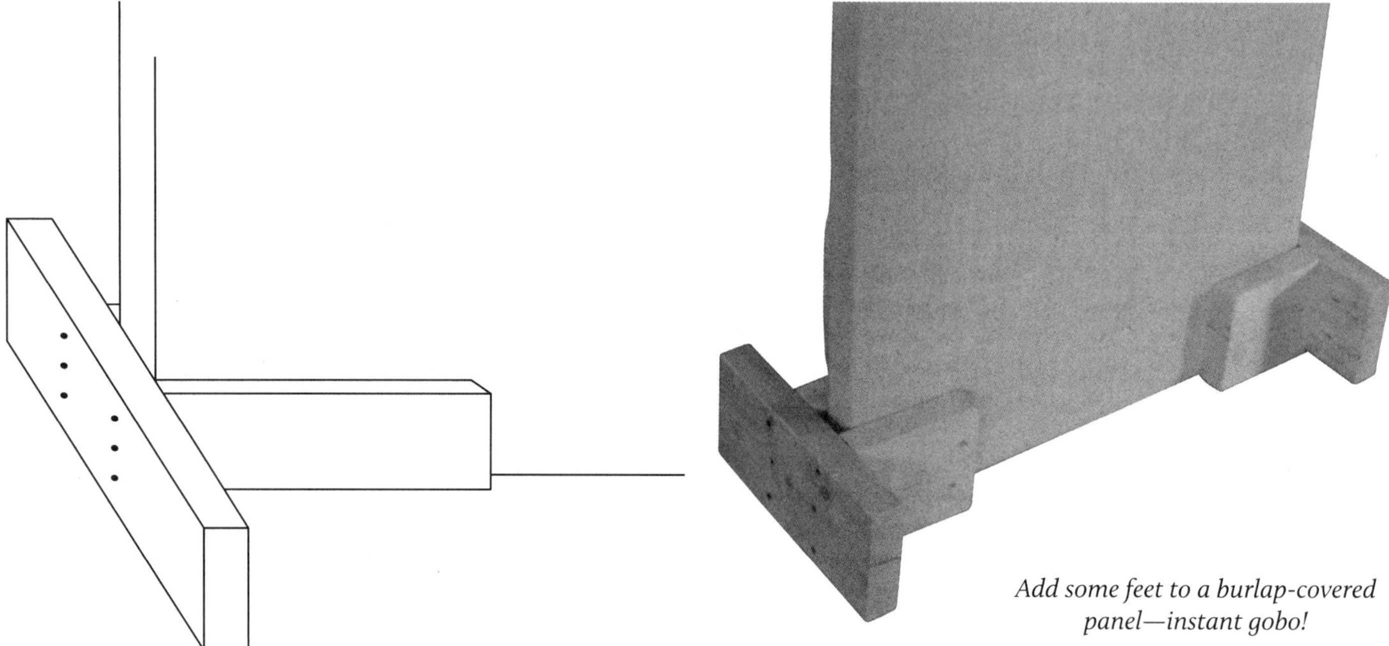

Add some feet to a burlap-covered panel—instant gobo!

3. Vocal Booth

There are several online articles regarding DIY vocal booths. Some are all-out rooms that are fixed installations, while others are nothing more than a few pieces of foam surrounding a microphone. This project is an idea I came up with after looking through all these and deciding what I thought was a good compromise between cost and performance.

Materials needed (for one vocal booth):

- (2) 2x4x8 boards
- (2) 1x4x8 boards
- (12) L brackets and wood screws
- (4) to (6) Medium-sized hinges
- Burlap fabric – at least 2 ½ x 6 ½ feet
- Miscellaneous fabric (for back sides) – at least 2 ½ x 6 ½ feet (or 3 sheets that are at least 2 ½ x 2 feet)
- 2x4 sheets of 2-inch thick mineral wool
- Staple gun and staples
- Electric drill
- 20 feet of chain (for hanging plants, etc.) with links that can be pried open and re-closed with pliers
- Six smaller screw hooks (for hanging panels from chain)
- Six larger screw hooks (for hanging items from ceiling)

1. Rip (i.e., cut lengthwise) the two 2x4x8 boards down their length to create four 2x2x8 boards.
2. Using project #1 as a guide, build three square sound panels—using the stained wood and front border approach—that measure approximately 2x2 feet (in other words, just use one ripped 2x2x8 board to make one frame) and stuff them with the two-inch thick mineral wool, cutting off the excess and saving it for later projects.
3. Attach panel A to panel B with two hinges on the front side (or three if necessary) so that they will fold (almost face to face). Then attach panel C to panel B (the other side) the other way (see photo).
4. Add small hooks onto each end of their top boards.
5. Using 6 larger hooks that are screwed into the ceiling at the appropriate spots (i.e., make sure to hit a stud!) and several same-size chains (made from the longer chain), you can simply "hang" the three-sided booth from the ceiling. Adjust the individual chain lengths as necessary depending on your ceiling height. For a typical eight-foot ceiling, 1.5 feet should be about right.

For bonus points, place the booth beneath a panel mounted to the ceiling!

With just a little careful measurement, some chain, and some screw-in hooks, you can easily hang an effective vocal booth anywhere.

Studio Talk: Glossary

In this glossary, we'll take a look at most of the terms you'll come across while recording. The process can usually be divided into four basic categories: *initial tracking*, *overdubs*, *editing*, and *mixing*. (Note that many of these terms will apply to several of these categories.)

Initial Tracking

The initial tracking usually involves laying down the rhythm instruments—most often the drums and bass, and possibly a rhythm guitar and/or keyboards. Here are some terms you'll come across with regard to the initial tracking stage.

Project/Song

This is simply the title of the song file or project file you're working on in your DAW. Within it, you can make many types of settings that will be specific to that song, including:

- Time signature
- Tempo
- Sample rate
- Bit depth
- Etc.

Things like time signature and tempo will affect the click track and playback speed of MIDI instruments, whereas the bit depth and sample rate will affect recording quality and file size, etc.

Track

A *track* basically corresponds to one recorded performance that you can manipulate via volume, panning, EQ, etc., without altering the rest of the tracks. Since each instrument is on its own separate track, you can then mix them however you want—i.e., the first guitar can be loud while the second one is soft, etc.

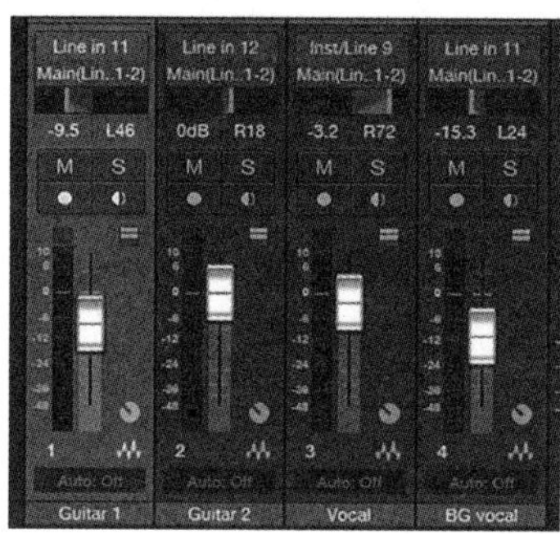

Tracks 1 (Guitar 1) and 4 (BG vocal) are turned down quieter than Tracks 2 and 3.

Tracking

This is simply a term for recording instruments on tracks. "Honey, tomorrow we'll be tracking the guitars, so take an extra long lunch (but bring me something back)."

Arm/Disarm

Arming a track means that you've put it into record-ready mode. When a track is armed and you press record, that track will begin recording. When you don't want to record on a track anymore, you *disarm* it.

Click

The *click* (or *click track*) is a metronome sound that allows performers to play in time. "I need either more click or less acoustic in my headphones please!"

Take

A *take* is an attempted recording of a part. Each time you try to record a guitar solo, for example, it's a new take. "We're rolling. This is take 58. Maybe we should have rehearsed a bit more?"

In editing, several takes are often "comped" together to create one superior performance.

Basic Tracks (or Bed Tracks)

The *basic tracks* or *bed tracks* refer to the song's foundation, usually including the drums, bass, and rhythm guitars/ keyboards.

Mic (Miking, Mic'ing)

Short for microphone, *mic* can simply be a short form of the noun "microphone," but it can also be a verb meaning to set a microphone up for recording a sound source. "Not now, mom! I'm miking the piano!"

Off-Axis

This refers to the relationship between a sound source and a mic. When a mic is not pointed directly at a speaker or instrument—and instead is angled—it's said to be *off-axis*.

Bleed (Leakage)

This is a term used to describe when the sound of one instrument is also being picked up by a microphone that's meant to record a separate instrument. If, for example you're recording acoustic guitar and vocals together, the sound from the guitar will likely *bleed* into the vocal mic (and vice versa) unless you do something to minimize it.

Gobo

A *gobo* is a moveable absorption panel that's generally used to isolate performers and/or cut down on ambient reflections and/or bleed. For example, if you want to record two guitar players playing together in the same room and reduce the amount of bleed between the tracks, you can place gobos between them to help absorb much of the sound. Check out the Appendix for instructions on how to build some yourself on the cheap.

Live/Dead

These terms refer to the acoustics (sound properties) of a certain space. A *live* space is one in which there are many echoes and/or much reverb (garages, gyms, large bathrooms, etc.). A *dead* space has very few reflections. This would include carpeted rooms with lots of thick curtains or a child's room with the largest collection of stuffed animals in the world.

A-B

When you "A-B" something, you compare one sound to another. This can be the sound of two different microphones, two different guitars, two different mic positions, etc. It's often useful when miking up an instrument for the first time. You can record quick samples with two different mics and then *A-B* them to see which one sounds best.

Phones (Cans)

These are both short (or slang) for headphones. "Which pair of cans do you want?"

Channel

This is often confused with track. This was easier when dealing with tape, because you could say (roughly) that a track pertained to the tape, whereas a channel pertained to the mixer. The gist is that a *channel* does not contain any audio. It's simply a *signal path* through which the audio can pass.

One analogy is to think of a series of adjacent homes on a street in which the garages represent the tracks (on the tape or hard drive), the cars represent the audio signal, and the roads through the neighborhood represent the channels. Four different cars (audio signals) could drive down the same main street (channel 1, let's say) to get to the homes and park in garages (tracks) 1, 2, 3, and 4, respectively, *if they went one after the other*. But they wouldn't be able to do that at the same time because the road (channel) is only big enough for one car (signal) at a time.

This is the equivalent of recording a song by yourself one track a time, using the same channel on your interface but sending the signals to different tracks in your DAW each time.

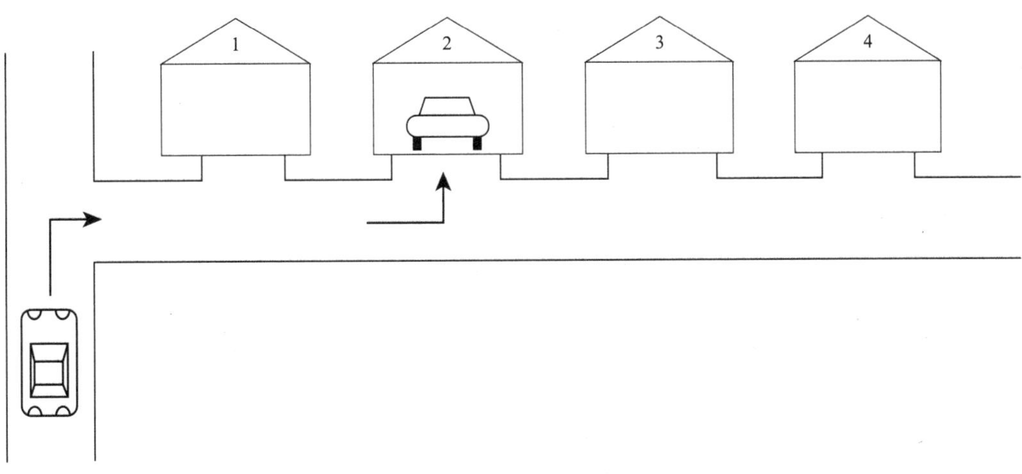

But if two cars took two *different* roads (channels 1 and 2, let's say), they could both arrive at garages 1 and 2 at the same time. This is because the cars aren't driving on the same road.

This is the equivalent of two people playing at the same time, each using their own channel and then recording onto their own track.

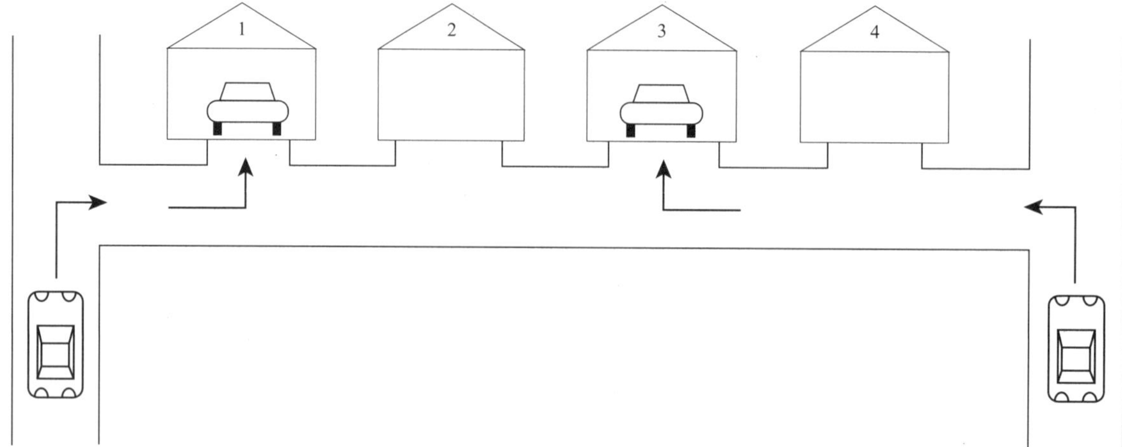

Routing

This term is often used when discussing channels and tracks. It refers to where an audio signal is sent. "Are you routing the guitar to track 5? I'd prefer track 7, because that's my lucky number."

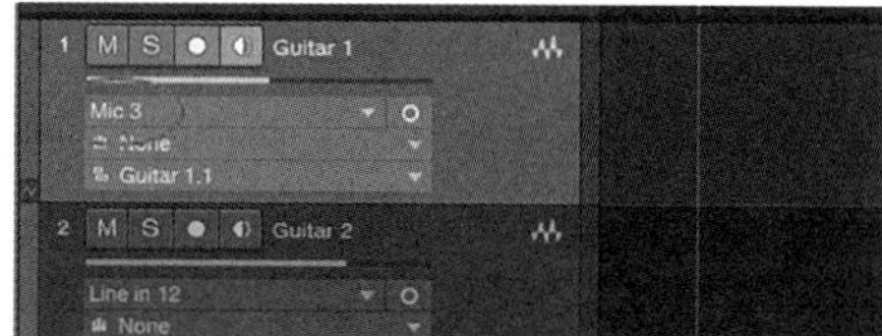

In this instance, the mic 3 input is routed to Track 1.

Assigning

This is basically synonymous with routing. "Channel 1 is assigned to track 4, and channel 2 is assigned to ... um ... nothing. The cord came unplugged."

Signal Path

The *signal path* is a term describing the electronic route the signal takes within one piece of equipment (mixer, for example) or several pieces of equipment.

Signal Chain

The *signal chain* is a list of each piece of equipment through which the signal passes en route to the recorder (DAW). This can also refer to the virtual path inside a DAW. "The weakest link in my signal chain is my compressor, so I'd really like a new one."

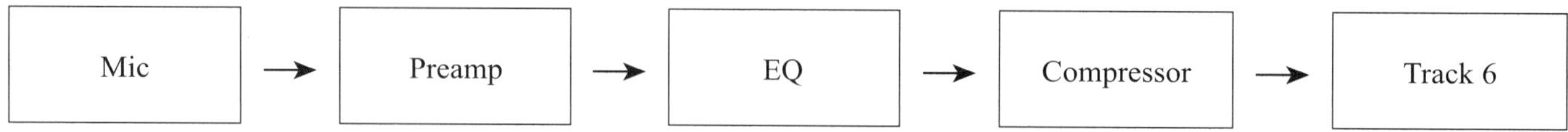

Submixing

Again, this greatly has to do with channels. If you only have the ability to record two tracks at once (for example, your interface has only two inputs), but you want to record more audio signals (instruments) than that simultaneously, you'll have to *submix*. A simple *mic mixer* can make this idea fairly clear.

Nady RMX 6 Mic/Line Mixer

A mic mixer (which is just a basic form of a *mixer*) is a device that allows you to plug in several different mics (usually four or more) and then mix those signals to one or two outputs.

Submixing can also occur virtually within your DAW. For example, many people submix groups of instruments so they can control their volume as a group with one fader and/or process them simultaneously with compression, EQ, etc.

Panning

The subject of *panning* deals with the stereo field. You can *pan* an instrument to appear only in the left speaker (known as *hard left*), only in the right speaker (*hard right*), or anywhere in between.

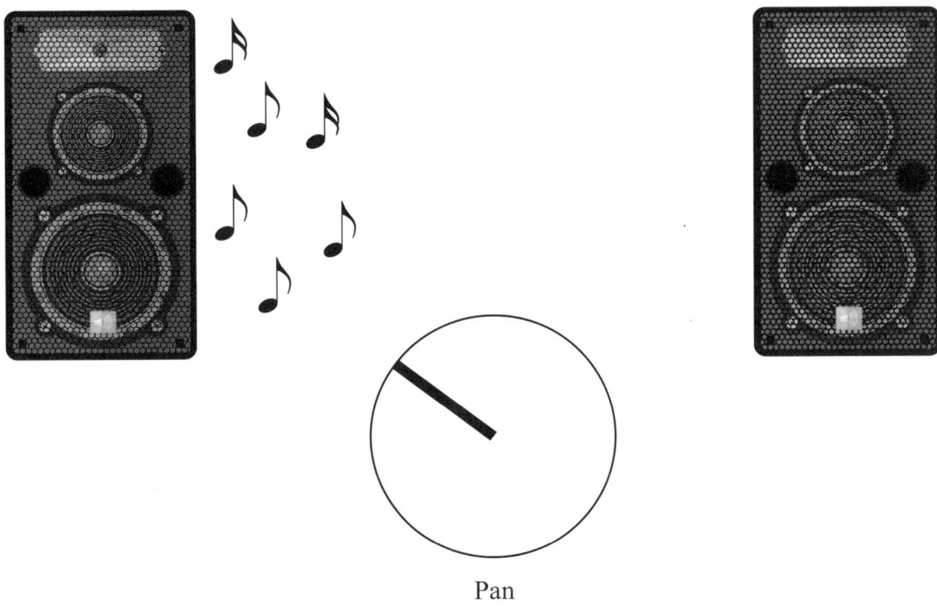

Pan

Console/Board/Desk/Mixer

All of these terms refer to a *mixing board* (or *mixer*), which was a must-have in the days of analog recording (although it was combined with the recorder in portable 4-track cassette studios). The function of a mixer is to take in several distinct audio signals, mix them together in various ways and/or process them along the way, and send them out various outputs.

These days, most DAW software is configured to mimic the look of a mixer, and it performs all the same functions "virtually" in the box, only it's controlled with your mouse. A *control surface* allows some physical control of a DAW's virtual mixer without using the mouse.

Studio One's "virtual" mixer.

Insert

When you *insert* something, this usually means placing a piece of equipment in series with the signal. For example, if you want to apply compression to a vocal, the entire vocal signal will usually pass through the compressor and come out the other end effected. On a mixer or preamp, they're usually in the form of a 1/4-inch TRS ("tip-ring-sleeve") jack, which conducts two signals. Using a special insert cable—a Y cable with one TRS plug and two TS ("tip-sleeve," or standard instrument cable) plugs—the signal will leave the mixer/preamp, and travel through the "send" cable into the device (compressor, let's say). It will then leave the output of the device and travel back to the mixer via the "return" cable and continue on down the signal path.

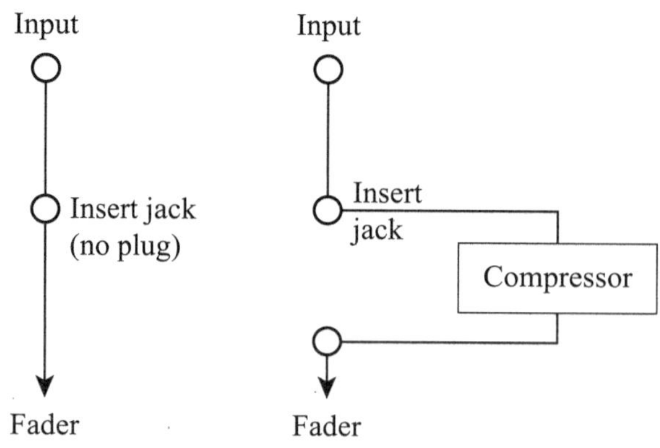

Insert cable: Note the two rings on one plug (TRS) and the one ring on the other two plugs (TS).

Meter

A *meter* shows a graphic representation of a signal level (or signal levels). In the old days, VU meters (with the needles that bounced left and right) were mostly used, but now you usually see virtual peak meters on a DAW. Several plug-ins, however, feature virtual VU meters just for the aesthetics of it.

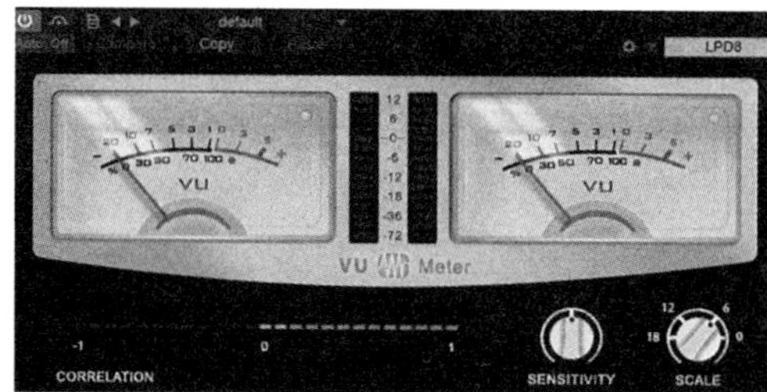

Monitor

The word "monitor" has a few different meanings with regards to audio recording. As a noun, *monitor* refers to your control room speakers as well as, of course, your computer screen. When you *monitor* (verb) something, you listen to it. As an adjective, a *monitor mix* is one that's usually meant for listening as opposed to what's being sent to the final two-track stereo recorder.

Cue Mix (Foldback Mix)

Cue mix refers to a mix of the instruments separate from what's being heard by the engineer in the control room. It's most commonly used for the performer(s) in the studio room. A pro studio will have the ability to generate different cue mixes for several different performers simultaneously. Setting up a cue mix requires numerous outputs on your audio interface, however: one for each separately generated mono mix, or two for each separately generated stereo mix.

Main Mix

The *main mix* is the final destination for most signals. It's represented by two main (left and right) meters that indicate the signal level that will be "printed" to the final stereo file upon rendering (see "Mixing" section). In digital recording, you don't ever want the main mix to clip (go above 0 dB), as this results in an unpleasant, unmusical distortion.

Headphone Amp

A *headphone amp* is a device that allows you to listen to music with several sets of headphones simultaneously, each with their own independent volume.

Art Headamp6 Pro Headphone Amplifier

Wet/Dry

A signal (such as a guitar) is said to be *wet* when it has effects, such as reverb, delay, tremolo, phasing, etc., applied to it. (Some people use the term "wet" specifically with regards to reverb only as well.) If a signal has no effects whatsoever applied to it, it's said to be *dry*. Most people choose to track (record) signals dry and add the desired effects later during the mixing process, as this allows you control over how much reverb, delay, etc. you'd like to add to the track. "That guitar track is dry as a bone!"

Recording "Wet"/Printing Effects

Sometimes an effect is integral to the sound of an instrument or particular performance to such an extent that it's difficult to record without it. One example is a guitar part that uses a timed delay effect. (U2's The Edge is famous for this.) In this instance, the delay effect is usually present while the track is being recorded. This is called recording wet or *printing the effect*.

Timbre

Timbre (pronounced "tamber") is somewhat analogous with tone. It's the quality of a sound that allows us to distinguish between, say, a piano and a clarinet even when they're playing the same exact note.

Direct Box (D.I. Box)

A *direct box* allows you to plug in a high-impedance audio signal, such as that from a guitar's output jack, into a low-impedance input on an interface or a mixer. Without running through a direct box, the signal from a guitar or bass is much too weak and will result in an inferior tone. Nowadays, many interfaces have 1/4-inch inputs specifically designed for guitar/bass input, which is roughly the equivalent of running through a direct box. The advantage of a dedicated direct box is that it can also be used in a live situation.

Radial StageBug SB-1 Active DI

Trim Knob

This is usually a knob on a mixer channel or interface channel that determines the input level into the channel. This is sometimes also referred to as *gain*.

Fader

A *fader* is a sliding *potentiometer* ("pot," or variable resistor) that's moved up and down to control the level of its corresponding track. A DAW has *virtual faders* that you move by dragging the mouse or with an external control surface.

Distorting/Overloading/Clipping

This refers to when a signal is being recorded at too high a volume, and it's distorting the input. In the digital domain, *clipping* does not produce a pleasing effect and is therefore avoided at all costs during tracking.

Note that there are several places this distorting/clipping can occur. If, for example, you like the distorted sound you get when you run your bass through an external mic preamp with the gain cranked, you can still record that signal at a useable level in your DAW by turning the output level of your mic preamp down and/or the input level of your interface down.

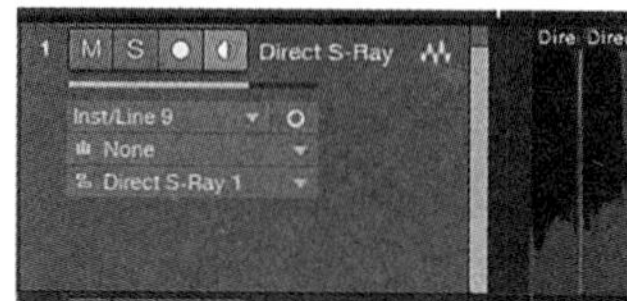

Clipping is a big no-no in digital recording!

Attenuate

This is simply a fancy word meaning to reduce the level of a signal, which basically means "to turn down." "Don't make me attenuate your track!"

Pad

This is a feature found on many mixers, mic preamps, interfaces, and microphones. It's usually a switch that, when engaged, attenuates the signal by a preset amount. It's particularly useful when recording sources that are exceptionally loud, such as a cranked amp or bass drum.

Phantom Power

This is a DC voltage that's necessary to power most condenser mics. Many interfaces and standalone recorders come equipped with at least one or two channels of phantom power. If yours doesn't, however, you can buy external phantom power supplies.

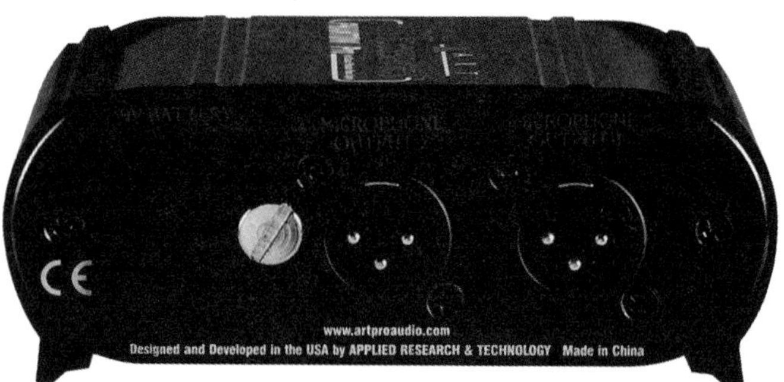

ART Phantom II Pro Phantom Power Supply

Phase Cancellation/"Out of Phase"

Two signals are said to be *out of phase* when, though they sound full and rich on their own, their combined sound results in a thinner, weaker tone. This is the result of their two waves working against each other—i.e., one's crest is mostly occurring during the other's trough. You may run into this phenomenon when using multiple mics for the same source or when combining a DI bass track with an amped one, for example.

Mute

To *mute* a channel/track means to silence it. Sometimes you may be hearing a noise/buzz when you have several mics going at once. By muting the channels one by one, you can track down which one is causing the issue. Muting is also used during mixdown when you want to concentrate on a certain group of instruments instead of listening to all of the tracks at once.

Solo

Similar to muting, but kind of the opposite, *soloing* a track effectively mutes all other tracks so you hear only the soloed track. This is also a common way to track down a buzz or refine an instrument's sound during a mix. Note that you can solo several tracks at once.

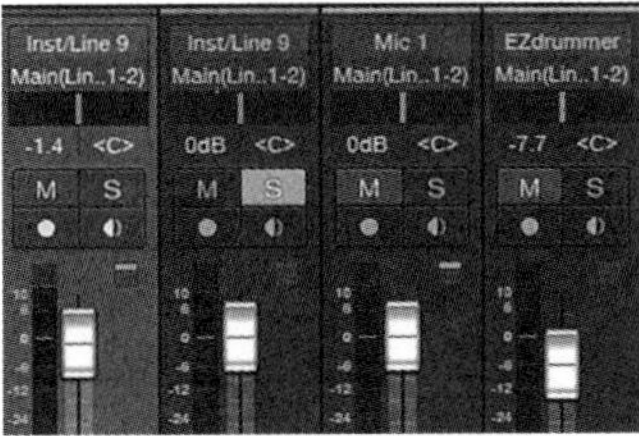

Transport

On a tape recorder, this referred to the collection of buttons (play, record, etc.) that controlled the tape motor. On digital recording equipment, it refers to the same collection of virtual buttons on a DAW.

Scratch Vocal

Sometimes when a band records the basic tracks together, the singer also records a *scratch vocal*: a temporary vocal track that acts as a placeholder until the real vocal is recorded.

Scratch Guitars/Keys/Etc.

Along the line of the scratch vocal, sometimes scratch versions of other instruments are recorded during the basic tracks with the intent on spending more time on the tone and performance later on.

Overdubs

After the initial tracks are done, the *overdubs* usually come next. If the basic tracks can be thought of as the frame of a house, the overdubs would constitute the walls, floors, and ceilings. Overdubs usually consist of tracks added one at a time, although they can also include several instruments playing together. A brass section or string section would be a good example of this. If you're a one-man operation, and you're recording a full-band pop song arrangement, you'll spend a good amount of time on overdubs.

Rough Mix

A *rough mix* is a quick, decent-sounding mix of the instruments recorded thus far so you can play along with them while you overdub new tracks.

Punch-In/Out

A *punch-in* (or *punch*) is the act of only recording a part of a track instead of rerecording the entire track. If you like your guitar solo, but you hit one bum note, you can punch in just long enough to play a new (better) lick there and then punch out. "Can I punch that last lick, please?" Nowadays, of course, all aspects of the punches can be automated, including...

Pre-Roll and Post-Roll

The *pre-roll* is the amount of "runway" you get before punching in. Let's say you're in auto-punch mode and have your punch-in point set at the beginning of the chorus and your punch-out point set one measure later. If you have your pre-roll and post-roll set at five seconds and press record, it will start playing from five seconds before the chorus. It will then automatically punch you in at the chorus (whether you play anything or not), punch you out at the end of measure 2, and then stop five seconds after that.

Pop Filter

A *pop filter* is a device mounted to a microphone stand and placed between a singer and mic that prevents certain syllables (letters like "p" and "b") from causing a "pop" in a vocal track.

Samson Audio PS05 Metal Microphone Pop Filter

Proximity Effect

Proximity effect is the interesting increase in bass frequencies that occurs as you get nearer to a microphone when singing. Generally speaking, eight inches or so from a condenser mic is a good place to start if you want to avoid it altogether.

Vocal Booth

A *vocal booth* is generally an enclosed area that's been treated acoustically to sound very dead (few reflections). This allows the vocal to sound very present (or "up front") in the mix. Usually, any ambience that's added to a vocal track (reverb, delay, etc.) is done artificially after the fact during mixdown.

There are also "portable vocal booths" of varying sizes and complexity. Some of these are quite expensive and basically constitute a temporary room, while the more affordable options can consist of a semi-circle frame with absorptive foam mounted to a mic stand. You can also check out the Appendix for DIY options in this regard.

Virtual Tracks

Virtual tracks are featured on most standalone recorders these days, and they allow you to store alternate takes for each track. A typical standalone recorder may feature 16 tracks, each with 16 virtual tracks. Only one of the virtual tracks can be played back at a time, though. A common use for virtual tracks is to record several different takes of a guitar solo, for example, to see which approach works best.

Editing

Editing usually refers to the manipulation of tracks with regards to time and pitch mostly. This is really where digital music production shines when compared to analog. It's the equivalent of using an old school typewriter and correction fluid vs. a word processing program. You can literally do on a computer with a few mouse clicks what could you take you hours or more with the traditional tape-splicing methods of the analog world.

After all the tracks and overdubs are recorded, many people will sit back and listen to the song as a whole, paying special attention to the performances with regard to accuracy in timing, intensity, pitch, etc. If the bass player really rushed the first note of the chorus, it's a simple matter on a digital system to move that note so that it's in time. You can also rearrange the song at this point. If you decide, for example, that the song should start right on the verse instead of the intro, you can do that with a simple click of the mouse.

Waveform Display

Each track is represented in your DAW graphically by a *waveform display*. This is a horizontal beam that shows what the audio wave looks like. When editing, you can zoom in on these when necessary to perform precise edits.

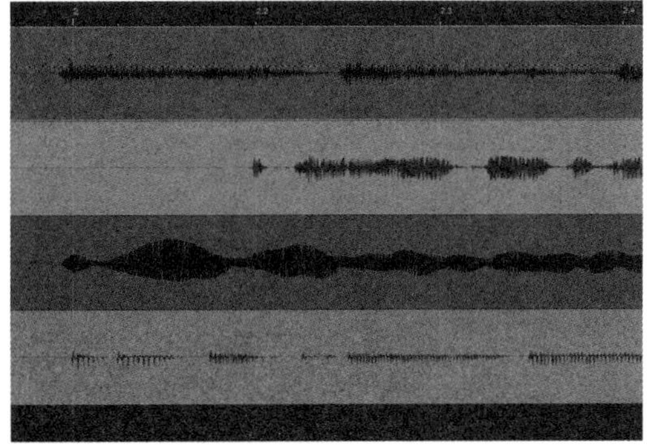

Waveform display in Studio One.

Edit Point

An *edit point* is simply the precise spot along the timeline at which an edit is going to be performed. "The cut will start at this point."

Split (Cut)

When you *split* an audio file, you cut it into two separate files, which can then be manipulated individually. If you wanted to move one ill-timed bass note, you would split it before the note starts and after the note ends. You could then move that one note forward or backward along the timeline so that it's on the proper beat.

Trim

Trimming a file refers to lengthening or shortening the beginning or end of a file. If, after the above split example with the bass note, the end of the edited note spills over onto the beginning of the next note, you can trim the end of the edited note so that it ends right before the next note. It's also common to trim the beginning and ending of a track to get rid of any unwanted extraneous noise in the recording.

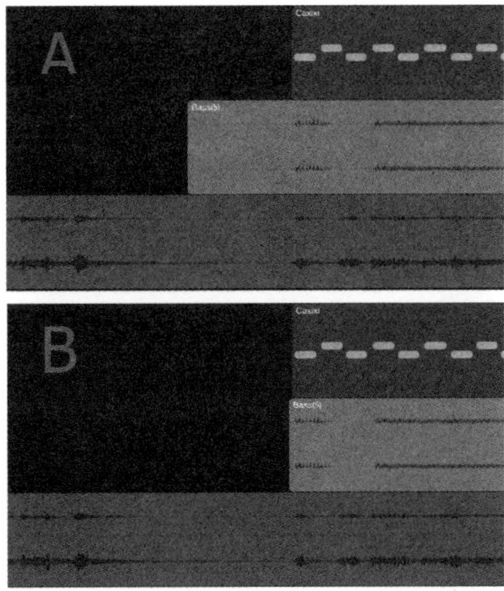

In screenshot B, the extra noise at the beginning of screenshot A has been trimmed.

Copy/Cut/Paste/Move

These terms are analogous to those of a word processor. If you want, you can select a part of the guitar track (the verse riff, for example), copy or cut it, and then paste it to another location or to a completely different track.

Glue/Join

When you *glue* two files together, they become one single file and can therefore be manipulated as such. This is kind of the opposite of split. This may also be known as *merge* or *join*, depending on the DAW.

Comp

Short for composite, a *comp* is a complete track that's been assembled from several other individual tracks. A very common practice with vocals, for example, is to record, say, four complete takes of the vocal. Then you go back and pick the best lines from each take, comping together the final vocal take.

Import/Export

Occasionally you'll want to *import* other audio files into your song. For example, you may use this function with drum loops. You can also *export* a track, section of a track, section of the song, etc. to another file (an mp3, for example).

Grid

The *grid* is a system of light vertical lines that help make it clear where you are within your song. You can set the grid so that it shows measures only, beats, or eighth notes, etc. Or you can arrange it via time. It's kind of like a piece of graph paper under your waveform display. For the purpose of editing, it's very helpful when aligning certain tracks, etc.

Snapping

Snapping is a function that works with the grid. You can enable snapping so that, when you drag an audio file, its edge will "snap" to the nearest beat, eighth note, etc.—whatever you have it set for. When doing larger scale edits, such as the form of the song, this is invaluable.

Quantizing

A common term when using MIDI instruments, *quantizing* refers to the rhythmic correction of a note's timing. If you record a MIDI drum pattern, for example, and the hi-hat pattern is rushing and dragging a bit, you can quantize those notes (assuming you're recording to the click) so that they will snap to the nearest rhythmic point (eighth note, 16th note, etc.) of your choosing.

If you want the drum track to still sound human, you can also specify the *percentage* of quantization. Instead of every hi-hat note moving all the way to the nearest eighth note, you can tell them to move only 50 percent of the way—or 85 percent, or whatever. This way, you can leave as much or as little of your human performance in as you'd like.

Undo/Redo

If you make an edit (say, move a note) and don't like it, just click *undo*, and it's back the way it was. *Redo* will re-perform the edit. Most DAW programs have a ridiculous amount of undo levels, so you can pretty much undo your whole life if you'd like.

Fade In/Fade Out/Crossfade

You can easily *fade in* or *fade out* a file at either end, and you have complete control over the duration of the fade and the envelope shape. Also, if you have two files that are overlapping, you can *crossfade* them if you'd like, so that the first one will begin to fade out while the second one begins to fade in.

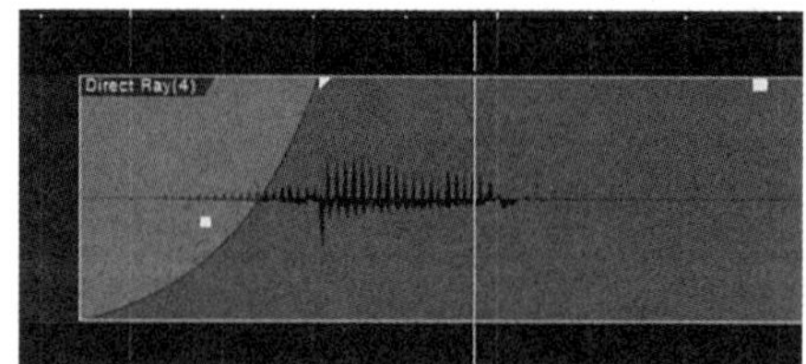

This track will gradually fade in.

Crop

The term *crop* refers to the choosing of a specific take when you've recorded several takes on one track. If you have, say, four different vocal takes on one track, and you decide you like take 3 during the verse, you can crop to that take, and it will become the chosen take to play from then on. The other takes will no longer be shown, but they will not be deleted, and you can still access them later if you so choose.

Time-Stretch

Stretching a file usually refers to the act of lengthening or shortening it while changing its speed as well. For example, if you have a guitar lick that normally lasts five seconds, you can stretch it so that it lasts five and a half seconds. The pitch will remain the same (although you could change that in a setting), but the phrase would sound as if it were played slower.

One of the most common uses for stretching is drum loops. If you have a drum loop (typically a stereo track of a one- or two-bar drum pattern that you import into your project) that was recorded at 96 beats per minute, but your song is 94 beats per minute, you can stretch the drum loop a bit so that it will line up with the tempo of your song.

Keyboard Shortcuts

A *keyboard shortcut* is fairly self-explanatory. Many of the most common functions in a DAW can be accessed with a keyboard shortcut so you don't have to click the mouse for everything. In many DAW programs, you can customize these yourself, so you can assign your own shortcuts for virtually any function.

Mixing

In the mixing step, we make decisions about all the instruments we've recorded and how we want them to sound together, including:

- Volume (level)
- Panning
- EQ
- Effects (reverb, delay, compression, etc.)

Once these decisions are made, the main mix is then rendered to a stereo file so that it can be played anywhere.

"In the Box"

This refers to something that's happening within the confines of the DAW software and not using any external signal processing. For example, if someone mixes a song entirely *in the box*, it means that they use only the virtual mixer of their DAW and only software plug-ins for their effects.

Equalization (EQ)

Equalization is the shaping of a sound by boosting or cutting certain frequencies within it. The frequency range is generally divided into four basic areas: bass, low midrange, high midrange, and treble. There are several different types of equalizers, the most common being graphic, sweepable, and parametric.

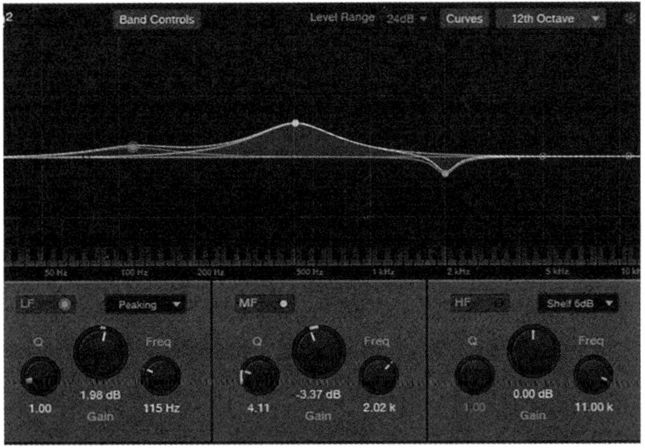

Studio One's Pro EQ plug-in is fully parametric.

FX

This is simply a shorthand way to write "effects," and it refers to any kind of audio effect, such as reverb, delay, etc. "That guitar is drowning in FX!"

Effects (FX) Send/Effects Loop

An *effects send* or *effects loop* is a signal path in which a portion (anywhere from 0 to 100 percent) of a signal, such as a keyboard track, is split from the main mix, sent through an effect (or series of effects) and then returned to the main mix to be blended with the original signal. This is the most common way that effects are applied to tracks during mixdown, because you can decide exactly how much of the effect (reverb, delay, etc.) you want to add to each signal.

Effects Chain

This is similar to signal chain, but it's only referring to a series of effects through which a signal is passing. "Exactly how many delays do you need to send your guitar through?"

Series and Parallel

These terms in recording refer to the way in which signals can pass through various stages. In a *series* path, one signal passes completely through a stage and then comes out the other end, continuing on. A perfect example of this is a typical guitar effect pedal.

In a *parallel* path, one signal is split into two. One side of it continues on, but the other side runs through an additional stage before being combined (mixed) again with the original signal. An example of this type of path is a typical effects loop (see above).

Automation

Back in the old days, if you wanted a track's volume to swell up or down during mixdown, you had to move the fader yourself (or get someone to help you while you took care of other things). Nowadays, virtually any aspect of a mixdown can be controlled automatically. *Automation* refers to the idea of the program making automatic mixing adjustments (volume, panning, effects, etc.) for you as the song plays.

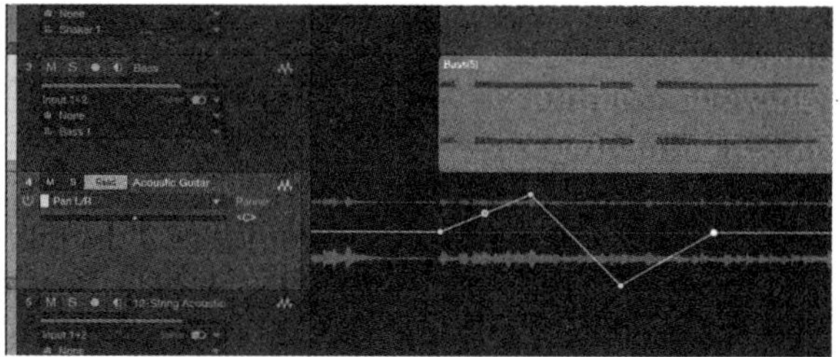

This panning envelope will make the track pan back and forth across the stereo field automatically.

Rendering (or Exporting)

When you *render* something (also called *export*) in your DAW, you turn it into a playable stereo (or mono) file on its own. For example, you can render a guitar track that has a bunch of plug-ins applied to it, such as an amp simulator, compressor, EQ, etc. All of those plug-ins eat up CPU power, and by rendering the track, you create a new file with all of those effects "printed" to it. The original guitar track with all the plug-ins can then be muted, thereby freeing up more CPU power again.

Another common use of rendering refers to creating the final mix of your song. In this respect, you can simply think of render as another word for "mix." When you're ready to print your final stereo mix of your song, you'll render it to a stereo file, using various settings that you'll specify (file type, bit depth, etc.). This will be the song file that you send to your friends for them to play on their stereos, mobile devices, etc.

Hal Leonard

The Name You Trust for the Best Music Publications

Whether you want to learn how to play a new instrument or need material to play at your next concert, Hal Leonard has you covered. Visit our website for thousands of physical and digital book and sheet music options.

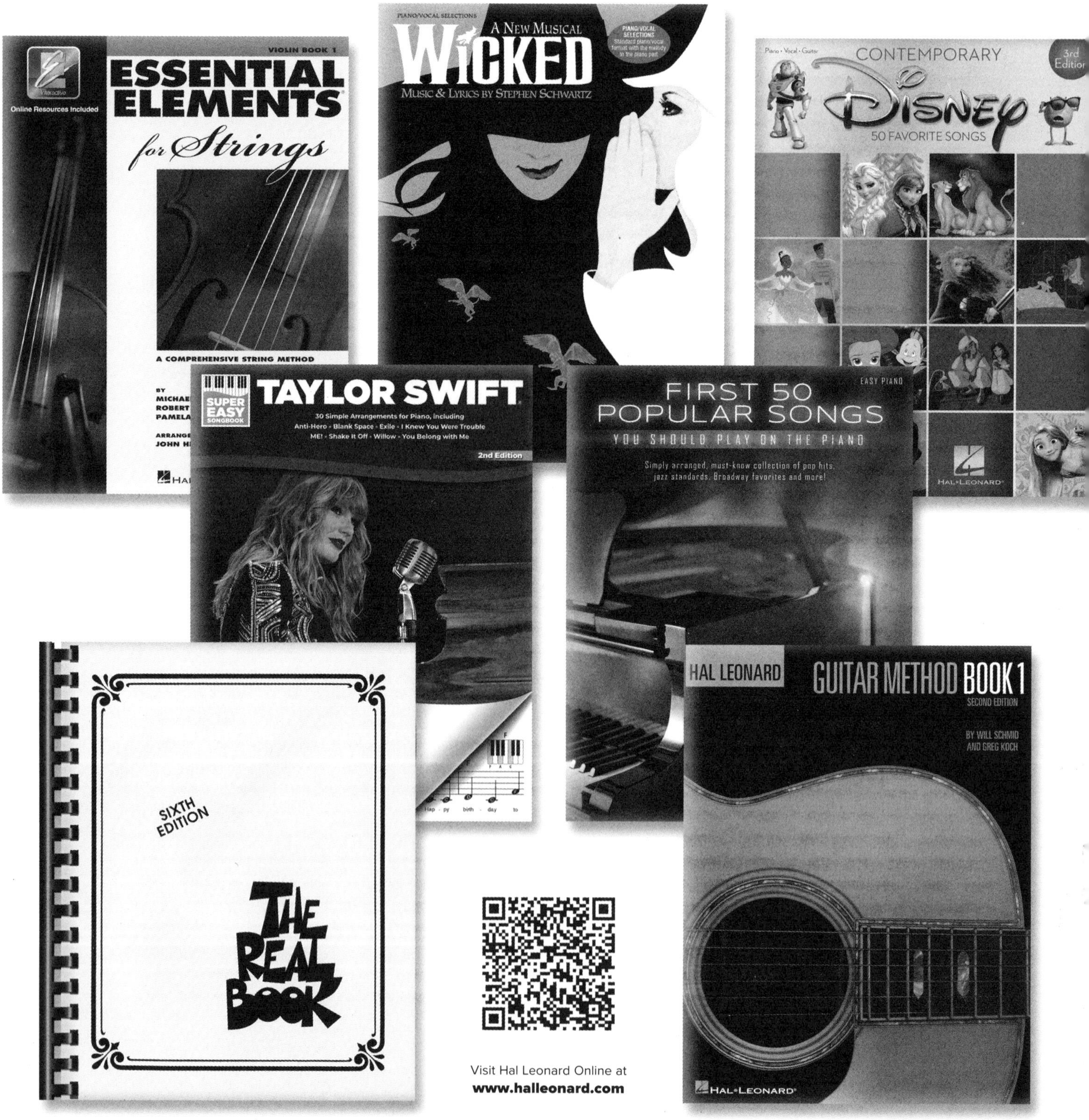

Visit Hal Leonard Online at
www.halleonard.com

HAL•LEONARD®
A Muse Group Company

02
3